THE UNITED STATES AND IRAN, 1946–51

The United States and Iran, 1946–51

The Diplomacy of Neglect

JAMES F. GOODE

Assistant Professor of History
Grand Valley State University, Michigan

St. Martin's Press   New York

First published in the United States of America in 1989

Printed in the People's Republic of China

ISBN 0-312-02723-0

Library of Congress Cataloging-in-Publication Data

Goode, James F., 1944–
The United States and Iran, 1946–51: the
diplomacy of neglect/James F. Goode.
        p.   cm.
Bibliography: p.
Includes index.
ISBN 0-312-02723-0: $40.00 (est.)
1. United States – Relations – Iran.   2. Iran – Relations – United States.
    3. United States – Foreign relations – 1945–53.   4. Iran-Foreign relations –
1941–79.   I. Title.
E183.8.I55G66 1989
327.73055 – dc19   88–8495
                                                                          CIP

To the Ehsani Family

Contents

Preface

What is all too apparent to students of recent United States-Iranian relations is the consistent character of that relationship during the many years prior to the 1979 revolution. No matter where one looks, official attitudes remained alarmingly similar. American envoys and military representatives displayed little knowledge or understanding of people and developments outside the narrow court circle in Tehran; decision-makers in Washington, Republican and Democratic alike, rarely questioned ties with the Pahlavi regime; Shah Muhammad Reza Pahlavi dominated politics, manipulating politicians and military leaders while pressing the United States to supply ever more weapons for his army.

One might reasonably ask how all this came about, and the following pages explain how the relationship established itself, not during the brief Azarbaijan crisis of 1946, nor in the sudden violence associated with the overthrow of Prime Minister Muhammad Musaddiq in August 1953, but rather gradually, quietly, in the years between. The story is complex, for in those early years one recognised another relationship, involving Britain rather than the United States. Until the early 1950s, Britain was the principal Western power at Tehran. During those early postwar years then, as the Cold War intensified, the Truman administration neglected Iran, partly because it assumed that the British, with their long experience in the Middle East, would maintain the Western position, while Washington concentrated on Europe and East Asia. It assumed too much. Matters degenerated into the oil crisis of 1951, forcing the United States to adopt a more active policy.

By the pivotal year, 1951, the US official attitude had begun to solidify in support of the shah. As the monarch increased his power, US leaders convinced themselves that he alone could guarantee stability at home and a barrier to Soviet expansion towards the Persian Gulf. With this idea firmly fixed, Americans thereafter rarely questioned their contacts with courtiers rather than opponents of the shah.

Here was neither malice nor conspiracy on the part of the Truman administration and its successors, but rather a misguided policy born of ignorance and anticommunist ideology. Assuming that stability would satisfy the Iranian people, Americans augmented royal power and as the years passed abetted the Pahlavi dictatorship, making straight the way for the explosion to come.

Acknowledgements

Many thanks are due to the librarians and archivists of Grand Valley State University, the Harry S. Truman Library, especially Dennis E. Bilger and Elizabeth Safly, Indiana University, the National Archives, Diplomatic Branch, especially Sally Marks, the Modern Military Branch, especially Ed Reese and John Taylor, the National Records Center, Suitland, the Public Record Office, Kew, and the University of Georgia. Their assistance, expertise and words of encouragement made this project possible.

I would also like to thank the diplomats and officials who shared their personal experiences and perspectives: Edward A. Bayne, the late General J. Lawton Collins, George McGhee, George Middleton, Peter Ramsbotham, Leslie Rood, William Rountree and Denis Wright. The family of the late Major General Robert W. Grow kindly gave me access to his diary and papers.

A number of institutions and organisations contributed financially to my research. I express my gratitude to the American Historical Association, Grand Valley State University, Indiana University, the National Endowment for the Humanities, the Harry S. Truman Library Institute and the University of Georgia.

Several scholars, Richard Cottam, Bruce Kuniholm, Lester Langley, Melvyn Leffler, M. Jeanne Peterson and David M. Pletcher, gave valuable time to read and comment on all or part of the manuscript. I thank them for their helpful suggestions. William Stueck of the University of Georgia was particularly generous in this respect. A special note of appreciation is due to Robert H. Ferrell who has suported this study from the beginning. I am proud to be the latest in a long line of younger scholars who have benefited from his knowledge, advice and friendship.

Finally, to my wife, Virginia, and my sons, Matthew and Zachary, thank you for your patience, understanding and interest. You make it all worthwhile.

List of Abbreviations

AIOC	Anglo-Iranian Oil Company (formerly Anglo-Persian Oil Company, now British Petroleum)
ARAMCO	Arabian-American Oil Company
ARMISH	United States Mission to the Iranian Army
CIA	Central Intelligence Agency
GENMISH	United States Mission to the Iranian Gendarmerie
ILO	International Labour Office
MDAP	Military Defense Assistance Program
NATO	North Atlantic Treaty Organisation
OCI	Overseas Consultants Incorporated
UN	United Nations

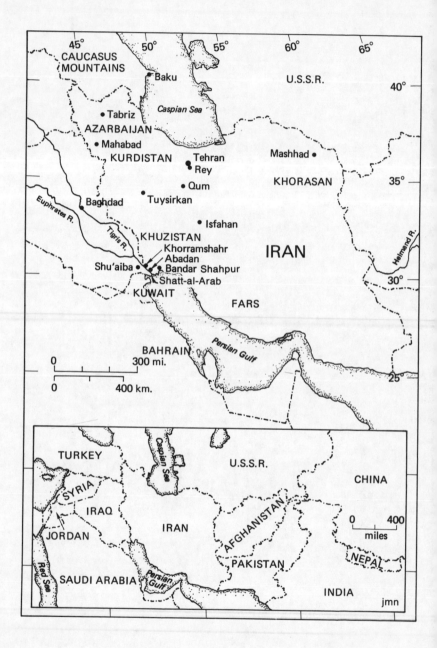

1   Beginning

After months of waiting, Ahmad Qavam al-Saltaneh, prime minister of Iran, ordered the imperial army into the breakaway provinces of Azarbaijan and Kurdistan in northwestern Iran. The year was 1946. Three columns moved forward cautiously, meeting no resistance as defenders fled in disarray. When news reached Tabriz, capital of Azarbaijan, mobs looted and burned shops and houses, and seized as many officials of the regime of Ja'far Pishevari as they could get their hands on. Soon the bodies of more than 500 unfortunates, lower-level bureaucrats and sympathisers with the regime, dangled from makeshift gibbets. The army reached Tabriz on 12 December, and received a hero's welcome. The movement to divide Iran had failed. Pishevari escaped to the Soviet Union.

In the developing Cold War, Iran momentarily caught the attention of Western countries, and then everything seemed resolved. With American encouragement and support, Azarbaijan and Kurdistan in early 1946 had passed into debate in the United Nations Security Council and the General Assembly. US and Soviet diplomats confronted each other. The Iranian army took the problem into its own hands, and news of Iran all but disappeared from American newspapers, pushed aside by crises in the Eastern Mediterranean, Western Europe, and – beginning in 1950 – East Asia.[1]

But this was not the end of trouble in Iran, for with the apparent victory of 1946 there commenced an extraordinarily involuted and, as it turned out, fateful chapter in the history of the country, and the new trouble many years later produced the bloody Iranian revolution commencing in 1978.

The beginning of the Iranian revolution years afterward traced back to the first decade of the present century, to the constitutional movement of 1906–11 that sought to reduce monarchical and foreign power by introducing a Western-style constitution and parliament. The overthrow of the Qajar dynasty after a coup by Colonel Reza Khan of the Cossack Brigade had followed. Reza initiated a movement to modernise and increase central government, while disregarding the democratic aspirations of the revolutionaries. The 'shah', as he was known after 1925, ruled with a firm hand. The founder of the Pahlavi dynasty undoubtedly had a commanding presence. He was well over six feet in height, and strongly built. His severe countenance and piercing eyes

1

turned the gaze of all but the most courageous. Intense, full of energy, he wasted few words. Instances of waste, negligence or lack of discipline triggered a fierce temper from which no one was secure. Physically and morally fearless, he did not shy from bloodshed in the interest of the nation. He could also be cautious, methodical. He suspected anyone whose loyalty had not been proved. But he was an uncompromising nationalist, working to end the capitulations that gave Europeans privileges. He especially sought to limit British and Russian influence. After a while he turned to Germany, the nation that had lost World War I and was not likely to dominate a weak Middle Eastern country, welcoming investment and advisers from Berlin.[2]

Years later, at the present time, it is a commonplace to remark on the ties between the Pahlavis – father and son – and the military in Iran, and indeed from the early days of the dynasty a relationship certainly existed. Reza Shah allied himself with the military, devoting time, energy and revenue to modernisation of the army. He ordered employment of foreign military advisers, construction of government factories for ammunition and small arms, and purchases of heavy weaponry abroad, especially in Germany. After World War II his son turned to the United States.

The rule of Reza Shah ended in disaster, for in the 1930s he misjudged the effect on Britain and the Soviet Union of his connection with Nazi Germany. In August 1941 as German troops drove into Russia towards the Caucasus, threatening the oilfields at Baku, the British and Russians intervened to remove any chance, however remote, of Tehran's military support of Germany. The country passed to the Allies. The invaders forced Reza Shah's abdication and exile, after 15 years on the Peacock Throne. His departure left Iran more securely in foreign possession than when his reign began.

The 21-year-old crown prince, Muhammad Reza, succeeded as shah in 1941, and the youth's situation was not enviable. Reza Shah's children had stood in awe of their father. In barely three weeks the crown prince had seen the removal of the patriarch. Almost no one paid attention to the young Muhammad Reza. Of medium height and slender build, he possessed none of the physical presence of his father. Visitors noted his intelligence and charm, but these qualities hardly sufficed. He appeared shy. Muhammad Reza spent the early years of his reign visiting hospitals, receiving ambassadors, handing out medals.[3]

The young shah nonetheless managed to carry on the military interests of his father. Reza Shah had established a military primary school in Tehran for the crown prince and his brothers, where students wore uniforms and devoted part of each day to drill. After returning to Tehran from five years of study in Switzerland in the early 1930s, the son had entered a military college organised by French advisers, where he studied tactics and strategy and graduated a second lieutenant in the spring of 1938. He took up his duties as inspector in the army, and pursued them until he succeeded to the throne. He considered himself a soldier.

The structure of power in Iran during the first years of the young shah's reign seemed as unchanging as during the reign of his father. Parliament, the Majlis, was controlled by landowners with an admixture of religious leaders and professional men, and proved utterly inadequate as an instrument of reform. Faction rather than party dominated, allegiances shifted, and only the handful of communist deputies, members of the Iranian communist party, the Tudeh, voted as a unit. Prime ministers and cabinet members came from a traditional élite whose members literally took turns in office. Power remained with the élite, the large landowners. The shah was the largest of the landlords, owning two thousand villages in the north of Iran, which provided an annual income of well over $1 million. Land was the basis of power and prestige, and although higher returns could come from investments in industry and commerce, men of wealth and ambition eagerly purchased land. Like all élites, the landowners wished to maintain the status quo, and while they supported the monarchy, they opposed anyone who contemplated reform – especially if the reform concerned their land. Conservatism was widespread among all classes of Iranians, and even peasants, pawns of the landlords, who would have benefited most from social and economic reforms, showed little knowledge of or interest in the world outside their villages.[4]

The very idea of government in Iran tended to militate against popular participation. The Iranian government did not consider itself the servant of the people. Nor did the peasants and tribesmen, who made up 80 per cent of the populace of 15 million, look to Tehran.

The trouble in the Iranian equation proved to be the landlords. Over the years the landowners became closely associated with city life, widening the gap between themselves and the peasants. The urban attraction had increased under the reign of Reza Shah, when centralisation of power at Tehran made it virtually imperative for landowners to maintain establishments in the capital. Landowners visited their estates less and less. Often they leased their lands to middlemen. Moreover, during World War II many landowners in the northern provinces migrated to Tehran to avoid the Soviet occupying forces.[5]

As the years passed a small but increasing and essentially new middle class appeared in the towns and cities between the mass of peasants and the tiny landowning élite. The traditional middle class had included bazaar merchants and clerics, who tried to influence the government with limited success. The new middle class included intellectuals, often educated in the West, together with businessmen, bureaucrats and students at Tehran University. They shared with their traditional counterparts a growing nationalism and a desire to end foreign influence. They supported changes aimed at a higher standard of living and a more responsible government. But the two elements of the middle class, old and new, did not always co-operate. And city dwellers despised the peasants who, with their seemingly uncouth and boorish ways, appeared little better than beasts of the field. Peasants in turn distrusted all who lived in town and city.[6]

With the end of World War II, Iran's economic problems worsened, and this result almost imperceptibly became the basis for hope of an increased American presence. The shah wrote to President Harry S. Truman in September 1945, recounting Iran's wartime sacrifices when the nation provided a route for *matériel* bound for the Soviet Union. The Allies had taken over the Trans-Iranian Railway and also used the few roads for convoys headed north, restricting transport of civilian goods. Thousands of free-spending American soldiers had filled the country. During the war years prices doubled annually. The shah stressed the need for postwar assistance. The economy was not modern. Industry had received more attention than agriculture, but the result was overstaffed and inefficient state-run factories – tobacco, sugar, textiles, cement. They served as symbols of modernisation, and could not compete with postwar imports. Private enterprise consisted chiefly of workshops using traditional methods. Less than 1 per cent of the population (100 000 workers) engaged in manufacturing. The Tudeh (communist) party made inroads among industrial workers, not only in the capital but in the textile mills of Isfahan. At war's end the communist-controlled Central Council of Federated Trade Unions had engaged in a series of strikes.[7]

During the war villagers seeking work had continued to flock to the urban centres, especially Tehran. The capital had mushroomed. Wealthy Iranians built ever more impressive houses on the higher slopes, the poor and new arrivals lived in hovels and makeshift shelters below. Services lagged. The water supply flowed from the mountains in open ditches, and slum dwellers received water that had been used and reused. Typhus and cholera were endemic.

The most intractable economic problem of Iran in 1945, however, appeared to be agriculture. Most of the population still lived as farmers or wandering tribesmen, and did not own land. Farming practices had changed little since ancient times. Farmers received fixed, often inadequate, shares of the crops, and in most areas enjoyed no tenure and could be dispossessed at the ends of harvests. Rural debt was very large. Only in good years could the land support the farming population; bad years forced people to the cities.[8]

Such was the scene as World War II came to an end and throughout Europe, the Middle East, East Asia, almost everywhere in the world, the winds of change brought hosts of problems. Gusts were blowing in faraway Iran. As we now can see, the Truman administration hoped that Iran, together with many other distant countries, might somehow pass from confusion to organisation without its government dissolving into anarchy.

Historically, of course, the United States had had few ties not merely with Iran but with the entire Middle East. Until World War II the missionary efforts in Lebabon, Syria and Iran, extending back into the early years of the nineteenth century, had represented the only continuing American interest. Missionaries had made few converts from Islam. They did establish schools and colleges to train leaders and serve as catalysts for modernisation. American ships of war visited Eastern Mediterranean or Persian Gulf ports, during local epidemics or spates of violence that threatened handfuls of American citizens resident in such places. In the years immediately following World War I the State Department pressed the British government to share London's oil concession in Iraq, and in the 1930s American oil companies entered Bahrain, Kuwait and Saudi Arabia. During World War II Washington did become involved politically, especially in Saudi Arabia, where it tried to stabilise the regime. The meeting between President Franklin D. Roosevelt and King Abd al-Aziz Ibn Saud in the Great Bitter Lake at Suez in February 1945 symbolised this concern. After the war the Truman administration interfered in the one place in the Middle East that diplomats and regional experts had hoped it could avoid – Palestine. The United States after 1945 continued to regard the Middle East as a place to remain apart from – an interesting area, to be sure, the source of Judaism, Christianity and Islam. The Americans took more interest in Europe.[9]

To the British government after World War II the reluctance of the United States to deal with Middle Eastern problems made considerable sense, and not merely because it was traditional American policy in the area but because of the increasing Cold War, the need for American support of governments in Western Europe, to a lesser extent in East Asia, against the machinations of Soviet Russia. Britain was in straits – diplomatic and economic. The war had exhausted the country. While Americans rested secure in belief that their nation was the most powerful on earth, that the American century had begun, the British exuded no such confidence, for Britain's power had declined dramatically. Labourites and Conservatives alike worried. They had sacrificed for years, only to see no relief after the war. Neither Winston Churchill, prime minister until July 1945, nor his successor Clement Attlee, showed any desire to confront the Russians alone. If the Soviets refused to negotiate, Attlee once said, the British would have to make the best deal they could. Britain had to promote a closer relationship with the United States. It could not handle the Russians by itself.[10]

What did the Soviets really want of the Western democracies in those early postwar years? As for what Churchill during the war had described as a mystery wrapped in an enigma, its purposes and policies were difficult to predict or, once something was discernible, explain. Perhaps they were inexplicable, for the first postwar years marked the last period in the life of the dictator of the USSR, who was to die in 1953. According to the testimony of his successor, Nikita Khrushchev, Stalin's pathological distrust deepened during those years, and he took his suspicions, always part of his outlook on his countrymen if not on nationals of other countries, into excesses for which there could be no justification. The Soviet Union had suffered a German invasion that wrecked a third of the country, and for such reason alone there was need to acquire a buffer in Eastern Europe against some time in the long future when troops might march from the West. And yet the Soviets' intransigence elsewhere, over solutions to almost any of the problems that threatened to divide East from West, was difficult to understand. The Churchillian description seemed accurate.[11]

After the Potsdam Conference of July-August 1945 the Cold War slowly commenced. Favourable American opinion of the Soviets declined. President Truman had gained a good impression of Stalin at Potsdam. He came to see himself as the 'innocent idealist', the participant who had been fooled. The Greek-Turkish aid programme announced in March 1947, which became known as the Truman Doctrine, marked American acceptance of some responsibility in the Near East.

When the Americans took responsibility for Greece and Turkey in 1947, it appeared as if they were learning about the importance of the area, but the British were not so sure, for simultaneous American intervention in the Palestine issue drove the British that same year to give Palestine's solution to a committee of the United Nations, a move that led directly to creation of the State of Israel. Meanwhile, the uneasy situation developed in Iran, for which the Americans did not seem to possess much understanding.

As the observer looks back over events in Iran in the years after 1945 he has a feeling that with more wisdom, or at least with more knowledge of Iranian conditions and especially of Iranian tendencies, the United States government could have helped prevent the descent into chaos in 1978. Perhaps Iran could have used its oil revenues for the benefit of all Iranians. The advance of Iran from a primitive state, at the turn of the century, into the modernities of our own time, might have been far less risky.

Historians like to find turning points in the movements of the past into the present, and these points often are imaginary, emerging from theories or literary explanations. And yet in the case of Iran in the years since World War II, a turning point surely came during the early years after the war. In 1946 the Iranian army expelled the Russian-supported regimes in the northwest. From that time until the Musaddiq period of the early 1950s, Iran lay open to change. Here was a brief moment, as it now seems in retrospect, when the United States could have encouraged constitutional democracy.

2 The Growth of Royal Power

At the end of World War II the people of Iran possessed a government beset by problems. The collapse of the Pishevari regime at Tabriz and the Kurdish Republic of Mahabad re-established central government control. But it exacerbated domestic difficulties–relations between the restored areas and Tehran, between the tribes and the army. There also was a struggle for power between Prime Minister Qavam and the young shah. Over all, so far as knowledgeable Iranians were concerned, hung the menace of the shah. Two American ambassadors did their best to confront Iranian problems or at least to handle them in a way that was in the American national interest, considering other problems besetting the United States and its allies at that time. And all the while the young shah of Iran was playing his own game, enlarging his power, seeking to dominate the politics of his country– in some respects with the best intentions, attempting to forward the Iranian national interest, in other ways looking very narrowly, even egotistically, upon his country's confusions and trying to dominate them because he enjoyed domination.

The initial Iranian problems to be sure had been Azarbaijan and Kurdistan. When government troops re-entered Azarbaijan in December 1946, the populace had welcomed them, but the Imperial Iranian Army quickly dissipated this goodwill. By mid-1947 inhabitants viewed the army as an occupying force. To military men the loyalty of the Turkish-speaking Azarbaijanis and local tribal groups remained suspect. Landlords driven out during the war returned, often with military escort; charges of extortion and corruption by government and military leaders abounded; poor harvests and Tehran's failure to carry out reforms increased antagonism. American officials in Tabriz claimed that for many Azarbaijanis, Pishevari was becoming a hero. Consul Herbert D. Spivack reported that people there held the United States partly to blame for the lack of reforms because America, they said, had ensured withdrawal of the Soviets and the overthrow of Pishevari and should see to it that the province, the only territory in the world ever won back from communist control, became a model of economic, social and political reform.[1]

Flushed with success after the brief campaign, the army wanted to disarm the tribes and settle them. Tribal leaders rejected the plan. The tribes were armed and occupied strategic, virtually inaccessible areas. The major tribes, Kurds of the northwest, Bakhtiari of the centre, Qashqa'i of the south, had become stronger since Reza Shah's abdication. The Qashqa'i under skillful leadership of their khan, Muhammad Husain, had all but driven the army out of Fars province. Tribal leaders distrusted the new army chief of staff, General Ali Razmara, and Kurdish leaders despised the commander of forces in the north, General Muhammad Shahbakhti, who despite pleas for clemency had hanged the president of the short-lived Republic of Mahabad in Kurdistan, Qazi Muhammad, together with his brother and a cousin. Army orders to surrender weapons therefore failed— a few hundred ancient rifles appeared, newer weapons remained hidden. The military faced the threat of a tribal coalition, which the shah knew, from Iranian history, might endanger the dynasty.[2]

Prime Minister Qavam, a wily leader, was not slow to take advantage of the army's difficulties, and concluded an agreement with the powerful Qashqa'i and Bakhtiari groups, offering control of local and provincial offices in return for support in the Majlis. Thanks to Qavam's success in keeping the army out of politics in the country's southern districts, the tribes enjoyed their largest representation in the Majlis since the early years of the century.[3]

Brought back to reality, the army made an interesting about-face in the autumn of 1947, reducing demands and shrewdly issuing tea and sugar licenses to tribal subchiefs; this threatened the control of tribal leaders, thereby undermining Qavam. Encouraged by the shah and his chief of staff, the leaders hastily established a *modus vivendi* with the military. Tribal support for Qavam began to slacken not only because of these friendlier relations with the army but also because, fortuitously, Qavam's imperious manner alienated tribal leaders.[4]

This was the situation in Iran, tribal affairs straightening themselves, when the shah determined to rid himself of Qavam. His dislike of his prime minister had arisen from several sources, both important and trivial: Qavam's alliance with the tribes; the prime minister's opposition to an expanded, better-armed military, an issue always close to the monarch's heart; his independence of royal influence; his veiled threats to the dynasty, symbolised by refusal on one occasion to remove his hat in the shah's presence; and his denial of a royal request to return Reza Shah's remains to Iran. Qavam had no illusions about his standing with the court, and although he tried in small ways to allay royal opposition, such as purchasing with government funds a private plane for the shah's personal use, he refused to abandon his independence. In particular he would not push for an American arms credit. Like many of his countrymen he feared that the army was more likely to use the arms against Iranians than against a foreign foe.[5]

When the shah began his manoeuvres to get rid of Qavam he turned for support to the Americans, especially to Ambassador George Allen, to whom he confided some of his concerns about the prime minister.

Allen seemed a close friend of the shah. He was an interesting person, in many ways an ideal member of the foreign service. Tall, athletic, young – indeed at 43 the youngest American ambassador – he had served an apprenticeship in Cairo and Athens before assignment to Tehran. The two men often played tennis together. The shah telephoned Allen to relate details of meetings with the prime minister and other leaders.

The ambassador sought to view the situation realistically. He tried to dissuade the shah from undermining Qavam, whom the ambassador considered an able and effective leader. Admitting that Iranian politics seemed far from ideal, too filled with intrigue, he argued in dispatches to Washington that the Majlis represented shades of opinion and might move the country in a more democratic direction. He encouraged the shah to exercise his constitutional prerogatives, which were considerable; he resisted royal arguments favouring increased power for the throne. Allen refused to be drawn personally into elections for the Majlis in spring 1947. Rumours in the bazaar linked the ambassador to the prime minister's 'party', but he said that the elections were a domestic matter and no concern of foreign powers. When delegations visited the embassy and argued for a more direct American presence, the ambassador admonished them to stay clear of foreign entanglements. US policy was to support Iranian independence, he said, not to seek a special position.[6]

At this point the observer from the vantage of later years, cognisant of all the criticisms and irritabilities that have wracked American foreign policy because of its apparent inability to measure local sentiment in developing countries, especially sentiment that is not easily visible in the local capital, will find it instructive to note that there actually was considerable information about provincial movements. For all its alleged bureaucratic, unimaginative tendencies the Department of State did really know a great deal about the factionalism of politics in Iran. The department kept watch on tribal affairs in Iran through its resident expert, Gerald F. P. Dooher, a colourful character of a type more commonly encountered earlier in American history and perhaps more often in the British diplomatic service. Dooher had come to the United

States from Ireland in 1917 at the age of three, and went to Iran during World War II. He was vice-consul at Tabriz during the exciting days of 1946, an experience that suited his bent for adventure. He served as political attaché in Tehran almost continuously from 1947 to 1950. He spoke Persian and throughout his residence sought ties with tribal leaders, who on the whole were pro-American and attributed to the United States much, perhaps too much, influence over the central government. From his office in Tehran he sent a stream of detailed reports to Washington analysing tribal affairs and local politics. American ambassadors valued his experience. The shah and Razmara became so suspicious of him that when he took home leave in 1947 they asked the State Department not to send him back, and he had to wait several months before being allowed to return. He was invaluable to the department for he could take the measure of what might have seemed almost impenetrable situations. Among other activities, he provided detailed analysis of hostilities in Fars province between the Qashqa'i and the imperial army and in Kurdistan between the rebellious Mulla Mustafa Barzani and the military. He interpreted the frequent changes in relations between Qavam and the court, and provided profiles on each member of the Majlis.[7]

It was difficult, however, for Ambassador Allen to measure Iran's complexities, even with the help of Dooher. Although Qavam's 'Democrats' controlled the new Majlis, within six months of the election a Qavam lieutenant, Reza Hekmat, led half the tribal deputies into opposition. At one point during the argument over Qavam, opposition leaders including the liberal nationalist Dr Muhammad Musaddiq took sanctuary in the royal palace, alleging that the government had rigged the election, a claim that probably was true. Musaddiq argued that Qavam remained in power only with American help, which was not true.[8]

Gradually the prime minister's position weakened, because of a controversial issue that provided ammunition for his opponents. Prior to Russian withdrawal from Azarbaijan in May 1946, Qavam had promised a Soviet oil concession in northern Iran. No one knows whether this was a *quid pro quo*, but it seems likely. Afterward the Soviets pressed him to bring the concession bill before the Majlis. The Iranian public was apprehensive, for although it opposed the concession it also feared the Russians. Qavam tried to elicit an American statement hostile to the concession, hoping to deflect Russian ire. In early 1947 the most he could obtain was private assurances that Iran must be free to decide the issue.

Fixing upon any American policy toward Iran proved difficult in the midst of this confusion, and became more difficult when the Soviets began to manoeuvre. The Near East division in Washington shied from any commitment to Iran, the United States having just assumed increased responsibility in Turkey and Greece. By late summer 1947 these same officers, equating the proposed oil concession with Soviet domination of northern Iran, seemed prepared for Iran again to bring the Russian issue to the United Nations. Secretary of State George C. Marshall and Undersecretary of State Robert A. Lovett tempered the Near East division's enthusiasm and in messages to Allen and to the Iranian ambassador in Washington, Husain Ala, advised that the United States could not offer an opinion on the proposed Soviet oil concession. Marshall knew that Stalin and Foreign Secretary Ernest Bevin had considered the issue at the Moscow Conference of Foreign Ministers in March. The secretary of state had raised no objection then. To do so afterward was awkward.[9]

At this juncture Allen perhaps made an error, departing from his generally judicious demeanour. In Tehran he expressed his personal opposition, telling the shah and Qavam privately that he believed passage of the oil bill would be contrary to Iran's interests. He made known a position that seemed to support the local view, rather than his department's. It is of course a well-known diplomatic stance for an envoy to make a personal position known, for if that position then fails he, the envoy, can be disavowed, or can somehow give the impression that his outlook had clouded for some reason or other, and that the outlook of his country had remained the same. Allen in this case seems to have acted on his own.[10]

During this issue with the Soviets, the American government found it difficult to elicit advice from the British. Actually Attlee and Bevin feared another Soviet intervention in Iran. Reflecting this view, the British ambassador in Tehran, Sir John Le Rougetel, cautioned the Iranians against closing the door in Russia's face. Bevin was disturbed by what appeared to be attempts by his Foreign Office assistants to thwart the Russian concession. He had given a commitment to Stalin in March that Britain would encourage the Iranians and if occasion arose would urge Tehran to abide by its undertaking, with the understanding that Russia would not again intrude in Iran's internal affairs. But Foreign Office officials tried to convince him to modify this position in order, they said, to narrow the gap between London and Washington. The foreign secretary was in a quandary. He could not abandon the principle that a concession should be granted, for Attlee pressed him to stand by the March agreement. To ensure that there would be no sly attempts to defeat the concession Bevin ordered Le Rougetel to remain in London until the Majlis voted.[11]

The difference between the British and the Americans was interesting. In principle Americans opposed the Soviet oil concession, but Marshall too did not want to anger the Soviets. From April to September 1947 the secretary resisted advice to tell the Iranians exactly what the United States thought: that a concession would 'seriously endanger the future independence and integrity of Iran'. Apparent British acceptance of a concession had led to rumour in Washington and Tehran that London and Moscow had established a secret accord similar to the spheres of influence agreement of 1907 between Britain and Imperial Russia. Rumour also had it that the British had encouraged a Soviet concession as insurance against an attack on the position of their principal economic investment in Iran, the Anglo-Iranian Oil Company. The British accused Ambassador Allen of contributing to the rumour. This was true. Allen half believed that the British were trying to protect the AIOC, and allowed his staff to pass on these unconfirmed reports.[12]

What with a confusion of counsel from the Americans and the British, and increasing Soviet pressure, everything seemed to focus on the Majlis, and the result was more confusion. Allen had accepted a speaking engagement at the Iran-America Society in Tehran for 11 September, 1947, and decided to support Iran's right to decide issues regarding its mineral wealth without foreign interference. He did not clear his speech with Washington, believing it contained nothing new. In the charged atmosphere of Tehran the speech appeared as opposition to the concession, just what Secretary Marshall hoped to avoid. Allen's words loosened the tongues of the Majlis opposition, and a few weeks later the deputies rejected the proposed Soviet concession overwhelmingly.[13]

All the while the State Department tried to avoid any hint that American companies desired Iranian oil. Officials denied permission for a representative of an independent American oil company to travel to Iran, and two officials of Standard Oil were cautioned to talk only with AIOC officials at Abadan. According to the chief of the Division of Middle Eastern and Indian Affairs, Harold Minor, the United States had access to enough oil in the region, especially after a contract between Standard Oil and the AIOC guaranteed a huge quantity annually. Minor himself believed the United States could safely support an Iranian oil policy of no more concessions. He even suggested that the AIOC make oil available to the Soviets to lessen any feeling of discrimination. The British rejected his proposal, informing the State Department that the AIOC had no extra oil.[14]

The oil issue like the tribal problem earlier then played itself out in a way that weakened Qavam and strengthened the shah. Qavam had little interest in the proposed concession to the Soviets, but its rejection exposed him to attack from Moscow, which guaranteed, as the shah surely had hoped, that he would never have Soviet support for a return to power. Deputies distanced themselves from the prime minister. Majlis speaker Hekmat abandoned him, with expectation of royal support for the succession.

And so at last Qavam had to go. In many ways he was the most expert, and certainly the most independent, of all the post-1941 prime ministers before Musaddiq, and his departure marked a turning point in the young shah's reign. Although Qavam was a schemer, not very honest, and without democratic convictions, he rendered an invaluable service to his country in the difficult days of 1946–47, a service that the shah would not admit. Qavam represented the last serious attempt of the traditional landed élite, many with ties to the previous dynasty, to limit the power of the Pahlavis. He had held the highest state offices before Muhammad Reza was born. Little wonder the prime minister considered the shah an 'inexperienced boy'. And yet youth and cunning outmanoeuvred age and experience. After a stubborn attempt to rally support the prime minister offered his resignation. He considered the move only a tactical retreat. He was wrong, for this marked the end of his career.[15]

Majlis rejection of the oil concession had greater significance than the departure of the prime minister, for it signalled the start of a two-year Russian propaganda barrage aimed at Tehran. The Soviets could not create a communist government in Iran as they had done in Eastern Europe, because the Tudeh party was small and weak and no Soviet troops occupied Iranian territory after May 1946, but Iranians knew that Moscow would do all in its power to assure a pliant regime in Tehran. Beginning in late October 1947 the Soviets pursued a policy of threat, combining radio propaganda, attacks in Tudeh party newspapers, official notes, border violations, recall of diplomats, closing of consulates and massing of troops along the border. Warnings began in the autumn of 1947, when the fate of the oil concession hung in the balance, and increased in intensity after its rejection. At first they were directed against Qavam, but after his fall they focused on ties between the United States and Iran. The Russians claimed that the United States planned to use Iran as a base against the Soviet Union, that American military missions controlled Iran's army, that huge installations were under construction, that United States army officers were busily mapping the border regions. Russian soldiers or irregulars skirmished with Iranian border guards, killing or wounding them or taking hostages. Where the boundary was not fixed it bulged steadily southward. To Iranians and their American and British supporters it appeared that the Soviets were trying to establish a case for intervention. Washington could not dismiss the possibility. Ambassador Walter Bedell Smith in Moscow thought that because Iran was remote and held limited interest for the United States, it would be a testing ground of American determination.[16]

Ambassador Allen went back to Washington in mid-February 1948 to become assistant secretary of state for public affairs, and John Wiley replaced him, in a change that proved unfortunate. Secretary Marshall and his assistants in faraway Washington could not easily have anticipated the effect of Allen's replacement by Wiley.

Ambassador Allen's successor considered diplomacy a genteel art, to be conducted in leisurely fashion, and whenever possible in the language he had learned in his youth. The son of wealthy parents, he had been brought up in Paris. He had entered government service as an appointments clerk in the Paris embassy in 1915 at the age of 22. He had served in legations and embassies throughout the world. In Tehran he lived in the reflection of this considerable experience. He rarely visited the chancellery, preferring to conduct relations from his residence on the walled embassy grounds. There, attended by poodles and Chinese servants, he paced the fine carpets of his office while subordinates gathered around and tossed out ideas for his inspection. He admittedly encouraged a collegial atmosphere at these sessions, and did much to knit together his young staff. But there was something of the dilettante about Wiley, whatever the background he brought to his duties in Tehran. He represented a diplomatic era that had vanished even before World War I, not to mention World War II. It was also not, one might say, an American way of representation, whatever the manner in which he encouraged his young assistants. The grand manner, the apparent belief that through a sort of communal atmosphere solutions to the extraordinarily complicated politics in Tehran might be found, limited the effectiveness of his mission.

Wiley took an immediate diplomatic stance against the Soviet Union. He waged a battle against the Soviets from the moment of his arrival. He encouraged Iranian officials to stand against Soviet threats while he deluged the State Department with communications calling for denial of Soviet accusations.

Officials at the department were busy with American policy towards more important areas of the world, and could hardly give attention to him. The department confusedly continued the policy of Allen–which, to be sure, had been for the most part its own policy. A department spokesman had denied Soviet charges in February 1948 before Wiley arrived in Tehran. The department suggested that Iran should prepare copies of Soviet notes and its own replies in case of emergency. During the UN session in Paris in October 1948, Undersecretary Lovett suggested that the chief US delegate, Charles Bohlen, might raise the issue of Iranian-Soviet relations only if Bohlen believed East-West relations would not be adversely affected. Secretary Marshall counter-manded even this timid approach and declared he did not want the Iranian-Soviet issue discussed. Marshall had an eye on the Berlin blockade, which had commenced in June, but acted also in response to British accusations that Wiley was prodding the Iranians to bring their case before the Security Council and seek revision of Article 6 of the 1921 Irano-Soviet treaty of friendship. The British feared that if Iran renounced the treaty, or even Article 6, the Soviets might take alarm, interpreting the move as an anti-Soviet action, and that could 'set things off'. They worried that Iran might decide to take steps against the AIOC to appease the Soviets. They wanted to prevent any communication with the Security Council concerning Soviet relations with Iran. Although Wiley telegraphed Bohlen to urge that no matter what the Iranians decided, the United States should denounce Soviet charges, the ambassador's crusade made little progress. The chief of the State Department's newly organised Division of Greek, Turkish and Iranian Affairs, John D. Jernegan, who supported the ambassador, wrote that the high command of the department might not share Wiley's view. By the end of 1948, Wiley knew that Jernegan was right.[17]

Secretary of State Marshall had good reason to downplay Soviet-Iranian relations. He knew that President Truman had determined to limit defence spending to $15 billion annually; it was imperative, therefore, not to increase commitments abroad. Marshall concentrated on strengthening Western Europe, encouraging European rearmament; this would right the power imbalance and dissuade the Soviet Union from political subversion or military aggression. The secretary did not consider Soviet aggression imminent, even after the provocations in Berlin in the summer of 1948. But he wanted time for the European recovery programme, the Marshall Plan, to succeed, believing that a revived Europe would stand as the first line of defence in any war with the Soviets. He did not want to dilute America's efforts in Western Europe by being distracted in Iran or at any other point on the Soviet periphery. Should Ambassador Wiley's warnings prove correct–which he doubted–the United States could use its leverage in Europe to keep the Soviets out of Iran.[18]

Curiously the Iranians seemed less concerned than Wiley over the Russian threat. Although the shah and his new prime minister, Abdul Husain Hajhir, told Wiley they had ordered the Iranian delegation in Paris to present the Soviet-Iranian situation, nothing happened. Other issues stood higher, even on the agenda of Iran's leaders. The shah's concern now was the rapid expansion of Turkey's armed forces with American aid, and for some of his officials of most concern was the Iranian claim to the British-held island of Bahrain in the Persian Gulf, or the continuing dispute with Afghanistan over division of the waters of the Helmand River. Wiley warned Hajhir that Iran would have to concern itself more with its neighbour to the north. His words had little effect. After centuries of proximity Iranian leaders had learned to deal more easily with the Russians than had the new giant half a world away. At the same time they wanted to believe that the West would not allow the Soviets to swallow their country. Iranians including the shah were not consistently anti-Soviet. Indeed, they argued as persuasively about the British threat to their independence.[19]

Ambassador Wiley seemed tantalisingly close to success in 1949. When Dean Acheson replaced Marshall at the State Department in January 1949, Wiley's call for action received a more sympathetic hearing. Ambassador Ala of Iran, who had orchestrated his country's appeal to the Security Council in 1946, was anxious to inform the UN of the sad state of Iran's relations with the Soviet Union. Wiley returned to Washington for consultation in February, and travelled to New York to meet the chief of Iran's delegation at the United Nations, Nasrollah Entezam. Lengthy discussions produced the Ala-Entezam proposals: if the Soviet Union appeared to pose a threat to the Iranian government, the latter would inform the United Nations immediately and ask for action; as a matter of routine Tehran would communicate with the Security Council to keep it abreast of developments. The proposals made clear that the UN Charter 'supersedes any prior arrangement under which the Soviet government might have had the right to unilaterally introduce troops in Iran'. These proposals, which the State Department supported, were in a letter to the Iranian foreign minister. But then the department drew back. No sooner had Wiley departed for Tehran than it cabled a warning that Entezam's letter did not contain the oblique reference to the treaty of 1921 agreed on at New York. It considered this inference the heart of the Ala-Entezam proposals, and suggested that Wiley discuss the matter with the foreign minister. The Iranian government, it became clear, wanted to extract guarantees of Anglo-American economic and military support before making an appeal to the Security Council. The department cautioned the ambassador not to push the issue.[20]

Wiley gained a small victory when Secretary Acheson made a radio broadcast, denying Russian charges of anti-Soviet activity in Iran and reaffirming support for Tehran. That, however, was all he received. Wiley had likened Soviet methods in Iran to those used in 1939 prior to the 'Red Anschluss' in the Baltic States, which he had witnessed, warning that another Soviet intervention in Iran was not a question of 'if' but 'when'. The department concluded that the ambassador was too wound up over the Russian threat and might have a demoralising effect on the Iranian government if he persisted with his warnings of imminent Sovict intervention. Acheson wrote a personal letter to Wiley and told him to line up with department policy on Iran.[21]

This, then, was the course of American policy under two ambassadors, Allen and Wiley, with the procedure of the former envoy far more attuned to Iranian realities than was that of the latter. During the manoeuvreings of the Soviet Union the one ambassador seemed quite able to calculate local needs. The other, despite long diplomatic experience, could hardly measure them, and seemed almost to take refuge in espying in Iran a major theatre of East-West rivalries.

During the elaboration of American policy, which in the main was to keep the lid on Iranian troubles, a slow development began that eventually, many years later, led to the revolution. Neither of the American ambassadors seems to have discerned what was happening. Nor for that matter did many Iranians. This was a gradual change in the shah's understanding of his constitutional duties, his cunning if shortsighted view of his personal opportunities in his own country, willingness to equate his personal position with the future of Iran, desire to use allegedly interfering foreign countries as fulcrums to increase his personal power.

United States officials not merely observed this untoward development but inadvertently transformed their policy to fit this new circumstance. American officials in Tehran and Washington possessed only the best of goodwill for Iran. They were uncertain how to advance it, and here the wish became father to the thought. At first they expressed concern about royal power, but felt confident they could guide the shah and that he would not abuse his prerogatives. They believed that under his rule Iran could become a stable, strong nation, a bulwark against

Soviet expansion towards the Persian Gulf. As the Cold War progressed, concern over communism then overrode other considerations. Whether in Iran or Korea, Greece or India, the struggle to contain the Soviets shaped American decisions. The increasing power of the shah fitted into the emerging global pattern of containment.

In the years between the fall of Qavam in December 1947 and appointment of Musaddiq as prime minister in April 1951, the shah pursued a determined and largely successful policy of enhancing his power. Never again would he have to accept a candidate for prime minister who was independent of the court. He did not approach his goal in a straight line, as his father had done, and experienced frequent failure on the way. Allen had sought to bolster the shah's confidence, and both he and Wiley reported periods, usually after some setback, when indecision gripped the young man and he seemed ready to slip back into the obscurity and inertia of his first years. The shah, as Wiley observed, was at a formative stage; he knew he was not his father, but had not yet decided what he would be. He wanted to build power, for in the late 1940s many Iranians considered him weak, and that was a precarious situation for an Iranian monarch.[22]

The shah worked relentlessly to develop his position as the most important figure in the nation. He enforced his will on parliament, where he gave the impression that he was about to undertake serious reform. Actually his plans for reform were inchoate and had low priority. The shah practised 'negative resistance'; not sufficiently strong to rule alone, he spoiled attempts by anyone else. He or members of his family acted to break up opposition. He destabilised the fragile political system, and stalemated attempts to deal with Iran's economic disorders.[23]

The Americans seemed to have little control, and less understanding, of what was happening within Iran. Jernegan had written Ambassador Allen in 1947 of his surprise at the perceptible increase of the shah's influence. During the war the shah had been close to a nonentity, the secondary figure that the constitution had envisaged. Allen encouraged the shah to remain aloof from politics because he was not strong enough; he questioned whether a monarch should be meddling, and worried where the shah would stop. Nevertheless, the shah manoeuvred. The election to replace Qavam became a contest between a former prime minister and conservative landowner, Ibrahim Hakimi, and Musaddiq who had led the struggle against oil concessions during the war. The shah ordered the president of the Majlis, Hekmat, to cast the tie-breaking vote in favour of the predictable Hakimi. All factions recognised that Hakimi's government could only maintain itself for a short period, and in June 1948 it fell. Royal favour passed to a former finance minister, Abdul Husain Hajhir, acknowledgedly pro-British, more importantly a protégé of the shah's twin sister, Princess Ashraf.[24]

Not always did the shah manage affairs deftly, and part of his trouble came from Ashraf. She was the most politically active member of the royal family, after her brother, but not skillful in intrigue–her interventions seldom remained anonymous. Even though she appears always to have had the interest of her brother foremost, she caused problems for him. The shah sometimes must have wished that Ashraf would take up residence in Paris, London, perhaps even New York. The queen mother opposed her ventures, and when she suggested that Ashraf go abroad for a vacation there was concern that these two strong women would divide the court. The premier wife of Reza Shah, Queen Nimtaj, was alert to attempts from any quarter to infringe royal prerogatives. Observers reported that she never tired of lecturing the shah to be strong like his father. Court politicians wondered how the monarch would govern if he could not control the women in his own family.[25]

Violent demonstrations by followers of Ayatollah Qasim Kashani broke out when Hajhir's nomination was announced in parliament. A political mulla who would come into his own for a short while under Musaddiq in 1951–52, Kashani was an Anglophobe, having been forced into exile by the British during the war. He described Hajhir as a British lackey. He sought American support, offering himself as a candidate. He would rid Iran of its problems, he told Wiley, by instituting a government based on Islamic law. After a hiatus of several weeks Hajhir received a vote of confidence, but only after the rejected Qavam had bowed to a royal request for support, with tacit understanding that his turn again would follow.[26]

The shah then decided to attend the Olympic games in England, with a view towards achieving some diplomatic success that might result perhaps in military or economic assistance. The proposed visit created much discussion. Times were not propitious. The British assured the Americans that London had extended the invitation in response to the Iranian monarch's request, and agreed to keep the State Department informed. Concerned at the thought of the shah piloting his own plane through busy European skies, the British provided transport. They knew also the favourable impression such a courtesy would make on Iranians. The Tehran press accused the British of trying to influence Iranian internal affairs, while members of the royal family and politicians argued that the shah should not leave the country when the weak Hajhir government required support. Qavam, General Razmara and the queen mother each approached Ambassador Wiley, asking him to use his influence, but once the shah made a decision he was inflexible. He turned aside all entreaties.[27]

The ensuing visit strengthened the shah's position both in London and in Tehran. He surprised British military men with the extent and soundness of his technical knowledge and strategic sense. While at Buckingham Palace he suggested an alliance between Britain and Iran. Admittedly King George VI dropped the subject, but the shah had broached it. He returned to Tehran after a several-week holiday in France and Switzerland, and, impressed by what he had seen, appealed to members of parliament to be more hard-working and patriotic and again called for social and economic reform.[28]

The shah's ambition increased with success. In 1945-46 the need for action against Pishevari in Azarbaijan and tribal difficulties there and elsewhere had awakened his desire for power. By discharging Qavam he had increased the court's influence over the weak cabinets of his successors. The great powers were playing out their rivalries elsewhere, the shah began to understand. He may have been well meaning, caught up with reform and economic development, desirous of bettering conditions for his people. He surely despised the chronic disorder, instability and corruption in his country. But he rarely considered the contribution he and his family made to such conditions. It is impossible to determine precisely the combination of motives that moved him, but his actions always blended a concern for his people with a desire to enhance his power, the impulses to benevolence and despotism reinforcing each other. He convinced himself that the situation would improve after he had gained control over the Majlis. Early in 1948 he informed the British and American ambassadors of a plan to dissolve parliament and call a constitutional convention.

What to do about the monarch's desire to dominate the Majlis? Washington opposed the scheme, arguing that the shah's powers, if wisely used, were adequate without taking the grave step of altering the constitution. The shah had no power to dissolve the Majlis. Any attempt would cause a reaction throughout the country. Jernegan agreed with Allen, now in Washington, that the Majlis was an important institution. Among other advantages it could deflect Soviet anger. The notoriously independent Majlis provided an excuse for inaction. Jernegan argued that the evils of the political system might give way to worse if the shah tinkered with the constitution. The State Department feared that the shah's attempt would defeat a proposed seven-year economic development plan that required Majlis approval. The British Foreign Office worried that public agitation would affect the Anglo-Iranian Oil Company's negotiation for a new contract.[29]

The shah seemed determined to go ahead. He assured the two Western governments that he had consulted all leading figures except Qavam, who was out of the country and whose influence he thought was in any case nil, and the mercurial Musaddiq who seemed to the shah not to be in full control of his senses. He threatened to abdicate. Wiley sought to argue him out of this position, pointing out how dangerous it would be if the threat became public knowledge. He observed privately that the shah was in one of his bouts of depression, when the duties of state seemed to overwhelm him. The ambassador reported that the shah, though promising as a ruler, was not yet mature.[30]

As months passed, the British became more conciliatory. By early 1949, Ambassador Le Rougetel was agreeing with the shah that the Majlis was ineffectual and that the government would remain paralysed without an increase in royal power. This attitude may have reflected frustration with the oil talks then underway between Iran and the Anglo-Iranian Oil Company.[31]

Providence, a recurring element in the shah's reign, now took a hand in increasing his personal power. At Tehran University on 4 February, 1949, an attempt on his life by a fanatical religious group, the fidayan-i Islam, resulted in a wave of pro-shah sentiment. Opposition leaders realised how narrowly the monarch had escaped. The shah received a superficial face wound. Police and soldiers fatally mauled his would-be assassin.[32]

Taking quick advantage the shah asked the Majlis to summon a constitutional convention, and proposed that he should have power to dissolve parliament and provide for a senate, a body envisaged in the 1906 constitution but never established. Under British and American urging he abandoned his plan to seek even more power, a veto over legislation together with authority to convene future conventions.[33]

At this point the seven-year plan for economic development came before the Majlis, and its passage was an obvious victory for the shah who supported it.

Ten days after the assassination attempt the Majlis acceded to the shah's request for a constitutional convention. The constitutional amendments thereupon became a reality. The ease with which the shah gained his objectives surprised both the Americans and British. According to the amendments the monarch would appoint half the members of the new senate, which would become a locus of royal power.

The shah already exercised the right to appoint the minister of war and court minister, the former with a seat in the cabinet; as commander-in-chief of the army he held not only military power but could use the army as an instrument for influencing elections in areas under its control. Since 1947 he had possessed direct control over the office of chief of staff. He presided over weekly cabinet meetings at which individuals were too awestruck or confused to take a forceful line. Once a month he met with Majlis deputies.[34]

The shah carefully did his best to play down his constitutional victory. He told Wiley he had sought only half as much power as that exercised by the king of Sweden. In a conversation in late December 1948 a well-known and outspoken deputy, Abbas Iskandari, had warned the American chargé, James Somerville, that the shah was a schizophrenic – half the son of Reza Shah and half democrat. According to Iskandari, the son of Reza Shah was in the ascendancy. His advice meant little to the Americans. Ambassador Wiley had spent a third of a century taking the pulses of diplomatic situations, and spoke French to the shah, and believed he could guide the monarch into respecting what the American represented as the policy of the United States. In Washington, Jernegan and Assistant Secretary Allen watched developments with a feeling for their secondary, even tertiary, importance as compared with the Berlin blockade and the developing negotiations in 1949 for the North Atlantic Treaty Organisation.[35]

The immediate postwar years thus passed in what for the United States was a policy of neglect towards Iran. Reluctant to commit its resources outside Western Europe, the United States instead contributed confusing advice. Washington wished to believe that the British, with a century of experience in the region, would prevent affairs from turning into a crisis. As Wiley summed it up, 'regardless of what has happened elsewhere, in Iran the British lion is still impressively Metro-Goldwyn-Mayer'. Admiring the shah's increasing control of factions, Americans duly accorded the monarch a new importance; he represented, they believed, one of the few reliable Iranian institutions. He symbolised stability. No one asked how he had increased his power, or guessed the long-term result. Mention of democracy disappeared from dispatches. Tightening lines of the Cold War and the strategic location of Iran reinforced the need to strengthen this link in the chain surrounding the Soviet Union.[36]

3 Military Aid

One of the most telling manifestations of American confusion in dealing with Iran after World War II lay in the handling of military aid. First the confusion appeared in management of two American military missions. Then it arose over questions of *matériel*.

At Iran's request Washington had set up two military missions during the war. Iran had asked for them in 1942 to balance the British and Russian presence and hasten military reorganisation. They remained after 1945 because the Iranian government wanted them and because Washington worried about what would replace them. But neither diplomats nor the military in Washington understood the predicament of the missions. The officers in charge of the missions were quickly drawn into the maelstrom of Iran's domestic politics where they were manipulated to advance Iranian factional interests. Moreover, there were the continuing suspicions of Iranian xenophobia – the feeling of almost all Iranians that the great powers were always pursuing their own interests.

Of the two missions, the United States Mission to the Iranian Gendarmerie (GENMISH) was by far more important than the US Mission to the Iranian Army (ARMISH). Under Article 20 of the agreement between Iran and the United States in 1943, the head of GENMISH exercised executive control over this internal security force of 25 000 men. He reported directly to the minister of the interior in Tehran.

Brigadier General H. Norman Schwarzkopf, head of GENMISH and the gendarmerie, was a man of considerable talent. He had organised the New Jersey state police in the 1920s and served as its superintendent for 15 years, and had headed the investigation into the Lindbergh kidnapping case in 1932, obtaining national and international attention. Later a disagreement with the governor resulted in loss of his position. Having served in France during World War I, he happily re-entered the army in 1941, and with his police experience he seemed qualified for the post in Tehran to which President Roosevelt appointed him. A hard-working, intelligent, dynamic officer, he virtually ruled the large Iranian force of internal security police. He did much to improve its training, discipline and efficiency. The gendarmerie took part in the 'reconquest' of Azarbaijan in December 1946, participated in government disputes with the tribes and sought to control smuggling.[1]

Did Schwarzkopf meddle in Iranian politics? One really cannot be certain. What was sure was the size and quality of his force, and its importance therefore in Iran. Surely anything that he did with the gendarmerie was likely to have domestic implications. Sooner or later his force was almost bound to become an object of attention by the highest officials, who would desire his downfall for reasons they would credit to his own behaviour.

Neither the general nor his Washington superiors recognised the strength of his opposition within Iran. The shah and the Iranian army's chief of staff, General Razmara, wanted to unite the security force with the Iranian army. Prime Minister Qavam, who doubled as minister of the interior, hoped to make the gendarmerie his personal instrument. The shah and his able and ambitious military chief had cause for concern for this reason alone, especially when relations between the prime minister and the court-army circle deteriorated in late 1946. Collapse of the Soviet-backed Pishevari regime in Azarbaijan in December 1946 removed the need for unity at Tehran and to some politically sensitive Iranians it became clear that the gendarmerie was going to get very close attention from leading figures in the capital. To make matters worse, Schwarzkopf cultivated friendship not only with Qavam but with deputies in the parliament who opposed the shah and Razmara.[2]

The American general did not foresee any move to oust him. Early in 1947 he confidently wrote that by the end of 1948, when the gendarmerie agreement would expire, he expected to have the force sufficiently organised to make American command unnecessary.[3]

Schwarzkopf's political insensitivity was extraordinary. Having arrived in Iran at the beginning of the reign, when the monarchy was at its nadir, he did not understand the increasing power of the shah. In 1943 he had virtually challenged the shah and army leaders, insisting on the gendarmerie's independence in matters of pay, promotion and discipline. With support of Qavam he won, but acquired enemies. Later he incautiously spoke against what he thought were moves towards despotic government. During an audience with the shah he insisted on the need to increase the gendarmerie to 40 000 men, and when the monarch expressed fear that the force would become the private army of the prime minister, he replied airily that the nation required such a force because his men had to do much of the work of the army in Azarbaijan and among the tribes.[4]

In retrospect one looks back upon General Schwarzkopf's work in Iran with a mixed feeling of admiration and consternation. The general found himself in a country that was passing suddenly from the nineteenth century into the latter half of the twentieth, that was about to develop economically and militarily in headless fashion. It was also an intensely political time. Anything he did was scanned and examined and analysed locally as if he, the general, were a politician. And that may have been his almost impossible dilemma – to be effective, he needed to consider politics. Given his background, his American belief in separation of civil and military affairs, he found such a role virtually impossible.

The shah and chief of staff waited patiently for the proper time to put their hands on the gendarmerie, and in January 1948, when Qavam had departed and the Majlis showed a willingness to accept an American arms credit and Ambassador Allen was on the point of departure, they acted. An intimate of Razmara, Major General Muhammad Sadiq Kupal, appeared at gendarmerie headquarters, announced himself as the new ranking Iranian officer, and began issuing orders. The American general beheld his authority vanishing.

What was the United States to do? When the ambassador asked for a meeting with the new prime minister, Hakimi, and argued that Kupal's action violated the GENMISH agreement, the Iranian assured him blandly that everything was all right. Allen consulted the shah, who admitted that the Iranian government did want to eliminate Article 20 of the agreement. The shah was talking about a change in an international agreement as if he were only asking for an emendation. The ambassador explained that the United States was prepared to alter it and even withdraw the military mission, but said that as long as the agreement was in force, both sides must abide by it. Disconcerted, he might have cabled Washington and obtained a virtual ultimatum, but he had been embarrassed by Schwarzkopf's control over the gendarmerie and welcomed the change, although hardly the method of effecting it. Schwarzkopf's Iranian friends advised patience, for they were optimistic that he would regain control of the gendarmerie. The general boasted to the new ambassador, Wiley, that he had 88 votes in the Majlis. Yet General Kupal continued to ignore him. The embassy tried to work out a formula to give the Iranians what they wanted while preserving a modicum of American prestige. One plan called for temporary reinstatement of Schwarzkopf, followed by reassignment to an important post in Europe, and a United States recommendation for revision of the mission agreement giving GENMISH an advisory status. And yet the mere communication of this proposal to Iranian officials was a confession of willingness to let the Iranian action stand.[5]

The failure of local American officialdom to recognise the situation for what it was–a direct challenge to American authority–may have been complicated by a rivalry between Schwarzkopf and the head of ARMISH, Major General Robert W. Grow. During the crisis over command of the gendarmerie, the ambassador, together with Schwarz-kopf and Grow, held a series of what they described as strategy meetings. But army professionals–Grow was Regular Army–tended to look down on officers like Schwarzkopf whose background was in police work and the National Guard. Grow had led an armoured division in Normandy. He had welcomed his assignment to Iran. He then had discovered that Schwarzkopf, who had spent the war in Iran, was far more familiar with local conditions. And as head of ARMISH, Grow commanded only a handful of men, while Schwarzkopf as head of GENMISH controlled a large force.

What is clear is that Grow during the meetings with Allen and Schwarzkopf considered ARMISH the more important of the two missions–indeed, he favoured elimination of GENMISH. The ambas-sador agreed, perhaps realising that the shah and Razmara would never again let the gendarmerie be independent anyway. Besides, Wiley thought its officers corrupt. Schwarzkopf, lulled by reassurances from his connections in the Majlis, argued that the government consisted of more than the shah and chief of staff. The embassy meetings ended in stalemate.[6]

Throughout the spring and early summer in 1948 the issue dragged on, with confusion within the embassy, resolution within the Iranian government. Schwarzkopf found himself almost alone in his opposition to the changing power relations within Iran. In a report to his Washington superiors he told how he had opposed the idea that the only result that mattered was a strong government in Iran: 'I said that there is no justification for departure from the U.S. principles of supporting democracy in independent small nations, nor acquiescence in Razmara becoming the Mussolini of Iran . . . the shah and Razmara are not the government as such, and I recommended . . . that the U.S. express strong disapproval of the conversion of Iran into a police state'. Many Iranians agreed, fearing a resurgence of autocratic power absent since the abdication of Reza Shah in 1941, and accused the court and Razmara of attempting a dictatorship. Newspapers attacked the decision to merge the two forces.[7]

Some opposition leaders seized on the gendarmerie issue to express scepticism about foreign advisers. There had been disappointments over the years, most recently during World War II with the Millspaugh Mission, led by the American financial expert Arthur Millspaugh who had sought to reorganise Iranian fiscal practices. Iranians believed that foreign experts changed once they arrived in Iran, forgetting who they worked for, and also often proved incompetent. Summing up a widely held belief, Musaddiq denounced the whole idea of advisers and missions, declaring in the Majlis that Iran had got on well for centuries without foreign assistance.[8]

Schwarzkopf in June 1948 received orders to leave for Germany. In Washington, US Army leaders had sought the advice of Allen, who had been reassigned to Washington, and who explained that he favoured the merger of GENMISH and ARMISH but feared it would support the court-army circle; hence the contract should be renegotiated to retain both missions and give GENMISH an advisory role. Allen said Schwarzkopf had been in Iran too long.[9]

Schwarzkopf left Iran without ceremony. Razmara had promised a reception. He never gave it, nor did he attend other farewells. The shah received the general in a brief audience but did not comply with a request for a photograph (Grow long since had received one). Schwarzkopf never received the Iranian honorary order for which he had been recommended. At the airport farewell no representative of the court, army or foreign ministry appeared, nor even an honor guard from the gendarmerie. Allen's successor, Wiley, seemed curiously detached from the situation, commenting loosely to the State Department that 'the General did not leave in a golden chariot'.[10]

In such manner the Schwarzkopf mission closed. The general had done well by the Iranian assignment, even if his political instincts had not been as well developed as his military talents. One adds hastily that no American officer could have plumbed the politics of Iran in the late 1940s. Grow was no supporter of Schwarzkopf, but he understood the latter's predicament, writing in his diary on 5 May, 1948 that 'Schwarzkopf gave me a long history of his fight with Razmara convincing me that Schwarzkopf has been too deep in Iranian politics but also that, as CO of the gendarmerie he could not keep out of politics'. As for the latter's trouble with Grow, the Pentagon should have settled it. Neither the State Department nor the Defense Department had served American interests well.[11]

The issue plagued United States-Iranian relations for another year. Iran refused to recognise Schwarzkopf's successor, Colonel James R. Pierce, who arrived with his status undetermined. Eventually the two governments agreed that the head of GENMISH should serve only as an adviser and transmit recommendations through the commander of the gendarmerie, not directly to the minister of the interior as before.

Razmara and the shah hence had achieved their goal. The gendarmerie in mid-1949 became part of the army in an arrangement announced as a one-year trial. The army's chief of staff took the opportunity to dismiss many of its members. But GENMISH did not experience a total eclipse, for the shah, suspicious perhaps of Razmara, allowed 5000 gendarmes to remain independent of the army, and promised to augment the force. GENMISH, which Razmara had hoped to eliminate, continued into the 1950s as a tiny but perhaps useful mission of 15 Americans. General Schwarzkopf served several years in Europe before his retirement, pondering no doubt the vicissitude that had led him there.[12]

Another postscript to Schwarzkopf's departure is worth relating. Success with GENMISH emboldened the shah to try to modify the ARMISH contract. Although in the autumn of 1947 the Iranians told Grow and members of the embassy that they wished to renew the contract as it stood, by the spring of 1948 no one doubted that the government expected change. The shah had conceived a grandiose plan to procure arms and instructors in Britain, and chafed under the ARMISH requirement of United States approval. Grow had engaged in talks with the Iranians, keeping the ambassador informed. Washington ordered Grow to cease his efforts, so that it could negotiate with the Iranian military purchasing mission then in the American capital. Negotiators thereupon took a much firmer line than with the GEN-MISH contract, believing ARMISH should be strengthened, not weakened.[13]

The American sticking point on the ARMISH contract proved to be Article 24, that a third country could not send military advisers to Iran without approval of the United States. This article ensured that Iranians would use American advisers and provided an excuse for inaction should other governments, Britain or the Soviet Union, press Iran to accept advisers. The Pentagon supported by the State Department refused to modify the article that permitted no foreign competition with the American mission. ARMISH had already had one bad experience with a British air mission at Tehran, a relic of the war years, whose members seldom had missed an opportunity to criticise American advisers. Actually, there was much truth in the British observations. The US military, faced with declining manpower, had had difficulty supplying personnel to its missions around the world. At the same time that the British military attaché in Tehran was reporting that members of ARMISH were 'not up to the mark', an American general in East Asia was coming to the same conclusion; Lieutenant General John R. Hodge, commander in Korea, admitted that the turnover of personnel was too rapid, that new mission members were young and inexperienced and came with little preparation for the 'bitter facts of life'. Earlier Lieutenant General Albert C. Wedemeyer had received similar complaints about the advisory group in China. Perhaps such problems were endemic. And yet it was necessary to protect the mission in Tehran from end runs by other nations.[14]

The ARMISH contract came to a decision in October 1948 and the Iranians backed down. At a meeting attended by the shah, Razmara, Minister of War Amir Ahmadi and Wiley, the ambassador expressed his country's determination to maintain Article 24 or, if Iran preferred, withdraw the advisers and replace them with 'clerks in uniform', who would spend time with balance sheets accounting for every penny of assistance. The thought horrified Ahmadi, who according to Wiley was one of the richest men in Tehran, 'showing what a thrifty soldier could do with an army salary'. Razmara agreed that Iran would renew the contract as it stood, through a simple exchange of notes rather than a Majlis vote. Razmara had made an important concession, for he was an ardent nationalist and Article 24 limited Iranian sovereignty.[15]

The United States government nonetheless lost in one respect. The Iranian military continued to make decisions without consultation, which put in question the whole idea of advisers. Razmara had frowned on allowing foreigners any influence. Grow, who understandably enjoyed good relations with the shah and the general, had made several approaches to the monarch, seeking to improve the Iranian army. He informed the shah that the single most important defect was corruption among higher officers and that the army's justice and inspection departments failed to carry out their duties. Junior officers of integrity did not advance, he said, because they refused to play the game. The shah had agreed and said he was at last in a position to make changes and would do so. He encouraged the general to come to him whenever he felt a situation demanded attention. But he did not act on Grow's advice, as the general reported to Washington. The shah gloried in thoughts of a big, well-equipped army and resented the general's constant reference to cost.[16]

The real weakness of the army remained its top command, for the shah was unwilling to dismiss corrupt and inefficient generals. Grow saw little hope for improvement.[17]

Behind all the negotiating, and its failure to reform the Iranian army, lay a fundamental fact, namely, that Washington did not consider Iran important. Perhaps the shah knew what the Americans only hinted at, that Iran would remain a minor military consideration in Washington regardless of the missions. Grow had complained in mid-1948 that no one from the Plans and Operations Division had visited Iran in two years. Grow read about the delegations to Greece, China and Korea, symbolising commitment. Athens welcomed missions headed by General Marshall, Secretary of the Army Kenneth Royall and the army's chief of intelligence, Major General Stephen Chamberlain. Marshall visited China, and Wedemeyer went to China and Korea; Secretary of the Navy James V. Forrestal and Secretary of War Robert Patterson visited East Asia. Iran seemed out of the mainstream.[18]

After Schwarzkopf's departure, Grow had only a few months to enjoy Tehran and then he too left. Schwarzkopf's going had pleased him and he informed the Plans and Operations Division of decided improvement in relations between the missions, relief on all sides, a new spirit of co-operation. Alas, the army assigned him to Fort Devens, Massachusetts, 'politely shelving him' according to the cynical Ambassador Wiley. The general, it appeared, had contributed to his own discomfiture. The army privately had accused him of disclosing highly classified information concerning policy in the Persian Gulf area to military and civil personages in Iran, of advising Iranians on political reform and of lacking finesse in dealing with Iranians. Wiley was upset by the thought that his own reports had been indirectly responsible for the general's removal, but the State Department assured him that the army had decided on the basis of Grow's reports. His successor, Major General Vernon Evans, arrived in Tehran in September 1948, preceded by what the ambassador described as 'the big Hollywood buildup', making him 'the greatest military personage since the late Napoleon Bonaparte'.[19]

Iranian leaders had played on differences between Schwarzkopf and Grow to achieve their national and personal goals. The shah, Chief of Staff Razmara, Minister of War Ahmadi rarely missed an opportunity to complain to Grow of Schwarzkopf's involvement in Iranian politics, of his attacks on Grow and ARMISH, of his attempts to obtain the larger share of American *matériel* for the gendarmerie. They made clear their preference for a single mission headed by Grow. The widening gulf between the two American officers contributed substantially to Schwarzkopf's recall.[20]

The departures of Schwarzkopf and Grow marked a change in American relationships in Tehran. General Evans and Colonel Pierce concentrated on military affairs; competition between the missions abated. Diplomacy became the preserve of the ambassador. All the while the shah continued to dream of a great military future for himself and his country. While his behaviour–tinkering with mission contracts, manoeuvring against American generals–was causing messages to pass between Tehran and Washington, the monarch was attempting to obtain more sophisticated weapons for a larger Iranian army. He expected the weapons to come from the United States.

In the tortuous negotiations for weapons in Washington there was insufficient frankness by the Americans, who would not admit to the modest plans they harboured for the Iranian military. In meetings and reports they seldom put cards on the table. This lack of candour was uncharacteristic, for Americans tend to assume that frankness will solve problems. Caution was due to fear of angering the shah and sending him to other sources for arms. Muhammad Reza Pahlavi was stubborn. Once he set his mind on an objective he abandoned flexibility.

Iran's military did present a sad spectacle at the end of World War II: low morale, poor discipline, inadequate *matériel*. Tribal opponents possessed better small arms. Faced with what everyone assumed would be a lengthy confrontation with the Pishevari government in Tabriz, Qavam in 1946 had asked the United States for arms. The State Department wrote supportively to the War Department, where the army's chief of staff, General Dwight D. Eisenhower, agreed that the issue was sufficiently important to declare surplus whatever *matériel* Iran required, regardless of the effect on reserve and National Guard programmes. The army eventually informed the State Department that it could make available a substantial portion of the items Iran requested. The State Department offered $25 million in credits.[21]

Events in Iran for a while put the whole issue in doubt. While the request had been moving through Washington channels, the Iranians took steps to feel out resistance on the borders of Azarbaijan, and pushed on to Tabriz.

With the provinces back in the fold, Qavam became less anxious for an arms agreement that would strengthen his army opponents. He knew also that it would antagonise the Soviets. And many Iranians wanted their country to maintain a neutral course. Deputies also recalled the strong-arm tactics of Reza Shah and shuddered at the thought of dictatorial rule. Critics hence argued that weapons from the United States would do little to enhance security from neighbours while making it easier for the military to intimidate domestic opposition. Qavam would have given up the arms credit if he had not feared the shah and the army. His course was to delay, in the time-honoured Iranian style of which he was a master, dragging out the issue, hoping it would go away.[22]

Qavam almost succeeded in his effort to avoid arms aid. American aid to Greece and Turkey under the Truman Doctrine in March 1947 helped his situation, for how could the Iranian government be asked to purchase arms when neighbours, no more threatened, received them as a gift?

At that juncture the shah raised the question of Turkey. He possessed a fine sense of the wrongs suffered by Iran, and associated many of them with Turkey. He thought it intolerable that Iran should have to pay for what he now described as obsolete weapons. As he also told Allen, aid to Greece and Turkey would prove unsound unless the United States included Iran, because the Soviets could turn the Turkish flank in Azarbaijan. In fact the United States might encourage such a move by strengthening Turkey and Greece. Offering this geopolitical wisdom, he could not understand why Iran, which had suffered so much during World War II, received less aid than Turkey, which had remained neutral and amassed a great treasure. In encounters with the Americans the shah displayed a profound distrust and fear of Turkey. He seemed more concerned over Turkey than over Russia. During this brouhaha Soviet propaganda scored a hit when Moscow claimed that the Americans in their newfound love for Turkey had concluded a secret agreement allowing the Turks to annex Turkish-speaking Azarbaijan. The United States denied the accusation, to little avail. Roots of Turkophobia were deep, for any Iranian leader could recall the centuries of conflict with the Ottomans, Turkish invasion of western Iran during World War I, the disaffection of Azarbaijan, and the continuing competition between Ataturk and Reza Shah in the 1930s. Perhaps this last weighed heavily on the shah. Nothing short of equal military assistance would have put his suspicions to rest.[23]

During this contention American officialdom in Tehran foolishly supported the shah. Grow argued that the Majlis would reject any arms credit and the United States should make a $50 million grant. The State Department recommended uncertainly that the army bring Grow back, to apprise him of its views and hear his arguments. Grow expected to see the Joint Chiefs and the president but, except for a brief meeting with Secretary Marshall, had to settle for his usual contacts who explained that the United States could not extend substantial military aid without an act of Congress, which was unlikely. At first Ambassador Allen opposed a grant, fearing it would exacerbate internal problems and suggest that the United States had forced weapons on Iran, but then he changed his mind. By the time of his departure from Tehran, he was encouraging the State Department to recognise Iran's commitment to the West.[24]

The State Department took every opportunity to explain its policy.

Loy Henderson, chief of the Office of Near East and African Affairs, told the Iranian purchasing commission that an arms grant was impossible because Iran had enough money from oil.[25]

The issue moved back and forth. Junketing congressmen assured the shah that they would vote for increased funds if the Truman administration recommended them. In early February 1948 the House Foreign Affairs Subcommittee on the Near East called for increased aid.[26]

It then appeared that the Iranian government would not present the proposed $25 million arms credit to the Majlis. Allen had encouraged Qavam to show a desire for reconciliation with the shah by presenting the legislation. Grow had urged the prime minister to take up the issue, but the Soviets kept up a propaganda barrage, claiming Iran an American puppet. Many Iranians did not want the credit. Not one newspaper came out unequivocally in support.[27]

Qavam's successor Hakimi now compromised. He suggested a credit of $10 million, arguing that the nation had enough oil money to purchase additional arms. He presented legislation for a reduced credit, on 17 February 1948, the day Allen departed. The Majlis voted 79 to 6 to accept.

The scene momentarily shifted to London, where in the visit of August 1948, mentioned earlier, the shah attempted to buy Vampire jets. It was doubtful that the British government could or would supply these planes or that Iranians could service or use them, but a penchant for the newest military hardware guided his thinking. Ambassador Wiley believed the British shared responsibility for the royal enthusiasm, for during the visit, he claimed, London officials did nothing to discourage the shah, despite general agreement that Iran had all the equipment its forces could use and London's promise to Washington to inform the shah of this evaluation.[28]

In Washington another development equally raised questions. An Iranian purchasing commission had been waiting ten months to conclude an agreement, but Major General William H. Arnold of the Plans and Operations Division now informed the State Department that much of the equipment available a year before had been committed, and the Iranians would have to take what was left. Secretary Royall also came under increasing pressure to withdraw an earlier offer to pay for repairing, crating and shipping equipment to Iran. The State Department had to go back to Congress for a loan to cover $16 million in handling charges.[29]

Involved in the above development was the issue of declining congressional appropriations for the US armed services. President Truman had set an $11 billion ceiling and although he raised it to $15 billion, the budget was barely adequate even then. Troops relied on surplus stocks. The army also added 135 000 men in 1949. Secretary of Defense Forrestal was at his wits' end trying to maintain unity among the services and fend off attacks from Congress and the Bureau of the Budget.

Warned that much equipment was no longer surplus, the Budget Bureau refused to advise the president to release the Iranian arms credit. Undersecretary of State Lovett responded with vehemence, arguing that Americans must honour a commitment. The director of the budget retreated. Along with many non-combat items the Iranians would receive fighter planes, light tanks, mortars and machine guns. The first shipment arrived at Bandar Shahpur in the Persian Gulf on 9 February, 1949, two-and-a-half years after Qavam's first approach.[30]

Reluctance to send arms to Iran thus had continued. Iran was not of first-line importance. Attention focused on Western Europe, the Eastern Mediterranean and East Asia. In a survey by the Joint Chiefs in mid-1947 listing the 16 nations important to US security, Iran's name did not appear. The Americans believed a large-scale military build-up unjustifiable, given Iran's poverty, unstable politics and backward army, which needed only to be strong enough to maintain internal security, thereby denying the Soviets a pretext for intervention. It was also a time before huge grant aid programmes. Until the Korean War a conservative Congress and budget-minded White House co-operated in belief that economic development would provide the key to Iranian stability. What little military assistance the American government provided was under supposition that it would free local revenue for economic development. But, of course, the Iranian armed forces increased while the economy stagnated.[31]

With signature of the North Atlantic Treaty on 4 April 1949, Iran did receive some renewed consideration in Washington. The likely reaction of Greece, Turkey and Iran had been the subject of a State Department Policy Planning Staff Paper a year before, on 17 March 1948, the day the Brussels Pact was signed between the Benelux countries and Britain and France, looking to the new military organisation. The paper recommended that the United States sign bilateral treaties with the Near Eastern nations to assure them of later support. Over the next year the United States and Britain discarded that idea in favour of a joint declaration reaffirming the area's importance. This decision itself fell apart only a few days before the proposed declaration was to be made.

The British ambassador in Washington, Sir Oliver Franks, informed Secretary Marshall's successor, Dean Acheson, that Foreign Secretary Bevin had decided not to issue it; he would make a speech in the House of Commons without mentioning Iran. The British cabinet did not want commitments outside NATO, and while it would reassure the Greek and Turkish governments privately, it refused the same for Iran. Franks explained that his country's ambassador in Tehran, Le Rougetel, had warned of Soviet anger should the foreign secretary mention Iran. Acheson decided to make a unilateral statement of support in a radio talk on 18 March 1949, and the president gave similar assurance at the signing of the NATO treaty.[32]

Accompanying the treaty was a Military Defense Assistance Program (MDAP), under which the United States would allocate funds primarily to NATO (Title I), with smaller amounts to Greece and Turkey (Title II), and aid 'intended merely to support the political orientation of the recipient nation toward the United States' to Iran, Korea and the Philippines (Title III).[33]

And yet even the token aid under Title III of the Military Defense Assistance Program became a subject of much acrimony. The question of aid to Iran presented a political as well as military problem. Acheson favoured military aid, and President Truman sided with him. But Acheson had to fight to keep the Bureau of the Budget from whittling appropriations. The bureau trimmed MDAP requests for Title II and Title III. Iranian leaders warned that they would reject the amount proposed, $12 million. During a meeting with Le Rougetel the shah dealt with the problem indirectly by threatening to cancel a proposed visit to the United States. The president of the Bank-i-Melli, Abul Hasan Ebtehaj, carried the message to Wiley that Iran must have parity with Turkey. The shah submitted a shopping list totaling $175 million. Prime Minister Muhammad Sa'ed announced that the shah and Razmara wanted enough equipment to supply 200 000 men, 80 000 more than presently under arms. This after the US military had argued that it would be wasteful to supply Iran with equipment unless for irregular forces in case of Soviet attack. The two nations eventually reached agreement on $10.7 million.[34]

By the end of 1949, Iranian and American views on military assistance thus were far apart. The shah and his military advisers wanted to expand the army, acquiring jets and heavy armour. They expected the United States to provide the same amount of aid that Turkey received. The United States saw no role for Iranians in opposing a Soviet advance except for guerrilla resistance. It wanted to limit equipment to what the army could use, and urged more efficient employment of American advisers.

In the tortuous negotiations over the military missions, and over *matériel*, one must conclude, the United States government did not do very well. Part of the difficulty was division of authority between the State Department and the military. Sometimes it did not appear that the right hand knew what the left was about. Beyond that problem was belief that Iran was unimportant in the Cold War.

In the early postwar years Iran lay on the periphery of American concerns. The Truman administration was doing its level best to meet the worldwide situation, a novel situation indeed, in which the Soviet Union had challenged American power. The major place for challenge, Washington easily calculated, was Western Europe, and in 1947–49 the result had been three major measures, the Truman Doctrine, Marshall Plan and North Atlantic Treaty. The measures had been taken by an administration without large public support, concerned in 1945 with problems of postwar adjustment, beset in 1946 by inflation and millions of striking workers, bedevilled beginning in 1947 by a Republican Congress; only the personal victory of the president in the 1948 election had enabled Truman to go ahead with NATO. It had been an almost hectic situation, in which the administration had stood against the Soviets and gradually won public opinion over to its side. In the course of such a transition it was simply impossible to face every problem in the world, and the Middle East and (as became evident in June 1950) East Asia could not receive the attention that, as everyone later saw, really was necessary.

4 Economy

As the young shah began to gain a feeling that his reign might prosper far better than did that of his father, that indeed the possibilities of life for the people of Iran in the years after World War II might be considerable, and to sense also his increasing importance within the Iranian scheme of things, not to mention the Middle East, perhaps even Europe and the world, he began to consider to what places, specifically, he might go for more of this world's goods, or for assistance in obtaining them. The sources of aid were, he quickly discerned, three. The first would be, obviously, the government of the United States. A second was the new economic institution of the post-World War II era, the International Bank for Reconstruction and Development, the very name of which seemed to promise dollars, millions of them, for the people of Iran. The third was the Anglo-Iranian Oil Company, controlled by that ogre of imperialism, namely, the government of Great Britain.

The United States seemed best able to assist the ancient nation of Iran headed by its youthful monarch. It was the richest country in the world. Furthermore, America lacked a history of interference in Iran. The shah and his officials were much concerned about the proclivity of foreign governments to interfere in Iranian affairs.

The shah and his ministers based their campaign for American aid on an Allied offer at the Tehran Conference in December 1943 of reasonable recompense for 'suffering and sacrifice during World War II'. Here, surely, the Iranians had a point. A report of an *ad hoc* committee of the State-War-Navy Coordinating Committee in early 1947 likened Iran to the spinal cord of the Middle East and concluded that under the 1943 declaration the United States was 'committed to economic assistance'. Allied troops in Iran during the war had commandeered transport and in a variety of ways forced inflation on the Iranian economy. Compared to the economies of Europe and East Asia, the Iranians had not suffered much, but this was cold comfort; Allied propaganda had related to them that their nation was the bridge to victory. Hence, rarely a week passed in which one of the Tehran newspapers did not carry a leading article describing Iran's many sacrifices and calling for repayment.[1]

Iranian requests to the United States at first tended to be general, seeking whatever assistance might be available. The shah expressed interest in a loan to finance the seven-year development plan, Qavam wanted $250 million in military and economic aid, the Iranian ambassador in Washington, Husain Ala, asked only for $100 million. Although an element of bazaar bargaining entered these requests, Iranian leaders of all persuasions considered aid both necessary and deserved. Iranians of course preferred grant aid. Loans aroused opposition from deputies in the Majlis who remembered the foreign borrowing of the Qajar dynasty at the turn of the century. The Qajars had used the loans to finance royal excursions to Europe. But if only loans were available, then the Iranians would have to make the best of them.

The initial requests of Tehran drew favourable responses. Ambassador Allen believed it was in the interest of the United States to see that Iran received economic support. In communications with Washington he argued for aid. He believed the Iranians were in the Western camp. American and Iranian interests, he wrote, were parallel. Then Undersecretary of State Dean Acheson, and Loy Henderson, supported him. Henderson typically was concerned that Iran might pass under Soviet control.[2]

But Iranian leaders did not understand the domestic awkwardnesses of American foreign policy. Apart from the Export-Import Bank, the State Department could not extend aid without securing legislation from Congress, and after the end of the crisis in Azarbaijan it seemed unlikely. Financing war-related reconstruction in Europe, the Export-Import Bank had reached its limits for borrowing. Congress was conservative, often hostile towards the Truman administration. And there was another problem. Americans by late 1946 believed that the United States had 'already fulfilled most of its postwar burden'. Negotiations for a postwar loan to Britain dragged on for months during 1945–46, because the administration pondered how much it could safely ask from Congress.[3]

The new 80th Congress of 1947–48 looked with jaundiced eye on foreign aid. In the congressional elections of November 1946, the Republicans gained control of both houses, for the first time since 1930. Senator Arthur H. Vandenberg, chairman of the Foreign Relations Committee in the new Congress, which took office in January 1947, knew the temper of his colleagues. He apparently advised Truman that to obtain constituent pressure on Congress for an appropriation for Greece and Turkey, he would have to 'scare hell out of the country'. After passage of the Greek-Turkish aid bill he declared that his committee could not entertain further aid requests.

Moreover, there was little support in the State Department for an

Iranian loan. At the State Department in January 1947, James F. Byrnes gave way to Marshall. The new secretary and his undersecretary after midyear, Robert A. Lovett, showed no interest in economic aid. They even believed that with the Soviet threat passed, the United States should leave Iran to the British. Besides, Iran possessed income from oil.

It is not difficult to understand why American officials declined to give money to Iran. Americans had little experience and few ties with the Middle East. To all except a handful, the Soviet menace had receded. The Tudeh party was small–perhaps it should have been larger. Inflation, food shortages and unemployment were local problems.

The Truman administration defended the decision not to extend economic aid to Iran, and Marshall stated this view plainly to Allen. The American people, he said, had been unenthusiastic about support for Greece and Turkey and might balk at Iran. In Greece and Turkey the United States was trying to maintain the status quo in the face of communist challenge. This was not the case in Iran. Above all, to aid Iran would provoke the Soviet Union, and tension between the two superpowers already was bad enough. John Jernegan, head of the Division of Greek, Turkish and Iranian Affairs, wrote that the department believed Iranian oilfields were as important as the Turkish straits but Iran's best course, he said, might be not to align itself with anyone.[4]

During this period Washington was besieged with inquiries from Third World nations seeking grants or loans–Latin America, India, Indonesia, the Philippines, Korea. Money was scarce for all areas outside of Western Europe, together with Greece and Turkey. Marshall especially was sensitive to the pleas of Latin American nations, but had to say 'no' to them. He flew down to Bogota early in 1948 to attend what he thought would be an Inter-American Conference, and found himself confronted with talk about a Marshall Plan for Latin America. Statesmen of the Latin countries informed him that their nations had participated valorously and importantly in World War II. They reviewed the manner in which the American dollar had inflated, diminishing the purchasing power of their dollar balances. As if this were not enough, rioting broke out, and for a day or two, until the minuscule Colombian army obtained control, Marshall himself was besieged in the American embassy. Again he said 'no' about a Marshall Plan anywhere save in Europe. The Truman administration introduced Point Four in 1949, hoping to satisfy the developing nations, but the programme got off to a hardly discernible start. Big-spending programmes came only in the 1950s when emphasis changed to military assistance.[5]

In this early period Iran also sought assistance from the International Bank for Reconstruction and Development–indeed, Tehran made little distinction between the bank and the United States, believing perhaps rightly that Washington dominated the bank. When the State Department recommended that Iran apply to the International Bank, Tehran assumed that an application was a formality.[6]

Having been terribly disappointed with the attitude of Marshall, the Iranians expected the bank to shoulder responsibility. But in the early postwar years the bank showed itself ill prepared to deal with the Third World. The bank's loan officer for the Middle East and Africa in 1948–49, Edward A. Bayne, had almost no experience in the area. The bank followed a cautious policy, determined to avoid the financial irresponsibility of the interwar period. It did encourage a co-ordinated development plan, and Tehran in 1946 invited an American engineering firm with experience in the region, the Morrison-Knudsen Company, to make a survey. In advance of its final report Prime Minister Qavam carefully announced a seven-year plan, in a New Year's speech to the nation on 21 March 1947. Complying to its own satisfaction with the 'American request' for a survey, the Iranian government showered the International Bank with requests that reached as high as $250 million. The bank responded that the projects were not co-ordinated and that the Iranian budget did not contain specifics covering local financing.[7]

The effort to enlist the International Bank consumed a great deal of Iranian time and energy. When Qavam resigned in December 1947, responsibility for the development plan passed to the governor of the Bank-i-Melli, Abul Hasan Ebtehaj, who induced a noted economist, Dr Husain Nafici, to return to Tehran to work on the seven-year plan. In a joint memorandum to their governments in January 1948, the British and American embassies enthusiastically endorsed the resultant Nafici Plan. The Iranians described it as Iranian, rather than foreign. They knew as well as the Western governments that foreign advisers would be necessary, but it seemed appropriate to show the plan originating with an Iranian expert. The embassies, too, were anxious lest Iranians consider the plan a foreign concoction.[8]

To maintain momentum in developing the plan, which would attract the International Bank, which would make money flow into Iran as if it were water rising from the ancient fountains of Babylon, Ebtehaj recruited a friend, Max Thornburg, and sent him to Washington. Thornburg was an American of special qualities, reminiscent of the international entrepreneur of another age who from bases in Switzerland or Morocco had been wont to arrange international financing. This, to be sure, had been long before there were such institutions as an International Bank. Like his professional forebears he combined intelligence and drive, qualities that often had led to demand for his services as a 'foreign industrial consultant'. Working from a private island in the Persian Gulf, Um as-Sabaan, given to him by the sheikh of Bahrain, he had travelled through the Middle East, seeking out investments, proposing plans. His specialty was oil. He had undertaken an economic survey of Turkey. His contacts were excellent. He appeared the ideal choice. He wrote Ebtehaj in late 1947 that American economic power was 'more than a match for all our potential enemies combined. This therefore is the strength that we must use. And we must use it where it is needed and when'.[9]

At first it appeared as if Thornburg could advance the Nafici Plan and thereby the likelihood of a loan from the International Bank. He explored possibilities in the United States of an advisory contract for technical assistance to Iran. In August 1948 his efforts resulted in an agreement with Overseas Consultants Incorporated, a consortium of American engineering firms. The International Bank endorsed these efforts but worried over commercial favouritism and the consortium's lack of international character. Overseas Consultants added a British engineering firm, Alexander Gibb and Company. The British firm was the only member with experience in the region, for Morrison-Knudsen was not included and the other American members had not even worked outside the United States. Desire to share in big contracts–this was the main consideration. The International Bank stressed that it would not commit itself to finance any Overseas Consultants projects, but agreed to look them over. The bank organised a meeting of the consortium's board to work out a code of ethics for contracts–an important consideration with $650 million at stake.[10]

At this point the interest of the British government began to rise, and here was another confusing, probably also confused, result of the effort by the shah and his government to bolster the economy in Iran. In 1946–47 the British government was probably at its lowest ebb economically in a century, what with the manner in which weather and failures of postwar economic plans had reduced British hopes from their modest enthusiasm of 1945. The British finally had arranged a loan from the United States for $3.75 billion in 1946, and it was to be a pump primer. Instead much of it frittered out (to change the figure) in payments for American wheat to feed the destitute millions of Germans, many of them refugees from the East, in the British zone of Germany. By 1947 the hopes of Britons for their country's economic recovery were almost dashed, and hat in hand they had gone to Paris that summer for a series of conferences over Marshall Plan aid. And yet with all of this lack of prospect at home, the British government 'thought large' abroad; and no one observing policy in Iran would have believed that it came from so small an economy as that of the British Isles. The British acted in Iran as if they could control the Iranian economy, and certainly behaved towards the Americans as if they had a right, drawn out of the nineteenth century perhaps, to do so.

When the British should have focused upon the dismal domestic economic scene, they dreamed of danger to their position in Iran–which was to say, danger to the Anglo-Iranian Oil Company. Iranian financing of the ambitious development programme here posed a problem. On behalf of the AIOC the Foreign Office stressed that the company would not make up any shortfall in Iranian development funds.[11]

In early 1947 the Board of Trade had expressed alarm over the Morrison-Knudsen survey, prophesying a day when British firms would be pushed aside in favour of American. The Treasury took up this theme, arguing that British interests in Iran should expand. The Foreign Office proposed that London face reality–the British had neither capital, material or experts to take the economic lead in Iran. The government recently had informed Alexander Gibb and Company, which had applied for a steel allotment to continue work on the Tehran municipal water system, that no steel would be available throughout 1948. The best course hence was to include a British firm in Overseas Consultants. When Ebtehaj visited London in November, Foreign Office officials emphasised that he should include a British firm, and he agreed. The State Department received requests from Whitehall as well. At the meeting of representatives from the Foreign Office, the Ministry of Fuel and Power, the Treasury and Overseas Consultants on 8 December, the British openly asked for a share in the consortium. It was shortly after this meeting that Overseas Consultants invited Alexander Gibb.[12]

In the early stages of the consortium the State Department maintained contact through its American president, Clifford Strike, and its vice-president, Thornburg. The department viewed the organisation as the best solution to policy in Iran–stability and progress through economic development. It was able to turn aside Iranian aid requests by including them in the larger programme–the fate of two Export-Import Bank loan requests in 1947 and 1948. It discouraged loans outside the plan.[13]

Initially things seemed in order. Overseas Consultants submitted a five-volume study, a blueprint recommending a series of small projects to establish a network of plants producing building materials and consumer goods, to improve roads, to spray the insecticide DDT so as to eradicate malaria. For later stages it would recommend hydroelectric projects, reforestation and heavy industry. A mission of technical advisers headed by Thornburg operated as liaison between Overseas Consultants and a Plan Organisation, set up by Iran. The projects required $650 million, and an act of the Majlis assigned oil royalties to this programme, the remainder of financing to come from the Bank-i-Melli and foreign commercial loans. Some disgruntled bureaucrats in Tehran ministries, by-passed under the legislation, opposed the Plan Organisation, but for most Iranian factions it appeared very attractive. The shah's half brother, Prince Abdul Reza, became its first director.[14]

A hint of delay then emerged. In January 1949 the loan director of the International Bank, William A. B. Iliff, told the British embassy in Washington that it would be some time before the bank would make any large loan to Iran. In March 1949 a vice-president of the bank, Robert Garner, visited Tehran, and Ebtehaj assured him that Iran would not need a loan for several years. Garner found this opinion congenial. He had come to the International Bank midway in a career in private banking and held conservative views on loans to Third World nations. He saw Iran as a credit risk, which for far more complex reasons than Garner possibly could have imagined, it indeed was.[15]

The British and Americans continued to advise the Iranians to undertake inexpensive economic reforms: agricultural demonstration centres, local manufacture of building materials, well-drilling, village health centres, vocational schools – admittedly parts of the first stage of the proposed three-stage development plan. This advice had its advocates in the American embassy in Tehran, and in the State Department, where Dooher had recommended small-scale health and education projects rather than the large projects the Iranians seemed to prefer. Ambassador Wiley advocated small, highly visible projects carried out by the United States and Iran to improve the situation in Azarbaijan. According to Wiley, the shah and prime minister were interested.[16]

The American position concerning the International Bank did not alter during the next years, despite changes of cabinets in Iran. The State Department urged Iran to abandon attempts to do things on grand scales, and instead to 'think small'. Eventually the Iranians began to sense that nothing of importance was going to happen in their campaign to draw large loans from the International Bank.

If during this postwar era the United States Treasury proved tight-fisted and the International Bank essentially refused a large loan, there appeared no alternative for the Iranians but to turn to the Anglo-Iranian Oil Company.[17]

The AIOC had begun operations in the faraway year 1909, after buying concession rights granted a few years earlier to the 'father' of oil extraction in Iran, William Knox D'Arcy. An Australian, the ingenious D'Arcy had never set foot in Iran. His new company had built a refinery on Abadan island in the Shatt-al-Arab in southwestern Iran, across the river from what was then Ottoman-ruled Iraq. When in subsequent years the British navy converted its ships from coal to oil, the government in London quietly became the majority shareholder in AIOC, an arrangement for which the first lord of the Admiralty in the Asquith cabinet, Churchill, was largely responsible. The company grew during the next two decades, until its royalty payments provided the largest single source of income for the government of Iran, as well as handsome profits for all its European shareholders.[18]

The history of the AIOC, alas, gradually became entangled with Iranian nationalism. During the constitutional revolution of 1906–11 the clergy, the bazaar merchants and intellectuals had joined–each for its own reasons–to oppose foreign influence and the rule of the Qajars. With overthrow of the Qajar shah and withdrawal of Imperial Russian troops in 1917, Iranian nationalists then looked on Great Britain as the remaining principal foreign influence and considered the AIOC the symbol of its power. Reza Shah's accession in 1925 defeated the hopes of liberal nationalists, who entered upon a long period of sullen opposition. They considered him a tool of the British, or at least open to foreign influence. But Reza was a nationalist too, and became increasingly hostile towards the AIOC, arguing correctly enough that D'Arcy had received his concession from a corrupt government. In 1932 he cancelled the concession, partly as a response to declining royalty payments tied to devaluation of the pound and declining world oil prices. The British government brought the dispute to the League of Nations. But before any action the parties compromised, neither relishing the confrontation. Reza was anxious to maintain the flow of money for his development projects. Under the agreement of 1933 the concession area became smaller, royalties higher, Iranian employees more numerous. The Iranian share of profits climbed to an annual average of 15–20 per cent, in line with agreements in other Middle Eastern states. A satisfied Reza extended the concession to 1995.[19]

The Abadan refinery and oilfields in the southwest of Iran expanded greatly during World War II. Native workers increased to more than 55 000, and their standard of living was high relative to that of the Iranian population. Beginning in 1945 the company, encouraged by Foreign Secretary Bevin, improved housing and health. AIOC officials were proud of their achievements. A report by a delegation of the International Labor Office (ILO) in 1950 found much to praise. Yet the company's approach was paternalistic; workers were not consulted, and were expected to be grateful. The ILO report, a balance of praise and concern, pointed to need for worker representation. A parliamentary delegation from London had discovered that few company officials had either training or preparation for industrial relations and collective bargaining.[20]

Far more serious for the AIOC was the rising local nationalism, which had begun in the last year of the war, reached its first crest with rejection of the Soviet oil concession in 1947, and rose to a sudden height in 1951. When the Majlis rejected the proposed Soviet concession in 1947 with American support, the threat to the British increased.[21]

Iranian officials were emboldened to think that the United States would support Iran against the British oil company if a struggle developed, a reasonable prediction. The AIOC provided a target for Iranians disposed to take potshots. As time passed the number of Iranians wishing to do so increased.

The AIOC exercised influence in much of Iran. Some Iranian officials, especially those in the southwest near the oil concession, showed greater loyalty to the company than to their superiors, passing confidential information to the AIOC or urging it to adopt a stronger line towards dissidents in order to show the way for the government in Tehran. The company did little to bolster its reputation. The concession area resembled a foreign enclave, isolated from the nation. Within that enclave the company was a law unto itself. British employees lived apart from Iranian workers, with better pay and housing.[22]

The issue of Iranians in top jobs was sensitive, and the Iranian government claimed the AIOC had changed the 1933 agreement on this point. The oil company, it said, had agreed to raise the numbers of Iranians in engineering and administrative positions, but over the years interpreted the agreement as a percentage, which hid the fact that because of expansion in work force, foreigners in high-level jobs were far more numerous than in 1933. Even on a percentage basis results were disappointing: of 200 top employees in 1949, 18 (8.6 per cent) were Iranians; of the middle-level 1000, 393 (36.4 per cent) were Iranians. Prime Minister Hakimi, unprepared to negotiate with the oil company in early 1948, pointed to the company's failure, while former Prime Ministers Murtiza Quli Bayat and Muhammad Sa'ed spoke of breach of contract.[23]

The company had no programme to publicise its work in and for Iran, unlike the Arabian-American Oil Company, its American analogue to the south, established in Saudi Arabia. Company contacts continued to be with a few officials in Tehran. Often the basis of this relationship was a cash retainer. The Iranian government had no power to examine company books to ensure that it was receiving its share of profits, or to interfere in any way with operations.[24]

The company had one legitimate complaint against the Labour government: it limited AIOC dividends to shareholders. London controlled the size of payments to Iran under the agreement of 1933. Iran received 20 per cent of dividends. In 1947 it was a much smaller dividend than the company might have paid in the absence of government regulation. Chancellor of the Exchequer Sir Stafford Cripps refused to compromise, despite pleas by directors and former Foreign Secretary Anthony Eden.[25]

From the Iranian point of view this situation was intolerable, but there was a good deal more. During World War II the British navy had bought oil from the AIOC practically at cost, while oil in Iran sold at world prices. In postwar years the price of oil per barrel rose from 50 cents to $2, but royalties paid to Iran stayed the same. Meanwhile, the British government took a handsome harvest in excess profit taxes, introduced during the war and continued by the Attlee government.

On Britain's side, the AIOC was as important as the company was to Iran. Britain's stake in Iranian oil was by far its largest overseas investment. The AIOC annually returned tens of millions of pounds to the Exchequer. Experts differ on the total; there is no disagreement that Britain received far more than did Iran. The oil industry was one of the few bright spots in the otherwise dismal postwar economy.[26]

Wiley frequently wrote to the State Department, expressing concern over the AIOC's *imperium in imperio*. Whereas the British government acted decently and was well intentioned, he reported, the oil company operated with 'bland and ignorant disregard of international considerations'. As ambassador in Colombia, he had observed oil companies. He was confident that activities blamed on the British embassy were the result of efforts by the company. According to him it was common knowledge that intelligence operatives trained in Iran during the war had become part of the AIOC hierarchy.[27]

The eventual turning of the Iranians to the AIOC – after failing with the US government, and with the International Bank–was a natural recourse, urged on by Iranian nationalism, and all might have gone well had it not been for the personality of the chairman of the AIOC in the post-1945 years, Sir William Fraser. Sir William had helped negotiate the agreement of 1933. Not known for breadth of outlook, he entered the post-1945 world unprepared for adjustments in the oil industry. A flinty Scotsman, he had taken over the company in 1941, and after the war continued to believe that it could maintain its monopoly. Paradoxically, the Labour government, so energetic in nationalising other industries, failed to change the policy of its predecessor with respect to the AIOC. The two seats allotted to government on the board continued to go as rewards to superannuated government supporters, men who had little interest in or knowledge of oil. Fraser hence had a free hand to pursue whatever policies he deemed appropriate, maintaining the fiction that the AIOC was a private venture in which government happened to have an interest. One British official remarked wryly to an American colleague, 'I think in their hearts this (Labour) government considers AIOC revenues as dishonest–like living off a whore's earnings'. Labour's attitude oddly did not change until the crisis of 1951, and then only after Iran had nationalised the company. Fraser was contemptuous of 'the gentlemen of Whitehall', and never admitted the political responsibilities of his company in Iran. Perhaps for that reason not one director of the AIOC had visited Iran in the two years prior to 1951.[28]

British officials worried but did nothing. Bevin in 1946 dismissed Sir William Fraser's contention that the AIOC was meeting all Iranian labour law requirements. This was not enough, he said; the company must excel. He worried about nationalisation, for how could a Labour government argue against it? He suggested a company jointed owned by Britain and Iran, which would give Iran greater interest in the status quo. But the strike against the AIOC, which prompted Bevin's concern, ended in late summer of that year, and more pressing problems distracted the foreign secretary. In May 1947, following a meeting of officials from the AIOC and ministries in London, Foreign Office officials refused to discuss increasing royalties. A note to Tehran advised the Iranians to approach the company, not the government, and cautioned that the company could not solve Iran's budget problems. Privately there was feeling in London that any increase in royalties should have a *quid pro quo*, such as extending the area of the concession.[29]

The Iranians then took the initiative. When the Majlis finally rejected the proposed Soviet oil concession in 1947 it called on the government to enter discussions 'with a view to securing Iran's national rights'. Observers agreed on the factors that prompted the call. Iran's oil profits were declining, and news of lucrative agreements between American oil companies and Venezuela whetted Iranian appetites. In addition there was Qavam's machinations. He claimed not to have inserted this obnoxious clause in the law of the Majlis regarding oil concessions, insisting also that he had removed the name of the AIOC from the statute. But he saw advantage in the measure. He probably assumed that he would be able to reach a quiet settlement and announce that he had preserved the nation's rights.[30]

In the increasing contentions between the AIOC and Iran, one problem soon led to another. Qavam's fall late in 1947 put the issue in less experienced hands. The caretaker government of Ibrahim Hakimi did little. Abdul Husain Hajhir became prime minister in midyear and undertook immediate action. With assistance of French advisers the Iranian government drew up a 50-page memorandum of points for discussion with the AIOC, and Minister of Finance Muhammad Ali Varasteh presented this document to a surprised company delegation headed by Neville A. Gass at their first meeting on 26 September. The British were not prepared for wide-ranging talks. After two weeks the discussion adjourned to give company officials in London a chance to study the proposals. Talks were to resume within three months.

The British government now divided over policy. Ambassador Le Rougetel had warned against delay, fearing that it would result in greater concessions. Gass reported that the Iranians desired a revision of the 1933 contract. But London could not decide what the company should offer. The Treasury determined not to give back any of the excess profit tax, believing that increased production would expand royalties and thereby satisfy Tehran. Fraser agreed; Middle East nations could take care of themselves. Sir Orme Sargent, on behalf of the Foreign Secretary, recommended that the company offer a gift of £10 million to Iran. Chancellor of the Exchequer Cripps warned of the precedent for other concessions – and besides, increased royalties were a gift. Everyone agreed that whatever the solution it must not require consent of the Majlis. The Iranians should not think lightly of contracts.[31]

The chief AIOC negotiator, Gass, did not help the confusion. He had returned to London with a list of Iranian demands, but he did little with them. In discussion with government officials he referred to a few of the points, and the rest remained obscure. The ambassador in Tehran considered them all 'cockshies', not serious, especially the demand for Iranisation of employees at upper levels.[32]

The Americans knew little of this negotiation. Le Rougetel argued that it should be kept secret from the United States. The Foreign Office agreed, noting that the Iranians probably kept the Americans informed.[33]

While debate in London went on, events in Tehran – the fall of the Hajhir government and the attempted assassination of the shah – delayed further talks until mid-February 1949. The British lamented that Iran had no oilmen to act as advisers. They complained about satisfying the Iranians. They believed the Iranians wanted to cash in. Fraser agreed to go to Tehran in April 1949, provided he could negotiate with the Iranian prime minister. The new government of Muhammad Sa'ed moved cautiously, appreciating how sensitive the oil question had become. The finance minister, Abbas Quli Gulshayan, tried to draw the Majlis into the talks so that it could share responsibility, but the best the government achieved was parliamentary permission to continue negotiation.[34]

Attempts to induce Bevin to intercede with the AIOC were without result; he praised the terms the company was offering. Privately he urged the company to give the Iranians a more equitable arrangement. But he was overburdened and in failing health, and could not supervise details. It is unlikely his admonition led to a sweetening of terms when Fraser travelled to Tehran, for the chairman knew that the Treasury expected the AIOC to be hard-nosed. The company did agree to revise the 1933 contract; the Iranians, it seemed, would accept nothing less.[35]

For reasons not clear, the Iranian government now drew back from most of its demands. Prime Minister Sa'ed was ill – worn down by negotiations – and viewed the agreement as temporary relief from pressure, knowing that a final decision would have to come from the Majlis. The result on 19 July 1949 was the Gass-Gulshayan agreement, long and complicated, understood only by experts. It allowed Iran a 25-to-50 per cent increase in royalties, depending on production and profit, and reaffirmed the company's title under the 1933 contract.[36]

Thereafter the Majlis debated the oil issue, and the company was confident it would ratify the agreement. The Iranian government blew hot and cold, one day assuring the embassy the Majlis would approve, next day expressing doubt. This was part of the government's strategy to obtain what had eluded it. The AIOC did not weaken, and as Iranian opposition increased, foreign oil companies watched, for a failure could set regional patterns; negotiation in Iraq came to a halt pending the outcome in Iran.

In all the postwar economic negotiations with Iran neither the United States nor Britain acquitted itself creditably. American officials did everything possible to avoid doing anything, calling on such surrogates as Overseas Consultants and the International Bank, neither of which was equal to satisfying the demands of Iranian leaders. The Americans hoped the problem would go away. They relied on Britain and the Anglo-Iranian Oil Company. But London did not welcome change in Iran, especially when it promised to reduce oil revenues needed at home. London did not take Iranian requests seriously, supposing that Tehran could be satisfied with minor alterations. Division within the Labour government allowed Sir William Fraser to resist reasonable Iranian demands.

And so nothing came from the great economic expectations of the Iranian government – nothing from the United States, nothing from the International Bank, nothing from the AIOC. The shah, government spokesmen and journalists, all had raised expectations, in speeches, reports and editorials extolling economic and social reform. The future, in words, had seemed golden. Then the words turned into more words of negotiation, and eventually into nothing.

5   A Royal Visit

For several years after World War II, down to the end of 1949, American assistance to Iran was quite limited. Washington advocated inexpensive internal reforms and a moderate strengthening of Iranian security forces. The Department of State concentrated on Western Europe, hoping to limit commitments in other areas. The department considered the Marshall Plan the necessary end of foreign aid, not the auspicious beginning.

All the while the shah became increasingly attractive to US policy-makers who considered him the best hope for a stable, progressive Iran.

But the shah had become frustrated. He had failed to obtain economic assistance from either the United States or the International Bank, and the Majlis had sidetracked the supplementary oil agreement that promised a sizeable expansion of revenue. Most important to him, his military force seemed minuscule, wholly incapable of delaying a Soviet advance.

Faced with these setbacks, the young man on the Peacock Throne planned a breakthrough in relations with the United States – one that would increase his popularity in Tehran, raise his local reputation for achievement. He had in mind a trip to Washington. He came to believe that in a face-to-face encounter he could convince President Truman of Iran's urgent needs.

The shah looked forward to the trip, his first to the United States. He had been anxious to visit the country ever since President Roosevelt offhandedly, as was FDR's wont, invited him during the Tehran Conference. Not until 1949 did the time seem propitious, with the monarchy more secure and conditions approaching stability. Early in 1948 he had expressed interest in going to the United States after his visit to London, scheduled for the late summer. The State Department had discouraged him because the new Hajhir cabinet required constant royal support. The sultry Washington weather, the department said, also militated against an August visit. An alternate date of late March 1949 seemed more appropriate. After the assassination attempt in February 1949 the two governments agreed to postpone the visit until November of that year.[1]

President Truman and his advisers in 1948 had reasons to delay the shah's proposed visit. One was a good political reason. During the campaign of 1948 the president had no time to entertain the 'king-of-kings' when his own sovereign, the American people, seemed likely to reject his administration in November. Beyond the rush of political speeches and appearances that autumn, however, Truman faced an apparently unending series of international crises. The German question, including the Berlin Blockade, had drawn his attention from such areas as the Middle East and East Asia. Secretaries Marshall and Acheson necessarily based their diplomacy on Western Europe, considering that to lose even a part of the continent would be a blow to American prestige everywhere.[2]

It is clear, of course, that American statesmen in the late 1940s and early 1950s had only begun to sense the subtle transformations in the Third World. Marshall and Acheson, preoccupied with Europe, had given little consideration to areas outside. Insensitive to world change, they failed to appreciate or sometimes even notice that Third World nations were edging away from the great powers towards their own policies.

Acheson, who took office as secretary in January 1949, was especially ill-prepared to deal with change outside Europe. He lacked any feeling for the importance of Asia. His knowledge of the Middle East was limited, which may explain his willingness to support Britain there. Perhaps he never had much respect for Third World peoples, believing that anyone seeking American help should rely on will and effort and that Asian countries assuredly showed little of those. According to the Acheson biographer David McLellan the secretary's respect 'went to those who were effective, to those who grappled with and solved difficult day-to-day problems and who faced the stubborn realities'. Iran, an oil-rich nation, had wallowed in despair, an unworthy candidate for American assistance. Acheson looked on visits to Washington by Third World leaders as attempts to pry commitments out of the United States. He preferred diplomatic channels, which could postpone decisions. The secretary in 1949 would have been happier if the shah had decided to stay at home.[3]

Then that year, marking the end of the Berlin Blockade, with no discernible sign of the approach of the Korean War, with the forthcoming nuclear contest with the Soviet Union understandable only in mid-September when it became clear that the Russians had tested a nuclear device, gave a sort of respite to the international crises of the past. The Truman administration, newly inaugurated, turned to budgetary problems. Fiscal considerations weighed more heavily than threats of communist advance. In the early postwar years President Truman, a fiscal conservative, had done all he could to maintain a balanced budget. In 1947 and 1948 the budget surpluses helped reduce the national debt. These balanced budgets, sought in vain by his predecessor, helped the president dampen inflationary pressure. The Republican 80th Congress had threatened to undo the administration's planning when it passed a tax cut in 1948, over a presidential veto. The $8.3 billion surplus of fiscal 1948 (July 1947-June 1948) became a $3 billion deficit in fiscal 1949. The president was deeply concerned. It was not a good time for the shah to seek assistance. It was widely believed in Washington that the 'Soviet Union was deliberately trying to scare the United States into spending itself into bankruptcy'. And so, even though the Soviets were making overtures to Tehran, the Truman administration was not going to be receptive to the shah's pleas.[4]

Ambassador Wiley nonetheless was an enthusiastic promoter of the shah's trip. Quixotically, he considered the shah's exposure to American culture far more important than aid. He sent a mass of letters and reports from the embassy detailing the shah's background, character, American attitudes towards the shah, conditions in Iran, and generally did his best to make the trip seem worthwhile. He fancied himself a royal tutor in things American, taking pains in meetings with the shah to discuss America's history, about which the shah knew little. After the royal pupil promised to read books on American history, Wiley asked George Allen to send works by Samuel F. Bemis of Yale University, and perhaps a few by Claude Bowers, the ambassador to Chile. Wiley proposed to inspire the shah through exposure to all that was best in America. Perhaps it would serve as a catalyst for progress in Iran. The trip might prove a turning point in the shah's life, in American relations with Iran.[5]

Looking back, it is almost amusing to envision the shah in early 1949, sitting on the Peacock Throne, reading a treatise on American foreign relations by the Yale expert, Professor Bemis, or paging the large-D Democratic books of Bowers, with their references to strange American events of long ago.

As mentioned, Wiley celebrated the shah's importance. Embassy opinion had altered since the days of Allen, who had maintained a healthy scepticism. Wiley's predecessor had been careful to separate assistance from reliance. He had seen democratic possibilities in the Majlis, if admitting that it neglected its duties. But Wiley's dispatches concentrated on the personal development of the shah, 'since we may expect so very little from others in this country'. They lamented the lack of able, honest men in Iranian public life, commented approvingly on the shah's hostility to the vested, selfish interests that dominated Iran, overlooked any connection between poor national leadership and increasing court influence, envisioned the shah as an anticommunist who espoused 'American' ideas on economic development. The shah, Wiley said, was 'more Western than Eastern'. He might replace Oriental complexity with a relationship more intelligible to Americans.[6]

State Department appreciation of the shah as a sort of Iranian catalyst was at first sceptical. Officials attributed the shah's ineffectiveness in reform to indecision or failure to understand what was required. The shah, they said, 'shared the national predilection for grandiose plans, extravagant speeches and fine façades with little genuine understanding or interest in the factors which constitute and maintain firm foundations'.[7]

And yet by mid-1949 Wiley's enthusiasms were beginning to make some converts. A few department members dreamily discerned a more mature shah, beginning to make good on statements of devotion to reform. They beheld Iran's seven-year economic development plan. They admired the shah's manoeuvring that had increased his control over parliament. They dismissed the idea that the shah could ever return to his father's dictatorial ways.[8]

As the time for the visit neared, opposition within Iran became evident. The press questioned the wisdom of the visit, and several papers made comparisons with trips by shahs of the Qajar dynasty that had brought debts and foreign meddling – a point on which Iranian opinion was hypersensitive.[9]

Another issue concerned some Iranians, namely, that the chief of staff, General Razmara, would remain in Tehran while the shah was away. The shah had no intention of sharing the limelight with Razmara. But risk was involved, as rumour circulated that the general meant to take control in a coup and make the shah a figurehead, or even depose him. The general had replaced almost all older officers of Reza Shah's day with men loyal to himself. The shah's young brother, Prince Abdul Reza, was particularly suspicious – perhaps because he had ambition for the throne himself – and missed no opportunity to warn his brother of Razmara. As insurance against a coup, just before the shah departed for the United States he appointed Razmara's bitter enemy, General Fazlollah Zahedi, formed aide to General Schwarzkopf, as chief of police.[10]

Minister of Court Hajir was assassinated on 4 November, ten days before the shah's departure, and the British ambassador encouraged Wiley to ask the monarch not to leave. Wiley was unsympathetic, having worked hard to ensure a successful trip.[11]

At last the time arrived. President Truman placed his presidential plane, the *Independence*, at the shah's disposal, along with an additional plane for baggage. The president on 16 November welcomed the shah at the military air transport field in Washington, and thousands of spectators watched the motorcade enter the city and proceed to the presidential residence, then Blair House – the White House was undergoing reconstruction and President Truman had moved across the street. Headlines in the *Washington Post* announced that the shah had come 'to observe the workings of democratic government in the greatest of the democracies'.

The shah remained in Washington only three days. On the first evening of the visit the president was host at a state dinner at the Carlton Hotel, a few blocks from Blair House. Afterwards came policy meetings, courtesy calls, tourist excursions, even a football game. From the capital he travelled to New York and thence to Detroit and the West Coast. In the Far West he toured military installations, beheld the Grand Canyon and Hoover Dam, and visited irrigation projects near Phoenix. He concluded with a holiday at Sun Valley and an unscheduled stay in San Francisco.

A grand visit it was. The shah came prepared to meet the American people who still thought of Iran as the fairy-tale land of the thousand-and-one nights. On Wiley's recommendation the court had engaged a veteran newspaperman and public relations expert to handle press relations, Henry Suydam, formerly spokesman for the Department of State. Suydam travelled to Iran to prepare the shah's speeches, arrange the itinerary, advise on tactics. Thanks to his ministrations, crowds greeted the shah everywhere. Glowing reports filled newspapers. The shah praised President Truman and complimented American women, cars, mass-production. He appeared not as an Eastern potentate but 'more like an earnest young army officer'. He seemed to enjoy being photographed as he slogged through mud or clambered up the side of a tank. He conjured visions of Western-style progress in Iran through land reform. He spoke the language of America.[12]

The substance of the visit was admittedly thin. Indeed it was farcical. Wiley had warned that the British had 'yes-yessed' the shah so much during the trip to England the previous year as to make the task of bringing complete reality to the shah's mind difficult if not impossible. The United States government was prepared, of course, to give him little. In talks with the president and secretary of state on 18 November the shah argued for military assistance because Iran's security must precede economic development. The Americans replied that economic and social reforms were essential to stability, and cited the downfall of

Chiang Kai-shek in China. The shah was impressed but not convinced. He said Iran would use oil revenue to carry out reform, including the seven-year plan.[13]

Nor did arms talks prove helpful. The shah regarded himself as an authority on military affairs, an illusion that caused continual complication during his visit. Wiley had written in exasperation that 'the shah thinks he is a soldier. He isn't!' General Evans had admitted that 'He doesn't know how little he knows about military details'. The shah nonetheless entertained plans for an army totaling from 200 000 to 500 000 – all combat units, with no attention to supply and service units. Meeting with the Joint Chiefs of Staff at the Pentagon he displayed his primeval ignorance. He began by explaining Iran's need for 150 medium tanks. On a large wall map he had brought with him he gave the American chiefs a lecture on strategic moves in event of a Soviet invasion. He expected the tanks to cover the retreat of his forces across the Iranian plateau to the security of the mountains 400 miles to the southwest. He supposed that dust clouds would screen his troops from enemy aircraft. Dust-coloured Iranian uniforms would further confuse Soviet spotters. The Russians would mistake wells dotting the countryside for fox-holes. The chiefs listened in embarrassed silence, asking occasional questions. The shah took their questions for agreement.[14]

The shah raised with Acheson the issue of a mutual defence agreement, a possibility the secretary had mentioned earlier. Acheson said it would be impossible to extend American commitments, although interest would be great if trouble came.[15]

The visit ended frostily. While the monarch was on his tour in the West, Ambassador Ala tried to extract something tangible from Washington. But even on the question of how the shah would return to Iran there was disagreement. Ala informed the chief of protocol that because of increased baggage and the need to pick up royal family members in Rome the shah had decided to charter a plane. Department officials interpreted this information as a scheme to persuade the United States government to transport the entire party, baggage and all. They considered such a caravan impossible, declaring privately that the cost would be prohibitive. Diplomacy might have sanctioned the added expense, but economy prevailed. The shah and his entourage departed the United States on a chartered KLM plane.[16]

The visit hence was no success. Acheson commented in his memoirs that the shah had too many plans beyond the capabilities of Iran – 'the visit turned out to be a disappointment for all' – and avowed that he always had opposed the idea of foreign statesmen trooping to Washington with pleas that they had to have something to take home.[17]

The visit did have one effect, although the Iranians never knew of it. After the shah had departed, the director of the Mutual Defense Assistance Program in the Department of Defense, General Lyman L. Lemnitzer, wrote to the State Department recommending against medium tanks, because the Iranians could neither operate nor maintain them. Lemnitzer and his State Department correspondent, James E. Bruce, agreed not to mention tanks in any negotiation. If the Iranians raised the issue they were to be dissuaded. If all else failed, the State Department would make the tanks available. The $20 million cost would have to come from the Greek aid programme. Under existing legislation the president could transfer it, and the winding down of the Greek civil war made the transfer feasible. To the relief of American negotiators, in a later meeting the Iranian commissioners agreed not to press for tanks, little realising how close they had come to getting them.[18]

In the United States the long-term effect of the shah's visit was profound, for it fixed on the blank public consciousness a clearer image of the shah that – renewed periodically – lasted for nearly three decades; he was 'a good guy . . . a charming young man . . . a monarch with the welfare of his people at heart'. The young monarch seemed to represent progress against the dark forces of reaction, xenophobia, privileged wealth. He was 'a liberal, forward-seeing, very human friend', also a paladin of anticommunism to a people increasingly concerned with the Red menace; having 'successfully resisted Red infiltration through his province of Azarbaijan', he had earned the right to be classed as 'a firm friend of the United States'. If the popular view remained at variance with official understanding of his weakness of character, it did not seem to matter. Ironically the trip Wiley designed to capture the shah for democracy achieved just the opposite.[19]

If in Tehran the shah received an enthusiastic welcome – triumphal arches, fireworks, a tumultuous progress from airport to palace – beneath the gaiety astute Iranians recognised that the United States was continuing to deny any obligations to Iran under the declaration of 1943. In a radio broadcast the shah exhorted his people to work for development of their country. But because of a disastrous harvest and now this failure to attract foreign assistance, the prospects really appeared bleak.[20]

The talks seemed to have made little impression on the shah. He again spoke of American assistance. Explaining that his plans had met with acceptance at the Pentagon, he asked the American ambassador about the Turkish bugbear and demanded to know what role the United States envisioned for Iran in a general war.[21]

The most portentous local result of the visit may have been its effect on the National Front of Dr Musaddiq, which had evolved out of disturbances associated with earlier elections. To protest the elections, 20 leaders of differing philosophies, including Musaddiq, had taken sanctuary in the grounds of the palace. Later the several groups joined to oppose the increasing power of the court-army clique. At first only the idea of opposition held them together. Not until the summer of 1950 did the oil issue intrude and become the front's rallying cry.[22]

Musaddiq had favoured a coalition of organisations rather than a popular party like those in the West. He argued for consensus rather than principle and discipline, which in any case would have been impossible to introduce in Iran at that time. Only groups – labour unions, political parties, student associations – could affiliate with his National Front. Two classes of Iranians accounted for membership in the affiliates, the traditional middle class (clerics and bazaar shopkeepers) and the modern middle class (intellectuals and reformers). The former were conservative, theocratic, mercantile, the latter modern, secular, technocratic, socialist.[23]

The National Front relied on the middle class, even though its leader was a member of the élite landowning class. The traditional middle class could be found in all urban areas, and exerted influence during elections wherever tribes, army or landowners did not dominate. The modern middle class tended to concentrate in the nation's capital, where university, industry and government offered employment. This was a legacy from Reza Shah, who had centralised power in Tehran. The National Front could rely on Tehran at election time, but that was not enough. The traditional middle class had to be consulted at every step, for it could deliver election victories in such urban electorates as Tabriz, Isfahan and Mashhad. During the first year of the sixteenth Majlis (1950–51), parliament provided the indispensable forum for the small group of eight National Front supporters. But the National Front's main support lay in the streets, where leaders often appealed directly to the people.

This handful of deputies would decisively influence Iranian affairs, for their tight co-operation compensated for numbers in a parliament where members prided themselves on independence, parties were rare and allegiances fluctuated. These eight deputies carried special authority, having been popularly elected, whereas their peers had been picked to represent special interests. The honesty of the 1950 election, said to have been freer in Tehran than ever before, owed something to the shah's trip. Having returned from talks with American leaders, the shah wanted to show Washington that his government was not corrupt like that of Nationalist China, and had restrained subordinates from their usual intervention. The new chief of police, General Zahedi, had welcomed the opportunity to assist the National Front and spite his opponent, Razmara.[24]

6   America to the Rescue?

The difficulty of American relations with Iran early in the year 1950 was that something seemingly needed to be done and yet no ranking American diplomat knew what it was nor wanted to find out. The very mention of the name Iran within the State Department raised talk of excess American commitments, the impossibility of solving all problems with money, the high cost of the Marshall Plan, the new responsibilities of the North Atlantic Treaty Organisation. The Democrats who had returned to office after the presidential election of 1948 talked so much about money they sounded almost like Republicans. The administration of President Truman, to be sure, was a bit on the conservative side. The president himself was a fiscal conservative; Truman for years had read presidential budget proposals and congressional amendments, and not merely knew what the small-point figures meant but had become convinced that the monetary outlays for the relief programmes of the Roosevelt administration and the huge cost of World War II had strained federal credit; he would have liked to see the government take up further burdens, but Western Europe had been enough and in all conscience, and with his experience in Washington for 15 years, he believed he could do no more. In 1949 his enthusiasm for helping people around the world had persuaded him to take up the idea of an official in the Department of Agriculture who espoused a plan to help the weaker nations and peoples of the world through technical assistance. Here was the idea that became Point Four, the fourth point in a series of recommendations in Truman's inaugural address of January 1949. Beyond that gesture, and it never was more than that, he felt the government could not go. The grandiose plans of the shah in faraway Tehran did not attract him.

And yet the problems of Iran kept arising, in reports from Ambassador Wiley and in comments by lower-level officials in the Department of State. Iran had been in an economic recession since 1947, the sort of sluggishness that had occurred in Western Europe and there received direct aid through the Marshall Plan. But in Tehran no Marshall Plan beckoned, and Iran slowly had sunk deeper into the morass. A low point in Iran's post-1945 economy was reached early in 1950. By that time the economy of Iran, never robust, had deteriorated so much that official Washington almost took alarm.

Reports predicted dire consequences if the United States failed to help

Iran, and emphasised 'psychological impact'. Advocates did not call for long-term commitment but for immediate money to reverse the torpid economy, restore confidence and banish the despair that threatened the American goal of a stable, secure Iran. Wiley repeated his warnings of Soviet machinations. For two years the secretary of state and his assistants ignored them, believing that local problems were a result of corruption and incompetence. As Acheson put it, no matter how much money or equipment poured in, Tehran would misuse it. When Wiley wrote about token aid, the secretary refused to listen. But by the end of February 1950 the ambassador had become insistent. Department officers decided to send the deputy director of the Office of Greek, Turkish and Iranian Affairs, William Rountree, on an inspection. This was in accord with the old government bromide that if there is a problem, give it to a committee or send out an investigator – in other words, stall for time, in hope that the problem will go away.[1]

The decision to send Rountree seemed sensible. An employee of the Treasury Department, he had transferred to the State Department, and during the war had served with the Middle East Supply Center in Cairo and later was economic assistant to Ambassador Henry F. Grady in the Greek aid programme. He was one of a handful of officers with experience in the region. He had a reputation for hard work and analysis. Arriving on 15 March, he spent two weeks in Tehran, interviewing everyone he thought might be of help – American military and diplomatic officers, British diplomats, members of Overseas Consultants, Iranian officials. He wrote a long dispatch analysing conditions and suggesting policy. His report made such an impression that when he arrived at his next stop, Istanbul, he found a cable asking him to return at once to the United States.[2]

Rountree had concluded that Wiley was describing conditions accurately, although perhaps not with detachment. Poor harvests, a result of drought, and the continuing insecurity in the breadbasket of Iran, Azarbaijan, had made food scarce, especially wheat, a staple of Iran's diet. And merchants had mountains of unsold imports. Theoretically Iran had enough money to pay its way, but parliament's refusal to vote the supplementary oil agreement that promised increased royalties, declining expenditure – perhaps calculated – by the Anglo-Iranian Oil Company, and a too-ambitious seven-year economic development plan, added to the financial woes. Tens of thousands of unemployed agricultural labourers had migrated to the capital, increasing the strain on an inefficient government. Over 30 000 people had obtained shelter in tent camps outside Tehran, and the government tried to keep them busy building roads and repairing railways. The Tudeh party had made inroads among labourers in the Abadan refinery and in the north at Tabriz. Despite a government ban, nothing could staunch the flow of Tudeh propaganda assisted by the Soviet embassy and radio stations across the border.[3]

Rountree's description started talk within the State Department, and in less than two weeks Assistant Secretary McGhee offered an analysis and recommendation. Reversing his position, McGhee now warned that 'the time of collapse may not be far away' and expressed concern that the Iranian government, frustrated in attempts to secure aid, might seek a *modus vivendi* with the Soviets or, worse, fall victim to a Russian-organised revolt. He attacked Iranian deputies, however patriotic, who had never learned about representative government and seemed to have few followers. Any aid programme would presume government reform; the United States must tell the shah whom it preferred to head the government. This was the first department memorandum since the Azarbaijan crisis to stress a Soviet threat.[4]

Acheson remained calm. He attended the undersecretary's meeting on 26 April, where McGhee's memorandum received attention, but opposed giving the impression that the United States might solve Iran's problems. The United States, he thought, should not become overextended.[5]

But it became evident that something should be done, and officials agreed to send an economic mission. They chose the ambassador to Greece, Grady.[6]

The troubleshooter for Iran, successor to Rountree, had a distinguished background and a wealth of experience that made him a favourite for solving State Department problems. He had been professor of international trade and finance at the City University of New York and at the University of California at Berkeley, and a dean at the latter institution. Highly regarded in business circles, he had chaired state and national committees, private and public. He had shown strength of character and a considerable managerial ability. After holding a series of posts during the war, he became chairman of the alternate members of the Cabinet Committee on Palestine and Related Problems in 1946, travelling to London with representatives from the treasury and war departments for talks with British officials. The Grady-Morrison proposal for settling the Palestine issue by dividing land and government among Jews and Arabs, with two autonomous provinces and a central government, caused such a stir that President Truman had to disown Grady, and later when Acheson suggested

Grady to head an economic mission to the Middle East the president objected because of opposition from people who believed Grady had dealt unfairly with the Jews on Palestine. Truman nevertheless respected him, appointing him ambassador to India, newly independent and turbulent in 1947, transferring him to Greece the next year when civil war threatened there.[7]

Grady's *modus operandi* was interesting. He possessed a remarkable ability to work, and in Greece surprised his juniors by his energy, leaving younger members of visiting delegations panting as he bounded up hillsides on tours of inspection. He liked to have around him men whom he trusted, and could choose men of ability. As one intimate remembered, 'his affable Irish manner belied a tough, determined character. He managed with a light hand . . . but he was very careful to preserve his position as top man and could be very rough with American generals, Greek cabinet ministers, and U.S. employees who stepped out of line. . . . He delegated but kept hold of the controls'.[8]

On personal matters Grady displayed the sensitivity of many high officials, and it mattered to him 'whether or not he was treated with proper respect'. Heaven help the junior officer who allowed the slightest peremptory tone to creep into a cable that came across Grady's desk![9]

The decision was not merely that Grady should undertake an economic mission to Tehran, but that he should replace Wiley. The latter had served two years, a long stint, and was due for reassignment. Besides, he would have been the first to admit his ignorance of economics and was by this point willing to leave, satisfied that the department was heeding his advice.

It was not easy to persuade such a personality as Grady to exchange Athens for Tehran, to leave a post where he had been successful for one that not merely was remote but promised difficulties. Grady had informed McGhee that his work in Greece was approaching an end, but did not have Iran in mind. When he returned to Washington in April 1950 to testify on the need for continuing aid to Greece, McGhee stressed to him the challenge and promised that the United States was prepared to commit $50 million from the Export-Import Bank and to increase military defence assistance. The department would raise the embassy in Iran to class 1. McGhee spoke to Acheson and persuaded the secretary to discuss the assignment, emphasising the president's wish that Grady accept. A few days later the meeting with the secretary took place, at which Grady told Acheson he wanted to be the first postwar American ambassador to Japan, a suitable assignment to cap his government career. The secretary promised to recommend this post when the time came. Grady interpreted the remark as a commitment, a *quid pro quo* for Tehran. Acheson did not see it as such, and said as much in a talk with the president shortly afterwards. Truman approved the plan to send an economic mission, submitted the ambassador's name to the Senate on 5 June, and made the appointment on 29 June. Grady returned to Athens to wind up, secure in the belief that he would have backing for an ambitious programme in Iran and soon be in Tokyo.[10]

But was the choice of Grady really a helpful move? A troubleshooter was what the situation seemed to require, and yet the Truman administration was not able, or willing, in its heart of hearts, to do anything serious about Iran's economic and military troubles. Grady was being persuaded to go to Tehran to resolve the needs of the moment, but to be more of a showpiece than troubleshooter. He would raise expectations. He could show his characteristic energy. He could not get the support of Truman and Acheson, two officials whose attention was riveted on the problems of Western Europe. Grady may have thought he could. If any American envoy at that time had a chance of doing so, he appeared to be the one.

Politics continued in Tehran. The capital buzzed about a successor to Prime Minister Sa'ed. As Wiley had noted late in 1949, Sa'ed's health was declining. Burdened with the Gass-Gulshayan oil agreement, the prime minister realised how difficult it would be to obtain passage of the agreement in the parliament, especially since neither he nor anyone else saw much advantage in it. He hoped to escape the problem by laying down his office and seeking sanctuary in the newly organised senate.[11]

The shah surprised odds takers when on 23 March he asked the veteran politician Ali Mansur to form a government. A royalist, Mansur had a reputation for being pro-Soviet and corrupt, which did not endear him to the Americans or to reformers in the National Front. No one could be certain why the shah called him, and most members of the court seemed surprised. The shah may have wanted to show independence of the United States, appearing to move Iran toward a more neutral policy; the department noted this possibility. In reality domestic factors were at work, and for the first time a cabinet was composed entirely of court supporters. The shah curtailed his recently announced anticorruption campaign. The new prime minister, a likely target, preferred to avoid this delicate issue, while the shah had lost enthusiasm anyway.[12]

American officials wondered how they could give aid if the shah insisted that corrupt politicians administer it. The department cautioned Wiley not to reveal any details of economic assistance, lest Iran assume the United States supported Mansur. Some officials thought he should let the shah know that Mansur was not acceptable.[13]

To counter opposition Mansur shrewdly lobbied for support in the

Majlis and even reached an agreement with Musaddiq, who offered short-term support in exchange for control over the order of debate. Musaddiq improved on his advantage when Mansur agreed to a special oil committee with five out of 18 places going to the front, far out of proportion to its strength in the Majlis.[14]

The shah's popularity thereafter declined. His enhanced constitutional powers served to weaken his popular support, for he seemed ill-prepared to carry out his responsibilities. He had refused to allow a strong prime minister or ensure free elections either for the constitutional convention in April 1949 or for the Majlis in November. When the promised improvement in government did not occur, the public blamed the court. In particular the shah incurred the wrath of the opponents of Princess Ashraf and her clique. In February 1950 the former prime minister, Qavam, sent an open letter to the shah from Paris, listing trends towards dictatorship and warning of popular resistance. In May, Musaddiq spoke in the Majlis and promised to support the monarchy if the shah ruled with popular backing.[15]

In the American embassy in Tehran there was little sense of the nuances of Iranian politics. The responsibility for this omission lay partly with Dooher and Wiley. The two men shared a love of politics and intrigue, and a desire to exert influence. The ambassador valued Dooher, perhaps stood in awe of his experience in Iran. By late 1949, Dooher had joined Wiley in support of the court-army clique, trying to convince Washington that General Razmara would make an excellent prime minister, that the shah needed the general to rule effectively, that deteriorating conditions demanded strong measures. As the embassy's strategy unfolded, Dooher spent his time with court politicians and military leaders, seeing little of the opposition. The Iranian press complained of Dooher's machinations. He and the ambassador had become isolated from opinion. The monarchy, they believed, offered hope of a progressive, Western-oriented Iran, which the people would naturally support because of the promise of a better life.[16]

At this juncture two high-ranking American officers bolstered the shah's feeling of self-importance. In the spring of 1950 came first the US Army's Chief of Staff General J. Lawton Collins, who visited Iran in early April. The Defense Department had been unenthusiastic about his mission, but responded to requests from the State Department. Collins held several meetings with military leaders, and the shah piloted him to the north for an aerial reconnaissance of Azarbaijan. The general worried that the monarch might miscalculate and fly across the Soviet border. But the monarch did seem interested in improving his country. Back in Washington, the general reported in favour of economic aid.

The chairman of the Joint Chiefs of Staff, General Omar N. Bradley, advised Secretary of Defense Louis Johnson that the chiefs supported economic assistance and MDAP grants.[17]

A month after Collins's departure, Lieutenant General James A. Van Fleet, chief of the Joint US Military Aid Group to Greece, came to attend ceremonies associated with reinterment of Reza Shah's remains in a splendid mausoleum at Rey, south of Tehran – a symbolic occasion for the Pahlavi dynasty, whose founder had died in exile in South Africa in 1944 and received temporary burial in Cairo. Van Fleet conferred with Iranian leaders, and discussed military affairs with the shah.[18]

Van Fleet might have noted that the delayed obsequies for Reza Shah had produced a mixed local reaction. At the train station the grief-stricken shah duly collapsed on his father's coffin and aides had to support him. The crowd that lined the avenues as the cortège passed responded solemnly. Yet in the Majlis, Dr Musaddiq objected to declaring the funeral day a national holiday and refused to permit the speaker to eulogise the late shah. In the holy city of Qum a hundred miles away, where an honour guard carrying the shah's remains had circumambulated the sacred tomb of Fatimeh, religious leaders had absented themselves. Two army battalions stood by to preserve order. In Qum had appeared the antagonism between pulpit and throne that dogged the Pahlavis.[19]

In faraway Washington, policy-making continued. State and Defense officials agreed that the head of ARMISH, Brigadier General Vernon Evans, should advise the Iranian army on war plans, and more important, accepted a delaying role for the Iranian army should the Soviets invade – all of which made possible the dispatch of medium tanks.[20]

The inclusion of Iran in war planning probably reflected other national security decisions as much as concern for Iran. The administration recently had adopted NSC-68, which acknowledged a Soviet design for world domination and urged preparation for inevitable crisis. The document recommended expansion of military capabilities everywhere. It increased the importance of nations like Iran, encouraging a larger share for them in defence of the free world.

Negotiation continued on the text of a bilateral agreement required before the United States could send MDAP aid. The shah wanted the agreement worded in such fashion that he would not have to submit it to the Majlis. Wiley supported this view, and in May 1950 the agreement took effect without parliamentary approval – a second time the United States had acquiesced in this sort of arrangement.[21]

Matériel did not begin to arrive until the following year, for firms that had converted to peacetime production in 1945 had to fill orders. NATO had priority, and there were problems of distance, and – after 25 June 1950 – the Korean War. By August 1950, France and Belgium had received only 5 per cent of MDAP allotments, a year later only half had arrived in Western Europe. To Americans in Tehran and even more to Iranian military leaders it seemed that Iran had to stand at the end of the line.[22]

In Tehran meanwhile a search commenced for a new prime minister, for rising domestic opposition to Mansur had disenchanted the shah. Privately he insisted that Mansur must get the oil agreement ratified, and as this seemed hopeless it sealed the prime minister's fate. Razmara was attracting attention as a successor. The press and much of the public, tired of indecision, increasingly mentioned his name, and declared that hard times demanded strong measures.[23]

Razmara was a capable, hard-working, puritanical officer who had managed to gain the shah's confidence and become the second most important figure in Tehran. He displayed none of the usual signs of wealth, and was apparently honest, unlike many of his contemporaries – power was his reward. An ardent nationalist, he had discouraged foreign attempts to gain influence in his country. More realistic than the shah as to the Iranian military, he preferred a small, efficient army – agreeing with the view of Washington. He was ambitious but rarely exposed his feelings. The only positions that could have satisfied his ambition were the prime ministership and the throne. He hid his designs behind a mask, saying he would accept office only if the shah insisted. As Wiley reported, the general was waiting for the moment, hopeful the oil issue would be resolved. While head of the army he had collected many enemies, but some had relaxed their opposition because of the national crisis. If he were to become prime minister, he believed he could put through a reform and lead the nation out of its confusion. He had conceived a Napoleonic plan, hoping for the same results he had obtained in the army, where he had made progress. He knew where he wanted to go and expected to make decisions and be obeyed.[24]

Observers concluded that the general would be the natural choice of Britain and the USSR, for he would establish a strong government to pass the oil agreement through the Majlis and settle border disputes with the Russians. In the conspiratorial atmosphere of Tehran, some whispered that Razmara had already obtained endorsement from London, Moscow and Washington.[25]

Americans promoted General Razmara as prime minister – and not only officials at the embassy. In June, Max Thornburg cabled the State

Department to ask whether the United States would support Razmara if he took measures to get reform underway; clearly Razmara had in mind extraconstitutional measures, perhaps jailing the opposition and ruling by decree. Thornburg had discussed this course with the shah, who seemed amenable but wanted American support. The department stalled, replying that Grady soon would arrive and evaluate the situation. By then it was common knowledge that the general was acceptable – an idea the embassy conveyed and Washington echoed.[26]

The problem of the prime ministership pointed in the direction of Razmara. Mansur was incapable of action. The elder statesmen – Hakimi, Sa'ed, Qavam – were ill or out of favour. Another candidate, Seyed Zia ed-Din Tabataba'i, was too closely associated with British interests, and the shah refused to agree to his demand that the court give a written guarantee of non-interference before he took office. Musaddiq's influence was rising, a development not appreciated, however, by Americans who dismissed the National Front as misguided, fanatical and xenophobic.[27]

The issue of Mansur's dismissal came down to timing. London was anxious to get as much as possible from him before he left office, and in mid-June Ambassador Francis Shepherd (who had replaced Le Rougetel) thought he saw a chance of getting the oil agreement through the Majlis. But the Americans were anxious to have Razmara's appointment coincide with Grady's arrival. On 17 June, the day before he left Tehran, Wiley told the shah he thought the time had arrived to elevate the new leader.[28]

On 26 June the shah confidently appointed Razmara. A few days before, the general had spent two hours at Musaddiq's house, but Musaddiq refused to compromise and remained free to harass the new government. On the day of appointment the general presented his cabinet to the shah. Razmara hoped to break the pattern that drew ministers from an élite; of humble origin, he wanted to appeal to intellectuals and reformers without concern for the upper class, and cabinet choices reflected this philosophy. He hoped to draw support away from the National Front. Despite street demonstrations and denunciations by Musaddiq and the front deputies, the new prime minister on 4 July won a vote of confidence (97–7). That afternoon he attended an Independence Day celebration at the American embassy.[29]

At last all the pieces seemed to fit. The United States had agreed to a slight increase in military aid, while the comings and goings at the embassy heightened expectation. A new prime minister, the strongest in several years, promised reform with the shah's support. An economic mission now appeared, its arrival coinciding with Razmara's assumption of office, headed by an ambassador whose name was synonymous with aid to Greece.[30]

That springtime and early summer of 1950 marked a poised moment in the affairs of the United States, a time of hope in Tehran, just before an event in East Asia turned American plans into confusion. The rancours of World War II, so deeply felt in Tehran under occupation by the Big Three, were beginning to disappear. The monarchy had found a strong premier, a man who seemed to respect the shah and yet had come up from the people, a man whose military position ensured support of that important group. As spring turned into summer in the dusty capital, the place where even in 1950, as reporters from Western countries had noticed years earlier, the city's water ran through the open ditches, the bustle of cars on the streets, of passers-by on the sidewalks, merchants in the shops, began every morning as usual and ran on through the day, halting for the afternoon naps that all Iranians enjoyed, during the height of the sun. Later the iron shutters on stores were pulled up, with a rumbling noise that itself almost betokened a renewal of economic life, and the day slowly blended into evening in the capital as the cloudless sky lost its blue and turned gradually darker into night. The lights came on and people continued about their business or pleasure. The capital seemed a lively place, symbolic of the survival of the country. Each day the tent people on the city's outskirts were at work on the roads and doing something constructive. Everywhere life appeared to be brightening a little. Iran thus could come into modernity through its own and Western efforts, perhaps led by the United States of America, advanced by the newly-appointed American ambassador, Grady, who already had revived another nearby nation.

7   The Grady Mission

The arrival of the Grady mission and establishment of the Razmara government coincided, alas, with the outbreak of war in Korea, which diverted attention from Iran and the entire Middle East. At the outset its effect was not quite clear. Throughout the summer the military situation in Korea was so confused that the Americans may have wondered what they were getting into. The State Department had been considering expanded economic aid to countries in the Middle East and South Asia. Now the last slim chance for an increase in aid evaporated. In a meeting with Acheson on 28 August, President Truman said Congress would not accept such a programme, given requirements in East Asia.[1]

Not only was Congress unlikely to approve new economic aid but it trimmed programmes already established. Congress reduced Marshall Plan funds by $200 million and cut by half the administration's Point Four request, a modest $27 million. If military spending required by Korea met little opposition on Capitol Hill, congressmen reflected public opinion when they said that the government should compensate as much as possible by reductions elsewhere.

Of course, Iran did not disappear from view. Although the economic crisis seemed less urgent now that Grady had arrived and Razmara had taken over as prime minister, there was continuing concern in Washington over Soviet plans for Iran and for other nations on the periphery. During the weeks following the North Korean attack American leaders anxiously tried to predict Russian policy. President Truman ordered the National Security Council to study how events in Korea were likely to affect nations bordering the Soviet Union and its satellites. The commander in East Asia, General MacArthur, assumed that Iran would be the next Soviet victim.[2]

American concern for friendly nations, following the North Korean attack over the 38th parallel in South Korea, deserves some explanation, for without sensing the feeling that looked towards disaster, it is impossible to understand the actions of officials in the summer of 1950. Only months later, when the Chinese intervened, did confidence in the ability of the United States to handle affairs, to preserve a modicum of the Western Allied position as it stood at the end of World War II, sink even lower.

Part of the problem with the North Korean attack was that it did not seem in any sense local – the Soviets simply had to be behind it. Years later, when Nikita Khrushchev dictated his reminiscences and the tapes were taken out of Russia and excerpts published in the West, it became possible to see responsibility. The Soviets had consulted the Chinese and then allowed the North Koreans to attack, for South Korea appeared to be an easy victim.

But the problem lay deeper than Soviet complicity. The grand question was what the attack might lead to. Would it be a feint, a gesture to force attention on Korea, whereupon the Russians would attack Western Europe? Did it mean the Soviets would move against other divided countries, Germany and Austria? Did it mark the beginning of worldwide hostilities, verging on World War III?

When the Truman administration at first had confronted the worldwide prospects in the spring of 1950 it had found trouble in many places, but the State Department and Pentagon believed that the Cold War was settling down. There was some thought that the election of Truman in 1948, in the face of what seemed impossible political circumstances, had confirmed the nation's foreign policy. In the year and a half from January 1949 until June 1950 the administration had relaxed and almost enjoyed the world, as well as the American domestic scene. There had been problems abroad, as when in late August 1949 the Soviet Union exploded a nuclear device. The administration met that problem in October by transferring, through presidential decision, $300 million to the Atomic Energy Commission, commencing an all-out search for formulas and designs for a hydrogen bomb; the American bomb was to be tested in 1952. The nuclear race, lay, however, in the future. For a year and more after the president's inauguration the prospect was still enjoyable.

Then had come the Korean War, which opened one Saturday evening when the president was at home in Independence, enjoying the quiet of the town in which he had spent his youth during the 1890s. The next day, Sunday, came confirmation of the attack, and Truman ordered his plane and flew back to Washington. For months thereafter, the war occupied American officials.

A report of the National Security Council dated 1 July became the official interpretation of Soviet policy towards Iran. It concluded that unless the Soviet Union had decided to begin World War III, which seemed unlikely, it would avoid aggression against states along its borders; more likely it would work through the satellites in Eastern Europe, as it had done in North Korea. Although Iran seemed a target, American fears were unjustified, for Moscow surely recognised the risk of world war should it invade Iran. Soviet troop movements in the

Caucasus and naval manoeuvres in the Caspian Sea were pressure tactics, nothing more. What should concern the United States, the report concluded, was internal subversion in Iran or a turn towards neutralism. In either case there seemed little the United States could do beyond bolstering neighbouring Turkey and Iraq.[3]

The study, with its emphasis on internal stability, enhanced the importance of the Grady mission, just getting down to work. Grady believed his assignment indicated a change in policy. Acheson saw the mission differently, likening it to that of Arthur C. Millspaugh during the war years: as an economic adviser Grady might persuade the Iranian government to set its house in order without further assistance. He noted the success of Grady in Greece without acknowledging its link with the sums made available under the Truman Doctrine. He saw the Iranian mission as a simple effort to bring economic progress.[4]

Grady opened his mission with the éclat that after World War II often marked ambassadorial beginnings. In the days before the war it was necessary for envoys to use available transportation, which meant long sea voyages and then trips by train – the railway stations were the points of ceremony. After the war the airports became the places. Grady flew in from Athens, and at the bottom of the ramp stood the staff of the Tehran embassy, as well as emissaries of the Shah of Shahs. In a long line to the airport waiting room stood Iranian soldiers and army officers, giving expression to the new envoy's importance.

With evidences of democratic simplicity, but enjoying the scene, the erstwhile university professor shook hands with his colleagues and walked slowly to his limousine.

The ambassador and staff set to work, and everyone felt hopeful as long as the administration acted quickly. On 17 September, Iran's application for a $25 million Export-Import Bank loan arrived in Washington, and in a cable Grady pointed out that the projects to be financed by the loan were well conceived and included agriculture and roads. He asked permission to present this loan as the first instalment of a $100 million commitment to Iran, on condition that the instalment was wisely used.[5]

The mission thereupon encountered its first setback, perhaps even a rebuff. The State Department refused to support the ambassador. Acheson believed Iran could not use such a credit wisely. Moreover, there was the Korean War. Money was beginning to pour out for the army, navy and air force, funds the Truman administration had denied ever since the end of World War II. Outlays were fuelling inflation – though the prospect of domestic shortages had perhaps brought on the inflation. The administration was in no mood to support large credits to Iran.[6]

Grady began to discern that he could receive no support from the British government, which had maintained a considerable importance in Allied policy towards such Middle Eastern countries as Iran. The Americans preferred to follow British leadership there – safer than venturing into issues with which the State Department had little experience.

But when Acheson travelled to London for a foreign ministers' meeting, officials recommended tying the Export-Import loan to ratification of the new Anglo-Iranian Oil Company agreement. The secretary discouraged the idea; the oil company was becoming unpopular in Iran, and he wished to avoid association between the United States and British oil. He encouraged the British to concede details in the dispute. He reminded Bevin of American advice that Iran should pay for its development – advice based on expectation of expanding oil revenue. The secretary had considered this revenue more important than any short-term assistance the United States might supply. The British thus were more concerned about their oil company than they were about diplomatic issues, especially American economic aid. Britain's economy was in an awkward condition. Iranian oil revenues were important.[7]

The London meeting could have been the turning point, the time when the United States seized the initiative on Iran. Washington had responded to the early Cold War crises of 1947–49 and did not rely yet on London for support in East Asia or over rearmament in Western Europe. Instead nothing happened.[8]

By mid-September the Near East division did press for aid to Iran. Assistant Secretary McGhee flew to London on 23 September to ask the British to guarantee Iranian oil royalties to service the loan. The British believed such a commitment would strain the pound. The loan might strengthen Iran's resistance to the new oil agreement. He did persuade the head of the Eastern Department to try to convince the Treasury. The chancellor of the exchequer, Hugh Gaitskell, refused, observing that if the United States wanted to get the credit for saving Iran's economy it should service the loan. Gaitskell offered to support a joint US-UK loan. Prime Minister Attlee agreed to guarantee convertibility of the Iranian oil royalties for one year to give time to find an alternative. He suggested that the two governments press Razmara to tighten exchange controls to prevent Iranians from sending dollars out of the country.[9]

The almost tentative proposal of co-operation did not satisfy the

Americans. The chief British delegate at the UN, Sir Gladwyn Jebb, reported that Acheson expected Britain to service the Export-Import Bank loan, and London made a small concession, agreeing to make $6 million available to Iran for purchase of agricultural and other machinery not sold outside the United States. In Tehran, Grady informed his British colleague that this concession was useless.[10]

At this point Acheson pressed the Export-Import Bank to grant a loan to Iran. The chairman, Herbert Gaston, had refused to extend credit without a guarantee of repayment, and the State Department engaged almost in arm-twisting before Gaston and the board overcame their scruples. Rountree and the director of the Office of Near East and African Affairs, Burton Y. Berry, with support of Assistant Secretary H. Freeman Matthews, persuaded Acheson to telephone the chairman, arguing that the Soviets would soon announce assistance to Iran, that the United States should make its commitment before the Russians. Acheson said he had talked to the British foreign secretary, and the Foreign Office would probably give a satisfactory answer concerning sterling-dollar conversion; but even if it did not the bank should act. The board of directors approved the $25 million loan.[11]

Anglo-American negotiations now became even more complicated. Acheson at first had reason for optimism regarding the British. He and Bevin had just completed talks in New York where they discussed East Asia and Germany. Compared to events in Korea and Europe, conditions in Iran assumed less importance, and yet recent meetings had been so amicable – at least as far as concerned Bevin and Acheson – that it is unlikely Acheson foresaw difficulty. Bevin and the Foreign Office would have accommodated the Americans on the loan. But the Treasury now refused. Attlee usually supported Bevin, and yet accepted Gaitskell's view, and relented only a little in late October when he offered Iran the $6 million.

The State Department informed Grady that the bank had approved the loan, and Razmara announced to the Majlis the crediting of $25 million to Iran's account, with expectation of more. The deputies applauded.

Optimism over the $25 million loan did not last. The cable from the bank announcing approval included a demand that Iran adopt measures to ensure repayment. Gaston had refused to allow for special handling. The State Department considered the loan political, as Acheson had indicated, but upper-level department officials, whether from inadvertence, lack of conviction, or pressing problems, had ceased to push the bank once the loan received approval. Grady soon received letters from friends in the department who accused colleagues of procrastinating. The ambassador began to understand that the Iranian situation, seemingly so urgent in the spring, had sunk again to low priority, and that commitment even to $25 million was conditional. Washington viewed the loan as a problem in banking, and years later Acheson captured the attitude: 'The Department . . . nagged at the lending agencies but could hardly fault their judgment that Iran in absence of some agreement with the Anglo-Iranian Oil Company did not look like a good risk'.[12]

As matters turned out, everything turned into complexity. The Export-Import Bank asked the Iranian government to send financial and technical experts to work out details. The bank insisted that the Majlis as well as the executive approve the loan and that the Iranian budget make provision for sums to cover interest, institute exchange restrictions and make overtures to the British government for sterling-dollar conversion. American experts must oversee projects, and Grady tried to convince the bank and the State Department that although these provisions might work, the Iranian situation demanded a minimum of red tape. Xenophobia was increasing, as the oil dispute with Britain was worsening. Facing an increasingly hostile parliament, Razmara was reluctant to submit an agreement; he seemed convinced that he had authority under the seven-year plan to borrow from foreign banks. The prime minister, it is true, originally had suggested submitting loan legislation to the Majlis, but as his troubles increased he changed strategy. Grady pointed out that even Greece, to which the United States had contributed hundreds of millions, had not complied with all American requests. He made little headway. The Iranian delegation reached Washington in early November, and negotiation dragged on as Iranian experts took exception to details in each of the 15 paragraphs of fine print the bank insisted on. The Iranians believed that less deserving nations had received far more from the United States, with far fewer conditions. They mentioned Indonesia, Afghanistan and Turkey.[13]

Patience in Tehran began to come to an end. During an interview with a Reuters correspondent on 27 November 1950, the shah criticised the United States for failure to provide aid, except obsolete military equipment at high rates of interest. He attacked 'carping criticism' regarding corruption and dictatorship, and returned to the theme of the unjust treatment of Iran by Washington compared to Greece and Turkey. The interview, which he gave without consulting the prime minister, caused a sensation in Tehran. Razmara rushed to dissociate himself from it, but the damage was done. It jeopardised any hope of getting a loan agreement through the Majlis.[14]

Grady's cables turned accusatory, claiming the Export-Import Bank's methods had discredited the United States government and that the State Department seemed to go out of its way to accommodate the British. The secretary and some of his assistants appeared out of sympathy; they were convinced that the ambassador had brought 'big money' ideas from Athens to Tehran. They thought he was obsessed by negotiation of the loan, whether the Iranians needed it or even wanted it and that this obsession arose from concern for personal prestige. Actually Grady had never advocated giveaway programmes. When he arrived he had recommended loans, and only as he became aware of the local financial difficulties did he modify his advice. After a change of mind in October, he returned to advocacy of loans. His attitude was conservative, no-nonsense. He was an unlikely advocate of extravagance. His disagreement with Washington arose out of misunderstanding as to the commitment for Iran. Coming from Greece, where the United States did have a commitment, he assumed that the department contemplated a similar policy, and in good faith promised economic assistance. He may have shown too much independence. There was little justification for the criticism he later received over the issue.[15]

All the while the direction of American policy wavered. The Americans seemed preoccupied with such issues as aid, and believed that somehow or other aid would help Iran towards stability. Perhaps the concern was understandable, for the Americans were torn between the ideal and real, the proposals Grady was sponsoring and the feeling of Acheson and his assistants that money to Iran would go down the drain.

American failure to consult the British on the Korean War made co-operation on Iran uneasy. At the beginning of October, London had been shocked to learn that General MacArthur possessed authority to cross the 38th parallel. American announcement of the Export-Import Bank loan on 6 October, again without consultation, worried the British. Then they learned that a large part of the agricultural equipment recommended for purchase with the loan was available in Britain, although American officials had assured them it could be obtained only in the United States. According to the British embassy in Tehran, Max Thornburg had drawn up the list with the intention of giving contracts to friends in America. In London negative impressions of Grady seemed confirmed. Ambassador Shepherd, not without a touch of boastfulness, reported that America's prestige had plummeted as a result of failure to provide assistance, and Iran had turned again to Britain as the leading Western nation.[16]

Grady again sought to push Iran's case and went back to Washington early in December for two weeks of talks. He warned department officials that after the shah's angry interview the Majlis might reject the loan. He raised the spectre of Soviet attack; Iranian soldiers – like their South Korean counterparts – would have to face Soviet tanks with the only weapons they possessed, their rifles; Iranians would fight if armed and trained. He did pry loose one shipload of Military Defense Assistance equipment. He succeeded in getting President Truman to write Gaston inquiring about the loan. But the bank's chairman adhered to the view that the loan must not be made loosely, and Grady returned empty-handed except for a wedding gift from the president to the shah.[17]

The two sides completed loan negotiations in early January 1951. But it was too late. Razmara had already crossed swords with the Majlis over oil, and no one expected him to submit the agreement. Washington officials believed the Iranian government had conspired to defeat the loan so it later could press the United States to extend more aid, but this fanciful view did not take account of the prime minister's difficulties. Once it became obvious that the Majlis would not accept a loan, even with a simplified contract, the Export-Import Bank agreed to make the loan directly to the largest commercial bank, the Bank-i-Melli. The Iranians instead suggested the Plan Organisation. So it went, through January, proposal and counterproposal. Eventually the project of a $25 million loan from the Export-Import Bank disappeared. In the course of its disappearance Grady returned to his idea of a $100 million loan. McGhee wrote Assistant Secretary for Economic Affairs Willard L. Thorp, at Grady's request, urging a grant of $25 million. Thorp and Adrian Fisher, legal adviser to the secretary of state, showed no enthusiasm.[18]

In the Iranian case one could excuse the Export-Import Bank for its practices – Congress had not designed it for crises, but in retrospect it is clear that the State Department must bear responsibility for the fumbling, and Acheson eventually acknowledged that he should have acted with decision. The Export-Import Bank had come a long way, and State Department officials had espoused grant aid that had seemed undesirable a few months earlier. The psychological moment passed. The loan fell prey to long-held suspicions in Tehran, London and Washington, a casualty to changing conditions. Grady felt vindicated. In later years, as uncertainty, disorder and violence swept Iran, he argued that the United States had missed an opportunity. Despite reports, missions and cables that argued repeatedly for assistance, the only American aid in 1946–50 proved the $25.8 million loan of 1947 for purchase of surplus military equipment. Such a statistic hardly reflected Iran's strategic location on the eastern flank of the great northern barrier.[19]

During this period another possibility of aid, less strictly American in origin, was the International Bank for Reconstruction and Development. As the proposal for $25 million from the Export-Import Bank wound its way through American, Iranian, even British diplomacy, and strangled to death in red tape, a proposal went to the International Bank. Prodded by the State Department, the International Bank sent a delegation to Iran in the spring of 1950 that recommended a loan for rehabilitation and expansion of port facilities at Khorramshahr in the southwest and also asked for two cement plants. The bank's directors accounced that they would only negotiate a $4 million loan for the port, and asked for more information on the cement plants. This tightfistedness angered Iranians, especially as $25 million of the bank's assets belonged to Tehran. When the Iranian commission arrived in Washington to discuss the Export-Import Bank loan, Grady and department officers urged International Bank officials to reopen discussions. The head of the delegation, Dr Ahmad Moqbel, arranged a meeting with the bank vice-president, Robert Garner, who suggested that as long as the Export-Import Bank had become involved in Iran's finances Tehran should go there. When Moqbel threatened to report Garner's views to his government, the vice-president assured him that these were personal views and said Moqbel should return in several days. Garner's attitude upset State Department officials and McGhee expressed displeasure to American representatives on the bank board. The bank agreed to reconsider, on condition that the United States ensure that Iran would contract no more foreign loans and take steps to arrange financing and institute budgetary and administrative reform. With nationalisation of the Anglo-Iranian Oil Company in March 1951, the bank suspended negotiation. Iran's relations with the International Bank became the butt of jokes in the Iranian press, and the humour masked considerable bitterness.[20]

Such were some of the troubles of Prime Minister Razmara. The National Front attacked him, especially after he tried to bring the oil agreement to a vote in parliament. Unaccustomed to sharing power he treated cabinet ministers like junior officers, and they turned uncooperative. In accord with the 'new look' in government, most of the ministers were young; they were inexperienced, unschooled in the bureaucracy, and even if they had remained sympathetic to the general's programme they faced problems trying to administer their departments. Razmara would have preferred to do all the work himself and frequently took decisions without discussion, increasing the chance for mistakes. To make matters worse, at the shah's insistence he brought Ghulam Husain Furuhar into the cabinet as minister of labour. An opponent of

Razmara's respected finance minister, Dr Taqi Nasr, Furuhar divided the cabinet and eventually drove out Taqi Nasr and took his place.[21]

The prime minister sought the dismissal of Abul Hasan Ebtehaj as head of the Bank-i-Melli. Ebtehaj was a trusted adviser to the shah, his wife was a lady-in-waiting to Princess Ashraf. Foreign bankers liked to work with him because of his forthright manner. But he had overridden the measures of successive cabinets in favour of tight-money policies. He had outmanoeuvred Dr Taqi Nasr for control of the Plan Organisation, and Taqi Nasr determined to put a stop to Ebtehaj's rigid control over finances. At Razmara's insistence the shah appointed Ebtehaj ambassador in Paris.[22]

Otherwise the shah gave little support to Razmara, nor did the latter ask for assistance, wishing to be his own man. Razmara had relinquished his post as chief of staff when he became prime minister, but left friendly officers in control, and the shah began to transfer many of the general's appointees and merged Razmara's former division with the imperial guard.[23]

One of Razmara's proposals advocated decentralisation of the Tehran bureaucracy, a laudable goal because the increase of the capital city's power, wealth and population was draining the rest of the nation. This too raised alarm. In a nation with many minorities politicians feared loss of control to the periphery. Musaddiq spoke against the measure, reminding listeners of independence movements in Azarbaijan and Kurdistan. Debates became so vitriolic that the beleaguered prime minister refused to attend parliamentary committee meetings and exchanged insults with deputies on the floor of the Majlis.[24]

As if all this were not enough, Razmara launched an anticorruption campaign. His 'purge' committee published a list of several hundred Iranians judged unfit for public service, and among them appeared some of the most powerful names in the country, including the speaker of the Majlis. The prime minister then attended parliament with three ministers whose names had graced the list, and Dr Musaddiq shouted at the ministers to withdraw. Razmara reluctantly – and far too belatedly – abandoned the campaign.[25]

Razmara did prove effective in dealing with the Soviet Union, although events played into his hands. Iranian-Soviet relations had been improving since late in 1949, when Russian propaganda attacks slackened. He took advantage of the new spirit to negotiate a trade agreement offering a much-needed outlet for Iranian products. Eleven captured Iranian soldiers returned, and discussion began over return of Iranian gold taken during the war. The Korean War brought careful

Iranian manoeuvring. Razmara avoided sending troops to East Asia. With United Nations reverses in Korea during November-December 1950, he openly proclaimed neutralism – although he added that Iran would fight to defend itself.[26]

The Soviet move to better relations with Iran was part of a 'peace offensive' to undermine support for the United States in Europe and Asia. The Stockholm Peace Appeal, a communist-inspired petition to outlaw nuclear warfare, attracted considerable strength in many countries, including Iran. The Soviets emphasised US setbacks in Korea to bring into question American military prowess. The propaganda could be formidable in Iran, given the proximity of the two nations.[27]

But Razmara's Russian policy created no friends in Washington. In the charged atmosphere of 1950, 'neutral' became an epithet. Although the National Security Council had concluded that the Russians would probably not act rashly, knowing that this might lead to World War III, there was the possibility of miscalculation, especially if Moscow believed the United States was unconcerned. In case of Soviet aggression the British would be in command in Iran, the American plan stipulated. The two Western allies would try to involve Pakistan and India, while the United States moved any spare US naval forces into the Persian Gulf. In such an emergency Iranian forces perhaps would delay the Soviets so that the shah and his government could withdraw to the mountains. Razmara's neutralism, which some Washingtonians called appeasement, meanwhile threatened to align Iran with the Soviet bloc. American officials beheld threats everywhere on the Soviet periphery, and Razmara's attempt to take Iran into the non-aligned bloc alienated them.[28]

In one sense any concern for Iran's position in Middle Eastern strategy became a modest 'plus' for Iran, though Razmara and his critics doubtless understood imperfectly how what they did or said might move the Americans. The CIA director, Rear Admiral Roscoe H. Hillenkoetter, concerned over Soviet 'softening up' of Iran, presented a detailed memorandum to the president on 27 July 1950 in which he argued that Iran would pursue a neutral course in the Cold War unless assured of American commitment to maintain its independence. The State Department, concerned about increasing Soviet-Iranian trade, asked the Department of Defense to find markets for Iranian rice in East Asia so that Iran would not become dependent on the Soviets.[29]

Razmara made no secret of his increasing resentment towards the United States. He ended Voice of America relay broadcasts over Radio Tehran. When ten Tudeh party leaders escaped from prison, it looked as

if he had arranged it. When the first shiploads of Military Defense
Assistance equipment finally arrived at Khorramshahr in January 1951,
he downplayed the occasion, refusing passes to correspondents who
wished to report the event. The port master met the vessels. To one of his
American advisers Razmara commented bitterly that Washington sent
him tanks when he needed wheat.[30]

Razmara faced daily attack in the Majlis. Dr Musaddiq used Korea to
support his argument against strongman rule. He claimed that after the
Americans withdrew most of their troops from South Korea in 1948,
they assumed that a military mission and rifles would be enough to
maintain the weak and undemocratic regime of Syngman Rhee. 'Once
again the Americans had to learn the lesson of China', he said, 'that arms
and American dollars are not enough in Asia to prevent the spread of
communism. What is needed is a regime firmly based on popular
support.' The analogy between Korea and Iran, Rhee and Razmara,
was clear.[31]

Razmara's neutralism strengthened American inclination to look to
the shah as the anti-Soviet bulwark in Iran. Washington decided that the
best way to show concern for Iran – and please the shah – was to expedite
the shipment of tanks and howitzers, which 'would point up our interest
in the Iranian people in an impressive way'. The director of mutual
assistance in the State Department, John H. Ohly, congratulated Major
General Stanley L. Scott on the fine work Defense had done in packing,
loading and shipping *matériel*, all in less than one week during
December 1950.[32]

Iran's economy continued to limp along. The first seven-year plan, a
casualty of financial stringency, came to naught. After the plan's
enthusiastic inauguration, the dispute with the AIOC restricted money
for it and later cut it off. The Iranian government transferred moribund
state industries established by Reza Shah, which used up revenues, to the
Plan Organisation. The national treasury made raids on Plan Organisation funds to meet budget deficits. Political in-fighting and turnover in
Plan Organisation personnel, together with Ebtehaj's exiling to Paris,
and grumbling by the Iranian public about corruption, all affected the
plan.[33]

Along with collapse of the seven-year plan came the demise of
Overseas Consultants. Like the Millspaugh mission during the war,
foreign advisers had encountered problems with Iranian counterparts,
who accused Americans of dictating, while the advisers claimed that
Iranians gave little support and showed an irrepressible preference for
showy projects. Some of the fault lay with Thornburg who had been

remiss in not maintaining ties with the embassy, once his consortium had negotiated the contract. In the beginning he had argued that Iran's plight resulted not from the antiquated landholding system or government inefficiency but from bad seed, poor roads and ill health – factors more manageable and less controversial. As conflicts between OCI technical advisers and Iranian officials became commonplace, Thornburg in an interview with the leading Tehran daily, *Kayhan*, expressed dissatisfaction that Iran had accomplished so little. He attributed the performance to young men with no experience and old men with titles. Iranians could achieve results if they would get on with the job. In America 'the test of a man's worth', he said, 'is not the degree or titles he carries around, but his ability to get some worthwhile task performed'. Such frankness hardly endeared him to local officials, and the Iranian government cancelled the OCI contract on 7 January 1951, much to the surprise of Thornburg, who claimed that Grady had him run out of the country because the ambassador was jealous of his ties to Iranian leaders.[34]

At first Grady had encouraged OCI directors not to abandon their enterprise, lest it seem that Americans were pulling out just as Grady's mission got underway. But in December when Grady met them again in Washington the situation had changed. Iran and the United States had signed a Point Four agreement in October 1950, and the need for private technical advisers no longer seemed urgent, or so Grady believed.[35]

By early 1951 it was obvious that the Grady mission also had failed. Many factors had contributed, only some of them American. The promise of 1950 gave way to disillusionment in 1951. East Asia had preoccupied Washington. Razmara had come to power with America's blessing, and turned anti-American.

Iran desired to be more than a pawn in the Cold War, and Razmara's neutralism emphasised this idea. Yet after six months the general had achieved only one of his three foreign goals – a *détente* with the Soviet Union. American economic assistance had eluded him. The dispute with the Anglo-Iranian Oil Company thereupon turned into crisis.

8 The Oil Crisis

Ambassador Wiley expected early Majlis approval of the supplementary oil agreement after its signing in July 1949, but public opinion turned against it, and during the months to January 1951 the contract did not come to a vote, for opposition seemed almost unanimous. The oil issue contributed to the fall of Ali Mansur in June 1950; he was unable to bring the supplementary agreement to a vote. His successor, Razmara, anxious to introduce reforms and strengthen control in the country, left the agreement in the hands of the special Majlis oil committee that Mansur had set up. Razmara beheld the agreement as a child abandoned on his doorstep and refused responsibility. Despite repeated committee requests for documents giving details of the negotiations, the government dragged its feet, and not until late October 1950 – four months after taking office – did Razmara inform the committee of his support for the agreement.[1]

At first the shah supported the supplementary agreement, probably hoping, like his father earlier, to maintain the flow of money. He sent his ambassador in Paris, Ali Soheily, to Portugal to visit the aged Armenian, Calouste Gulbenkian, the 'Mr 5 per cent' of Middle East oil and a long-time honorary Iranian consul, to learn Gulbenkian's opinion as to whether he should support the agreement. The British feared that a grudge from the war years would prejudice him. They need not have worried, for the 80-year-old oil magnate had always separated personal feelings from business decisions. He told Soheily that the contract was in the best interest of Iran. The old man declined a British offer to fly him to Tehran to give more advice. Conservative business instincts and his distaste for strident nationalism – the force that had driven his family into exile – determined his recommendation to the shah.[2]

Reassured by Gulbenkian and under British pressure, the shah urged Razmara to act, and with some changes Razmara was willing to go forward. The prime minister supported the proposed contract in a senate speech on 18 October 1950 and again at a meeting of the oil committee. The general understood that nationalist expectations necessitated some alteration in the contract. Earlier the Iranians had sought an additional 20 per cent of undistributed profits, but Razmara wanted no change in financial clauses; in secret negotiations with the AIOC he asked instead for other concessions: a higher percentage of Iranians trained and employed, a lower price for AIOC products sold in Iran,

Iranian government access to company books, official monitoring of oil exports. None of these concessions would have impaired company control.[3]

If only the British government and the Anglo-Iranian Oil Company had displayed a modicum of common sense and sensitivity towards developments in Iran, the measure could have become law. Prime Minister Sa'ed had made a secret trip to London in October 1949 to discuss revision of the agreement with his friend the chancellor of the exchequer, Sir Stafford Cripps, and with Sir William Fraser and the board of the Anglo-Iranian Oil Company. Sa'ed asked the British government to compensate Iran for substantial losses because of the excess-profit tax, dividend limit, and cut-rate oil sales to the Royal Navy. London responded that the problem was for discussion between the Iranian government and the AIOC. Unimpressed by warnings from its representatives in Tehran, the board of the AIOC in London had refused compromise.[4]

The AIOC refused all concessions. Company officers reporting from Tehran warned that National Front opposition would be difficult to overcome. Ambassador Shepherd wrote that the Iranians had never been happy with the agreement and without some changes, giving more control, they would not compromise – control was more important than money. But when the Foreign Office suggested that the company might consider more rapid Iranisation, Fraser rejected the suggestion, alleging lack of qualified Iranians. In reply to the shah's suggestion that the company publicise the proposed agreement, poorly understood by deputies, AIOC representatives said the task belonged to the Iranian government. When the shah offered new proposals, these too the company brushed aside, despite Foreign Office advice to take them seriously. British officials seemed divided, waiting for Fraser to find a solution. Bevin wrote in desperation: 'This should be settled; find out what will settle it'. The gap between the oil company and the Iranians widened.[5]

To Americans it appeared that the AIOC had decided to 'put the screws on the Iranians', insisting on all details of the supplementary agreement, refusing to lessen the stringencies of the government in Tehran until the Majlis acted. Americans also guessed that the company would not have continued its intransigence unless supported by the British government. The department recommended that American oil companies in the Middle East avoid acting like the AIOC. It urged them not to tie themselves to local élites but to make their activities known, gather information, inform themselves of popular sentiment. Companies should foster good labour relations and establish machinery for grievances, and must 'roll with the punches'; it would be foolhardy to be inflexible regarding royalties. Washington believed that the pragmatism of American companies made them preferable to those of other nationalities, an attitude that naturally irritated the British.[6]

Paradoxically American officials, at least until nationalisation, probably pondered the Iranian issue more than did authorities in London. As the year 1950 opened the State Department became an intermediary in the developing controversy. In separate discussions with representatives of the AIOC and the British government, its officials argued the fairness of Iranian demands. Assistant Secretary McGhee, recently returned from the Middle East, met in Washington with the new head of the AIOC in Iran, Richard Seddon. An oilman himself, McGhee had read the latest company report and concluded that the AIOC would hardly bankrupt itself by acceding to the changes Iran asked. Conditions were changing, he told his visitor, and the company would have to move with the times. Seddon politely thanked the assistant secretary for his views and departed.[7]

Throughout 1950 the Americans pressed the British. They tried to obtain a settlement, supporting a proposal by Ambassador Grady. The department urged the AIOC to make sizeable sums available to remove financial pressure on Razmara; this would free him to make reforms and ultimately settle the oil problem, perhaps with a new Majlis. The chief AIOC representative in Tehran, George Northcroft, showed amazement when Grady first presented this plan on 8 July, barely a week after arrival. The ambassador stood his ground, arguing that, like the United States in other areas, the oil company had a responsibility to preserve Iran from communism, even if it lost money. Northcroft replied that advances would only bring deterioration.[8]

The British government returned to its earlier suggestion that Washington and London unite in presenting an aid package to Iran, but Washington was now even more reluctant. Meeting in London during September, McGhee urged the British government to intervene with the AIOC to ensure a rapid settlement in Iran, and thus avoid disorder. At the suggestion of the Foreign Office he met with the board of the AIOC and argued flexibility and compromise. The directors were not interested, and one of them wrote Northcroft in Tehran, summing up McGhee's performance: 'It is dangerous when important people obsessed with the communist question express views on complex questions without proper knowledge'. Fraser missed these sessions with McGhee, for he ostentatiously took a month's vacation abroad.[9]

When McGhee arrived back in Washington empty-handed, Acheson cabled the Foreign Office expressing unhappiness. The British sent a vague reply. Bevin now was siding with the company and referred to Iranians as 'these tiresome and headstrong people', and told his assistants to wait for the Majlis to act. AIOC officials became adamant. When Max Thornburg appeared as Razmara's representative to urge compromise, Fraser said cavalierly that Razmara had had his chance but failed and would have to go.[10]

Ambassador Grady rightly was exasperated with the AIOC, for he realised that without a settlement a small Export-Import Bank loan would have slight influence on the Iranian economy. He suspected some collusion between London and Washington, for he knew how much Acheson valued British friendship and surmised that as long as he was in charge the United States would not press Britain. The importance of Anglo-American relations had increased after the outbreak of the Korean War followed by the decision, vehemently opposed by France, to rearm West Germany.

At the close of 1950 the AIOC still was calling the tune for oil policy in Iran. Despairing of accommodation or even any sign from London as to what should happen next, and facing increasing opposition in parliament, Razmara decided to withdraw the supplementary oil agreement.

At this juncture the Foreign Office became agitated over Razmara's financial troubles. It now proposed a sizeable loan.[11]

At last, too, Whitehall seemed prepared to press the AIOC. Officials suggested separating the AIOC's Iranian operations from those in other countries, for this would allow Iran greater control. In London company critics were becoming vocal. Sir Frederick Leggett, Labour's adviser to the AIOC and privy to board discussions, called at the Foreign Office to complain that board members were 'helpless, niggling, without any idea between them, confused, hide-bound, small-minded, blind and generally ineffective'. He and L. A. C. Fry of the Foreign Office agreed that the best solution would be a partnership between the AIOC and Iran.[12]

But differences among ministries hampered action. In early January the Foreign Office official in charge of oil, Peter Ramsbotham, advised setting up a working party on Iran composed of members from several ministries. His suggestions went unheeded, and precious weeks slipped by. If policy had rested with desk officers, action would have been taken, but as in all bureaucracies, the higher the official the less the urgency. In the Foreign Office officials temporised, almost as if they expected the problem to solve itself. Memos circulated. The Foreign Office faced criticism from the more conservative Treasury, which argued that the best course would be to let the company work out arrangements. Treasury officials considered the diplomats too eager to encourage a loan or advance on royalties.[13]

Because the ministries could not agree, Fraser and the board maintained their freedom of action. In late January 1951, without discussion in Whitehall, the AIOC decided to pay royalties at the higher rate established in the unratified supplementary oil agreement. The shah and Razmara received this news with relief, but asked the AIOC not to announce it for fear of opposition in the Majlis, where deputies would conclude that the government and oil company had conspired.[14]

Only later did another company move come to light. Evidently Fraser had sought to reopen negotiation on the basis of a 50–50 proposal, a compromise Iranians had rejected in 1949. Razmara refused to reveal this offer, and not until his death did the company publish it. The general may have believed that any arrangement short of nationalisation was impossible. More likely he anticipated that 50–50 would encourage the Majlis to demand more. He had sought non-financial concessions, which the company still seemed unwilling to negotiate.[15]

The National Front continued its role as a catalyst for nationalisation. The group of eight deputies elected in January 1950 and led by Dr Musaddiq displayed an uncompromising nationalism. Gradually the Iranian political scene played into the hands of the 65-year-old leader of the front.

Musaddiq, the forthcoming leader of Iran, was a fascinating personality. The scion of a prominent landowning family, with a reputation for honesty, patriotism, sound finance and reform – an enviable accomplishment in Iran – he possessed impeccable credentials for leading a national crusade. His father had served as minister of finance in many governments. The son had studied finance and economics in Paris, and received a law degree in 1914 from the University of Neuchâtel. In the years after his return he himself had served as finance minister, minister of foreign affairs, and governor general of Fars and Azarbaijan. But it was as a deputy in the Majlis that he found his *métier*. He had opposed establishment of the Pahlavi dynasty, with the result that Reza Shah had forced him into retirement in 1928. During this first part of his career he developed a dislike of the British, seeing Iran as a sacrifice to British imperialism. Exiled to Khorasan province in 1940, he remained there under house arrest until Reza's abdication. Returning to the Majlis in 1944, he opposed all foreign oil concessions, and led the fight to forbid discussion of concessions without parliamentary approval.[16]

Musaddiq cunningly arranged his election as chairman of parliament's special oil committee set up to review the supplementary agreement and make recommendations. Although only five of 18 committee members belonged to the front, others were sympathetic, and became more so as popular fervour grew. The committee reported unanimously in December 1950 against the Gass-Gulshayan agreement, forcing the Razmara government to withdraw it. The Majlis accepted the committee's report on 11 January 1951, and asked it to recommend a course. By an unhappy coincidence, at that moment news of the Arabian-American Oil Company agreement with Saudi Arabia, a 50–50 arrangement, reached Tehran. The supplementary agreement died instantly.[17]

Prime Minister Razmara wanted to dismiss the Majlis and hold new elections to obtain a more tractable body, but each day popular enthusiasm for nationalisation increased, stirred by the National Front, and so Razmara changed his mind. At first he procrastinated. He met with the non-National Front members of the special oil committee on 21 February 1951, and admitted that nationalisation was likely in the long run. Without revealing the AIOC's proposal he sought authority to reopen talks on the basis of 50–50. But a few days later he returned to the same group and denounced nationalisation in any form. Between these two meetings the British government and the AIOC had expressed displeasure that he had not maintained implacable opposition. The general's about-face weakened his support in the oil committee whose members rightly suspected British meddling.[18]

Razmara changed his mind again, and ordered experts in government departments to report on the practicality of nationalisation. On 3 March, armed with the reports of government-appointed advisers and engineers, he met again with the full committee. He argued that the time for nationalisation was inopportune and, in an attempt calculated to turn the tables, claimed that anyone who supported immediate nationalisation was a traitor.[19]

By this time the British appeared in an even greater muddle than the Iranian prime minister. Shepherd pressed Razmara for 50–50, privately telling his superiors that a bow to nationalisation seemed imperative. In talks with the Americans, London officials clung to the supplementary agreement. The company waited to see what would happen, confident it could manage. The British–AIOC and government – did unite on one issue, opposition to National Front participation in any Iranian government. To the shah they expressed this view repeatedly.[20]

Anglo-American relations deteriorated. After termination of the Overseas Consultants contract, Thornburg publicly blamed Iran's economic problems on the AIOC. State Department officials told an AIOC representative that after the company had bungled, nationalisation seemed a possibility, with all it would mean for loss of Iranian oil. McGhee complained to a representative of the Ministry of Fuel and Power that His Majesty's Government had erred in taking a hands-off attitude, because any dislike for the company in Tehran would attach to the British government. The Americans refused a British request to speak in Tehran on behalf of proposals for a settlement; they agreed only to support a compromise. The British had hoped to convince the Iranians of Anglo-American co-operation, but statements and press leaks from the Americans undermined the plan.[21]

The end to months of muddle in London and Tehran came suddenly and unexpectedly. On 7 March, four days after Razmara's confrontation with National Front committee members, the prime minister fell to an assassin's bullet.

The assassination itself came in a sudden act of violence. For days rumour of an imminent attempt had circulated in the tea houses of the bazaar. If the prime minister knew of it, he paid no attention. Straight to the centre of the bazaar – the Saltaneh Mosque – he went, to represent the shah at a memorial service for a leading cleric. Having just returned from a honeymoon on the Caspian coast, the shah had urged Razmara to stand in for him. Accompanied by a close friend of the monarch, Asadollah Alam, the prime minister entered the spacious courtyard of the mosque and made his way slowly through the crowd of mourners. He had taken no precautions and became separated from his bodyguard. He did not notice the bearded young man eyeing him nervously as he passed; in an instant this fanatic pulled a revolver and fired four shots. Only two struck, one in Razmara's neck, the second in his back. The prime minister collapsed onto the tiled floor of the courtyard and never regained consciousness.

The assassination was catastrophic for the work of Ambassadors Wiley and Grady. Both had done all they could to bring the general to power. Moreover, the general had proved worthy of support. No other leader possessed either the influence or interest in trying to hold back the rising opposition. For all his weakness as a political leader, Razmara had stood up to the National Front.[22]

As news of the assassination spread, American and British officials in Tehran, Washington and London exchanged hurried calls and arranged visits as if to recapture in activity the lost opportunities of bygone months. Suddenly Iran became too important to entrust to desk officers. Wise men took counsel together. But the initiative had passed to the other side.

Officials did not realise that for Iranians the AIOC issue had become more than a quest for royalties. It was a question of national prestige. Only seven weeks separated the death of Razmara and selection of Musaddiq as prime minister.

In Tehran it was first necessary to appoint a successor. After showing independence by rejecting the shah's nominee, the Majlis agreed to Husain Ala. He received no overwhelming endorsement, 69–27 with ten abstentions, followed ominously by a walkout of National Front deputies. Educated in Britain, Ala had held posts in several cabinets, recently serving as court minister, where according to Ambassador Grady he had intrigued with the royal family to undermine Razmara. He was known for being pro-American, anti-British. In early postwar years he had served as ambassador in Washington, presenting Iran's case before the United Nations Security Council in 1946. He had acted against orders of the Qavam government, refusing to withdraw the Iranian complaint after Russian troops departed, because the puppet Pishevari regime still ruled in Tabriz and Russian intentions were unclear. Ties with the West, of course, made him suspect to nationalists.

For a while Musaddiq temporised, seeming to be unsure of his course. Soon after the voting on Ala he announced National Front support, but only as long as the prime minister continued to carry out the will of the people – he must not bow to the British. Musaddiq preferred Ala to the wily Qavam or the pro-British Seyed Zia ed-Din Tabataba'i, who waited in the wings. Ala in turn consulted Musaddiq on his choice of ministers, and included Shams ed-Din Amirala'i of the front as minister of justice in his cabinet. To lesser government positions he appointed Hasan Arfa, Nasrollah Entezam and Fazlollah Zahedi, all enemies of the late prime minister.

But hardly had Ala received a vote of confidence than the British rushed to announce their position. Ambassador Shepherd delivered a strongly worded note warning against any attempt to cancel the oil concession. The Americans reproached the British for not consulting them. The Foreign Office argued for action.[23]

This pronouncement was the last straw. The Majlis voted unanimously on 15 March to nationalise the AIOC.

Five days later the senate concurred. Shepherd had urged several members to boycott the Majlis and prevent a quorum. The court also tried. But deputies would not absent themselves because they feared the consequences, said Shepherd. He gave too little credit to the popularity of nationalisation.[24]

At that point there was nothing more to do. Huge demonstrations broke out in Tehran and provincial cities. Strikes in Abadan and the oilfields of the southwest forced the AIOC to close the refinery. Three Britons and nine Iranians died in Abadan. The Ala government declared martial law in the oilfields and tried to resist the popular demand for seizure of all AIOC properties. The British attributed the rioting to communists. The State Department reminded London that the company on the new year had eliminated worker benefits in the fields, again without consulting the diplomats. The AIOC, Washington said, had almost ensured its discomfiture.[25]

Any possible change on the oil issue, any encouragement from London for the beleaguered Ala, vanished when the Labour government faced its own crisis in March-April 1951. In addition to the Iranian problem the Attlee cabinet encountered Egyptian opposition to troops in the Suez Canal zone. The two problems developed in tandem as Iranians and Egyptians encouraged each other. In Washington, British representatives argued that accepting Iranian nationalisation would lead Egypt to try the same at Suez. Britain's economy remained in a dismal state. The two stalwarts of the Labour government, Cripps and Bevin, resigned because of ill health, and Bevin died in April. Foreign relations passed to the inexperienced Herbert Morrison, formerly Lord President of the Council, who proved incapable of leading the Foreign Office. He seemed in a quandary when he wrote regarding events in Iran, 'So what do we do about it? It doesn't look as if we or AIOC have been too bright'. It proved difficult to get him to apply himself to Middle East problems; years later Attlee referred to his appointment as the greatest mistake of his career. And if this were not enough, Attlee in April accepted the resignations of the principal leftist representatives in the cabinet, Aneurin Bevan, minister of labour, and Harold Wilson, president of the board of trade. These two had opposed spiraling defence expenditures and the cabinet's decision to charge recipients costs under the previously free National Health Service. The prime minister spent April in the hospital with ulcers.[26]

With the government tottering, Attlee and colleagues could not afford the slightest compromise on Iran for fear that public opinion would turn against them. In the years after World War II the British had gone along with Attlee in abandonment of responsibilities in India, letting it take care of its own enmities. It did the same in Greece. It dropped Palestine into the lap of the United Nations. One might have thought departures from imperialism in Iran and Egypt would not have made much difference. Strangely there was a difference. For all their dislike of imperial duties, the British people were reluctant to have officials pushed around by the peoples of the Middle East. There was something irrational here, but the British public in 1951 was in no mood to compromise over the AIOC.[27]

Thus it happened that a Labour government showed itself more imperial than the imperialists. Actually, Socialist cabinets in France were displaying the same sentiments towards troubles in Indochina. Labour had determined long before to keep a presence in the Middle East – military force in Egypt, defence agreements with Jordan, Iraq and other Arab states, oil interests in Iran and the Gulf States. It resolved to maintain communications with Commonwealth nations farther east and guarantee oil supplies at home. This was Bevin's legacy to the Attlee government.[28]

In its last months of power the Labour government proved the epitome of intransigence. When news of strikes, riots and deaths in Iran reached London, the government responded not with encouragement and understanding for Husain Ala but with support for the AIOC. It blamed the rioting on Tudeh agitators or religious fanatics, emphasised benefits for Iran from the supplementary agreement; if Iranians understood the new contract they would endorse it.

Neither government nor company would accept nationalisation, and both hinted darkly of force. The admiralty dispatched the cruiser *Gambia* to Abadan to protect nationals and property, and announced that five warships were within range of the port. On 1 April, Defence Minister Emmanuel Shinwell cautioned Iran not to violate the AIOC contract because 'the sport of twisting the British lion's tail might produce undesirable reactions'. On the day after the rioting in Abadan, 13 April, while discussions with the United States were in progress, Morrison announced in the Commons that the British government reserved the right to protect lives and property, holding the Iranian government responsible. London secretly secured Iraqi permission to bring troops to the base at Shu'aiba for emergency evacuation of personnel from nearby Abadan if necessary.[29]

Public announcements complicated the situation in Iran, provoking the nationalists, increasing difficulties for the Ala government, adding no security to the AIOC position. Bluster was impolitic, for the cabinet had divided over suggestions of force to protect property, the military chiefs were reluctant, and although the defence minister and foreign secretary favoured a hard line, the new chancellor of the exchequer, Hugh Gaitskell, and the prime minister opposed it, not to mention the left wing. Unrealistic threats would provide Iranian extremists with a rhetorical position: they could mock Britain as a paper tiger, and complain of foreign interference and neo-colonialism.[30]

Washington too was unprepared for nationalisation. Although the State Department repeatedly had warned the AIOC and Foreign Office, it had no policy to fit its prediction. For almost a month after Razmara's assassination it waited to see if the British and Iranians would work matters out, a hope that reflected sensitivity to British prestige and experience and little understanding of the crisis. The United States needed Britain's support in Korea and in Western Europe.

The State Department responded to the assassination with a cable urging Grady to support the shah and authorising on-the-spot action by the ambassador, and another cable to McGhee, who was in New Delhi, asking him to proceed to Tehran.[31]

The Central Intelligence Agency admittedly showed concern. Deputy Director Allen Dulles telephoned McGhee's deputy, Burton Y. Berry, and on the morning of 13 March, Berry, Rountree, and Edwin Wright of the State Department met in Dulles's office with the deputy director and two CIA officials, Kermit Roosevelt and Frank Wisner. After presenting agency views on Iran, Dulles offered to carry out any policy the State Department set forth. The department asked the CIA to assign extra agents to Tehran and agreed that Roosevelt should serve as liaison.[32]

The special assistant to the president, Averell Harriman, also took interest in the situation. Harriman had travelled through Iran in 1942 on his way to Moscow, visiting the Abadan oil installation, and had some familiarity with the AIOC. He discussed the situation with Acheson and afterwards detailed to Berry his objections to the Near East division's policy paper on Iran, then under consideration by the National Security Council. He volunteered to see if he could find money for Iran. A week later he again visited Berry, and members of his staff requested copies of outgoing telegrams.[33]

Despite Harriman's reservations the president accepted the policy paper for Iran, NSC 107, on 24 March. The first since 1947, it had been long in preparation and failed to reflect developments. It steered clear of commitments. NSC 107 failed to come to grips with the issue of nationalism or the desire of Iranians to remain neutral in the Cold War.[34]

McGhee arrived in Tehran on 17 March, two days after the Majlis nationalised the AIOC. Interviews followed with the prime minister, and with the shah who received the assistant secretary lounging on a sofa in a darkened audience chamber. He appeared dejected, even frightened, quite unlike the monarch McGhee had met in Washington. He pleaded with McGhee not to ask any action against nationalisation; the issue was too popular. What McGhee could only have guessed was that the shah favoured it, believing that the oil company and the British government had brought on the action. No thought had yet emerged about carrying out the law and it was easier to unite on nationalisation without inquiring what it meant.[35]

McGhee came away convinced that the best solution lay in nationalisation, lip service to Iranian sensibilities. Later there might follow an agreement that would leave the oil concession intact, give the oil company and Iran a 50–50 division of profits, and include minor changes that would meet Iranian demands but have little effect on British control. Ala's selection as prime minister reassured him, and he continued on his travels, visiting Syria and Israel, and did not arrive in London until 1 April.[36]

McGhee's brief visit to Tehran was not soon forgotten. In talks with Shepherd he had criticised both the AIOC and the British government. The Iranians knew this. In London, Deputy Undersecretary Roger Makins dismissed the idea that Americans like McGhee sought commercial advantage in Iran and thought they only believed the AIOC had mishandled the situation, but he wanted the Foreign Office to impress on Washington the danger of spreading these views around the Middle East.[37]

After McGhee's departure relations between the embassy in Tehran and the State Department, affected by failure of the Export-Import Bank loan, continued to deteriorate. To Grady it seemed that his predictions of disaster were coming true. The department had failed to heed his advice and chaos threatened the Iranian government, with unknown consequences. Grady's energy and enthusiasm had evaporated with defeat of the loan scheme in February, a defeat he took personally. He blamed the British and high-level members of the department influenced by London. Chief among them, he believed, was Acheson. To friends Grady burst out in exasperation: 'I just cannot understand the general attitude of our government toward this vital spot'. In late April he indicated privately that he would be happy if the president relieved him. Not-so-diplomatic cables coming from junior officers in the department were asking him to stabilise Tehran during a crisis caused by the British. The British embassy in Tehran and especially Shepherd had been unco-operative. Grady departed for a week's vacation at the height of the crisis, astounding the department; he left Tehran for Beirut on 27 March, the day that communication with the oilfields ceased and the Tehran government ordered more troops into the area.[38]

Grady did settle one issue before going on vacation. He had had difficulty with Thornburg, who on news of Razmara's assassination had returned to Tehran from his island in the gulf, offering his services to the new prime minister, while making contact with Musaddiq and such National Front leaders as Husain Makki, a leading critic of the AIOC concession. He told Grady and McGhee he could help solve the oil problem. The ambassador reminded him of his public attack on the AIOC and the British in January, and doubted the British would welcome his help. The United States, Grady said, did not want any private American involved; if the Iranians considered Thornburg an unofficial representative, his likely failure would hurt American interests. The ambassador persuaded him to leave.[39]

While Grady rested in Beirut, McGhee was making good use of the remainder of his stay abroad. As soon as he left Tehran his thoughts turned towards a regional solution for the oil issue, and on 26 March he dispatched a long cable laying out proposals for a comprehensive, co-ordinated United States-United Kingdom oil policy in the Middle East to avoid country-by-country flare-ups. Diplomats in the Middle East had responded with enthusiasm, thinking they saw a plan to force the AIOC to be responsible. He wanted to discuss it during his visit to London, hoping for a joint declaration.[40]

But a lukewarm cable from Acheson pointed to shortcomings of McGhee's plans – Middle East nations, especially Iran, the secretary said, might conclude that the United States and Britain were working against their interests. This might revive a favourite communist red herring, Western control of regional oil. Acheson wanted to deal with the Iranian crisis before any discussion of regional oil policy. He recommended that McGhee urge the British or the AIOC to issue a statement expressing determination to abide by nationalisation and maintain production while negotiating a settlement.[41]

Acheson assumed a British acceptance of American views that was nowhere in evidence. Although the British cabinet had finally set up a working committee on Iran and informed the AIOC that it would exercise more control over the company, the Labour government had not accepted nationalisation, nor was it working with the Ala cabinet to find a solution. London wanted a 50–50 settlement or, barring that, a leasing arrangement. It sought American backing for whatever proposals it made.[42]

That the weak Attlee government shied away from nationalisation in April 1951 is not surprising. Responding to American pressure, the cabinet had endorsed an ambitious rearmament for Britain at estimated cost of £4700 million for 1951–54. This programme would require a higher per capita contribution than that of citizens of the United States.

The cabinet had divided, with Minister of Labour Bevan (who resigned that month) opposed to Gaitskell's proposal to secure economies of £23 million in the National Health Service. If such a small sum stirred emotions, what of the millions of pounds that might be lost on Iranian oil (£120–160 million annually)?

At the British government's request McGhee stopped in London on his way back, but got nowhere. He emphasised dangers for Iran and for the region. He found officials dazed by events, not believing nationalisation a reality, convinced that the Iranians would come round. They hoped the shah would take the initiative. McGhee made clear his doubt that the company could stand on its rights. He broached the subject of an Anglo-American statement supporting oil concessions throughout the Middle East based on some profit-sharing formula that would apply to all of the region. The British doubted that competitive oil companies would abide by an arrangement. He lunched with Fraser of the AIOC who revealed an obvious self-justification towards events in Iran. Anxious to return to Washington after almost two months, and knowing that talks had been scheduled there beginning 9 April, McGhee left after two days. Little had changed; the British would not accept nationalisation.[43]

The assistant secretary did confirm London's view that he was a brash young idealist. On instruction from the foreign secretary, Ambassador Franks in Washington expressed displeasure at McGhee's 'light-hearted' approach towards the Iranian crisis and suggested to the secretary of state that McGhee should not prescribe policies before the talks in Washington. One can only imagine Franks' distress at having to deliver this reprimand, for in addition to his ties with Acheson he had enjoyed a friendship with McGhee. He had served as the latter's tutor at Oxford when McGhee studied there as a Rhodes scholar in the 1930s.[44]

Over the Atlantic, bound for Washington, McGhee could only contemplate events, while back in London Foreign Secretary Morrison received an unexpected visitor, Lord Mountbatten. The former viceroy of India, no stranger to negotiating with Asian leaders, came to suggest that the government dispatch a delegation to Tehran to work out a compromise before the Majlis passed legislation putting an amicable solution out of reach. No doubt he had himself in mind. The foreign secretary replied that he could take no action before the Washington talks, and that the Americans preferred a private appeal to Ala rather than a delegation.[45]

Back after his two-month sojourn, McGhee exuded confidence before the House Committee on Foreign Affairs. In executive session on

10 April he assured committee members that the Iranian people thought – indeed hoped – that Prime Minister Ala would remain. He emphasised, as he often had, the need for the shah to rule to fill the vacuum. The image of the fear-stricken shah had faded. He played down Iranian criticism of Anglo-American consultation. He urged members not to take Iranian demands seriously, for leaders who pushed nationalisation probably did not know what it meant. It was a vague term in any case, and he could not believe they wanted to dissociate themselves from the company that had been in Iran for so many years. He recommended a formula that would salve nationalist consciences and keep oil flowing.[46]

The British attached importance to the forthcoming talks and made them a full-dress affair, hoping to impress Tehran with Anglo-American unity. Franks led the delegation, assisted by representatives of the Foreign Office, Ministry of Fuel and Power, and Neville A. Gass of the AIOC who had negotiated the supplementary oil agreement in 1949. The delegation came with a brief that cited the failure of the United States to support Britain. It would not accept unilateral modification of the concession. The Foreign Office had instructed Franks to ask for support for new proposals and for a guarantee, communicated to Iran, that the United States would not supply technicians or equipment to run a nationalised oil industry in Iran. The British also sought a joint statement that 'concessions should be regarded as binding'.[47]

McGhee headed the American delegation, assisted by the chief of the State Department's oil policy branch, Harold Linder, and representatives of American oil companies. Acheson and Harriman attended, although the secretary was preoccupied with hearings on the recall of General Douglas MacArthur from East Asia.

A press leak a few days before the talks brought out differences. Articles in the *New York Times* and *Wall Street Journal* pronounced nationalisation a reality the AIOC would have to accept. The British were furious, believing such sentiments would make the Iranians recalcitrant. Rountree denied State Department responsibility, but the Foreign Office knew that McGhee had given an interview the day before and the stories reflected his view.[48]

Talks continued for ten days, and produced a tangle of proposals. The British wanted support for the company plan to split profits 50–50 and work out a programme of nationalisation extending over half a century. They wanted American oil companies to sign no new agreements until the situation cleared. American participants viewed nationalisation as a *fait accompli*. As McGhee said, the United States had learned through experience in Mexico that the only course was to yield. Discussion became heated when McGhee warned Franks that the United States could not support Britain unless it offered Iran more. He suggested that the British state all their terms at once, not in stages. Franks responded that this was not the best way to proceed in the Middle East. He claimed that Britain had come part way and expected benevolence and quiet help, 'for in this matter there could be no neutrality'. The Foreign Office could not tell the Americans when British proposals would be presented to Ala. It pressed the United States for a joint communiqué. The State Department objected, lest it appear to support Britain's yet-to-be-determined proposals, but Franks insisted and the Americans gave way.[49]

Discussions ended on 19 April, with the British still refusing to recognise the changes in Iran. Acheson's frustration appeared during a meeting of Truman's cabinet the following day when he declared the situation more critical, and that the British had not met their responsibilities.[50]

The talks had importance not for what they achieved but because the Anglo-Americans set out their positions. The American dilemma had become apparent. Washington dared not push the British for fear of antagonising an ally during the Korean War. Yet it feared chaos and communist advance should the oil question remain. Ironically the British pursued a hard line, while advocating compromise in Korea; the United States opposed concessions in Korea but urged a flexible approach towards Iran. The perspectives are understandable, considering the levels of involvement. The United States had committed itself to the survival of South Korea, and the outcome might determine the future of Japan. It had no such stake in Iran, where a handful of American officers laboured to maintain a symbolic presence. Britain's economic investment in Iran was immense – loss of the oil concession would lead to a political storm at home and weakening of influence throughout the Middle East. It fought reluctantly in Korea to demonstrate its special relationship with the United States.

Britain did agree not to use force in Iran without consulting the United States. It was unlikely London would have used force unilaterally. The understanding reassured the State Department.[51]

Neither side seems to have considered the effect in Iran. 'There is nothing more pernicious to Iranians', wrote the editor of *Kayhan*, 'than a situation in which two foreign governments should get together outside of Iran to determine the fate of Iran's resources'. Ali Soheily, the new Iranian ambassador in London, protested talks that dealt with a domestic Iranian issue. Acheson on 17 April issued the first American statement concerning the oil crisis, denying the discussions had prejudiced Iran's interests, but did not suggest comparable US-Iranian talks. He encouraged Britain and Iran to discuss differences. The Americans believed this position reasonable, for consensus was the American way. Throughout the crisis that began in March 1951 they spoke of the problem as if it were a question of economics, confident that some formula would satisfy everyone. The statement by Acheson, however, did not convince Iranians, who gathered in crowds to protest before the embassy in Tehran. They believed nationalisation a closed issue, a legitimate exercise of sovereignty, not subject to foreign interference. From Tehran's perspective the only reason to negotiate with a foreign company was to discuss compensation.[52]

When the United States during the talks failed to convert the British to nationalisation, the last chance for a compromise in Tehran evaporated. Ala received a vote of confidence, 76–1, on 17 April, seeming to put him in a strong position. He and the shah accepted nationalisation. Like Razmara he was sceptical of Iran's ability to operate the oil industry in the short run. Had the British made a gesture, he might have been able to yield a little while maintaining the principle. In its absence he informed Shepherd that the 'new' proposals the British ambassador had secretly presented to him were far from acceptable. They offered equal division of profits, and a new British company with 'adequate' Iranian representation. Caught between British intransigence and National Front hostility, angered at not being consulted on the nine-point bill then before the Majlis for carrying out nationalisation, afraid of assassination if he did not do what it promised, Ala made a final visit to the British embassy on the morning of 27 April, seeking concessions. Failing, he submitted his resignation.[53]

Ala's departure from the government showed how rapidly the situation had deteriorated. Even before the Majlis chose his successor, Shepherd announced – with the bad timing and ham-handedness that had marked British diplomacy since the beginning of the dispute – that Iran could not depart from the 1933 oil contract and warned against hasty action full of serious consequences. This sally provoked Musaddiq into asking an immediate takeover of the oil installations to forestall behind-the-scenes attempts to thwart nationalisation.

Ala's resignation surprised the American government. The same day Acheson had informed the cabinet that the situation had shown improvement, and based his optimism on the British proposals, unaware that Ala had rejected them. The secretary of state expressed concern over Shepherd's statement, for he doubted that a nation could deny the right of another to nationalise, as the ambassador suggested.[54]

When the talks ended, the State Department considered a unilateral approach, including an immediate $15 million grant, increased military aid and promise of a larger grant to strengthen Ala. At an undersecretary's meeting on 25 April, McGhee made a determined but 12th-hour appeal for action.[55]

In Tehran the Majlis gathered to choose a successor. Musaddiq was one of the candidates and made passage of the nine-point bill a condition for accepting office. The Majlis on 28 April unanimously approved the bill, which among other things called for seizure of AIOC properties. Ambassador Shepherd asked Grady to intervene, but the American refused, having no instructions. On 2 May the measure went to the shah.

What Americans had feared since Razmara's assassination, transformation of dispute into crisis, had come to pass. Washington's influence, exercised spasmodically, had achieved little. Americans had impressed neither Britons nor Iranians with their tepid calls for moderation. The Truman administration had faced an unending series of crises since World War II, in Greece, Berlin, Korea, to name but a few places. Wistfully they recalled long-abandoned expectations of a peaceful and stable postwar world, a hope that now had receded. No one cared to predict the outcome of the Iran imbroglio but all agreed that Britain deserved a full measure of blame.[56]

The British now felt confident that their protégé, Seyed Zia ed-Din Tabataba'i, would succeed Ala. They had groomed Seyed Zia. In his 60s, at the height of ambition, he had waited 30 years for the opportunity. In 1920 asd a young mulla he had conspired with Reza Khan. After only a few months as prime minister, he had fallen out with his co-conspirator and fled the country. He returned in 1943, and established a reformist, anti-Soviet political faction, the National Will party, and a newspaper, *Rad-i Imruz*, which led opposition to the oil concession and to autonomy for Azarbaijan. He was a nationalist, reformer and devout Muslim; this latter characteristic set him apart form the more secular Musaddiq.

Shepherd had the task of convincing the shah that Seyed Zia would make a good prime minister, for he was independent-minded and his off-and-on-again relations with Reza Shah made him suspect. The Americans had doubts. They thought he could not work with the shah. Nor were they convinced of his abilities. Reluctantly the British had acceded to earlier American requests to support Razmara; now they argued it was time for Seyed Zia. Although Grady did not take up the latter's cause with the State Department, as he promised, this did not concern the British as long as Grady remained neutral. Seyed Zia worked to line up Majlis support. The shah had asked him to form a government in early March. He preferred to wait, he said, until after No Ruz, the Iranian New Year, 21 March. He told Shepherd he expected to be prime minister and wanted British fiscal advice. On 20 April he claimed support of 60 to 70 deputies but said he was waiting for the go-ahead from the shah.[57]

When the shah finally acted it was too late. On 28 April he ordered the Majlis speaker, Hekmat, to obtain a vote of inclination for Seyed Zia. The speaker returned to the palace an hour later to report that the deputies preferred Musaddiq. Stunned, the shah pressed the senate to refuse assent, but failed. Musaddiq became prime minister the next day.[58]

For the first time since the coming to power of Qavam five years earlier, the shah now had to accept an appointee not of his own choosing. He had the wisdom to bend with the rising nationalist wind. He and the conservative landowners in the Majlis consoled themselves in the belief that Musaddiq would find solution of the oil problem so difficult that he would soon resign.[59]

9 Conclusion

Musaddiq swept into office amid a national euphoria, for patriotic Iranians sensed victory within their grasp. At last they controlled the nation's most valuable resource, the goal pursued since rejection of a Soviet oil concession in 1947. The time for the Anglo-Iranian Oil Company to leave Iran had come. The new prime minister did not anticipate difficulties with the British government. He probably thought he could separate the Labour government and the company. During a speech he cited an exchange in the House of Commons regarding Burma's nationalisation of oil in which Foreign Secretary Bevin had dismissed any thought of hostile action. The precedent bolstered his spirits.[1]

Speaking for the first time as prime minister on 30 April, Musaddiq saw no obstacles to 'economic freedom and self-domination of the country's resources'. He called for unity, peace, order, and promised that through the greatest resource of national wealth – oil – the Iranian people, especially the deprived classes, would prosper. He had taken up his responsibilities, he said, only because the nation demanded it, and although his health was unequal to the burden he would sacrifice his life.[2]

Iranians continued to see Anglo-American differences as competition, believing the two nations were rivals in the Middle East and that American oil companies could hardly wait to take over at Abadan. The AIOC had received unfavourable publicity in the United States, and Iran's leaders, unfamiliar with an independent press, linked newspaper opinion with government policy. If the British raised difficulties, Tehran could surely turn to the Americans.[3]

But if Iranians were unrealistic, so were the British. After the Majlis vote of inclination, Ambassador Shepherd told the shah his country placed no confidence in Musaddiq and indeed regarded his appointment as a disaster. In a dispatch to the Foreign Office the ambassador recalled that Musaddiq's daughter was in a Swiss mental institution, and it seemed to him that the prime minister was not quite normal either. Geoffrey Furlonge, head of the Foreign Office's Eastern Department, privately set out the British attitude: 'A band of extremists have been enabled by intimidation to impose their will on the Majlis and to silence the voices of reason'.[4]

The Labour government had repeatedly refused to control the

company. Now the government and company sought excuses. In fine, the British beheld nationalisation as a fad. Shepherd complained about lack of American support. The shah too, he said, had failed to do his duty and asked the Majlis to suggest a candidate rather than proposing his own, as he had done earlier for Mansur and Razmara.[5]

But American policy had hardly been a triumph. The United States had supported Iranian independence after 1946, a policy announced when Washington adhered to the Tripartite Agreement during World War II. The affirmation became important as the Cold War intensified. Still, support rarely went beyond speeches, and the administration rejected any commitment if the Soviets invaded.

Like the British, officials believed Iran's political leaders were inefficient and corrupt, and would waste aid. Grants or loans must be hedged with restriction to make every dollar count. Acheson, Undersecretary James Webb and McGhee all propounded this view in face of opposing claims from Allen, Wiley, Grady and, of course, Iranian leaders.

If the Iranians really wanted reform they would find the money. What Iran needed was cheap, simple, effective reform, which Iran could pay for if it accepted a new agreement with the Anglo-Iranian Oil Company.

Military assistance was another matter. Such aid had the dual purpose of strengthening Iran's army and pandering to the shah. The loan the United States approved in 1947 paid for arms to secure Iran's internal stability. Before 1949 the US refused to grant further assistance, arguing that what the nation needed was economic and social development. Resolve weakened as the Cold War intensified. In line with policy in Europe and Asia that saw establishment of NATO and containment in Korea, officials in Iran accentuated defence. Objectives broadened when the Pentagon and State Department allowed American officers to comment and advise on Iranian war plans and provided *matériel* such as medium tanks to slow down a Russian advance.

The Defense Department lagged behind the State Department in enthusiasm for military aid. At the end of World War II the military chiefs acquiesced in the State Department's decision to continue the two military missions, and later in regard to quantity and quality of *matériel* the department had its way. The military despaired of correcting abuses in Iran's army and were content to leave the British responsible for Western strategy.

Washington wanted to influence the shah. Relations came to centre on him. Americans in 1947 had considered the wily old prime minister, Qavam, equal to the shah, but by 1951 the second Pahlavi had no rival. He would ensure Iran's alliance with the Western bloc, and he was a progressive who shared American ideas of economic development. During his visit to the United States he convinced the American people and thereafter they rarely doubted. Officials were familiar with his shortcomings, especially his indecisiveness, his bouts of depression, his penchant for intrigue, but dismissed them in the belief that they could guide him. As Wiley happily recalled, 'When the shah finally realized that I talked to him as a friend, he became at once eager to discuss his problems with me, and to listen with much interest to anything that I might say'. After Razmara's assassination, Webb cabled Grady that the shah was the only person who could provide direction and avoid a communist takeover, adding that 'the U.S. and Britain should support him in every feasible way and encourage him to act with force and vigor'. Less than a week after Musaddiq became prime minister, Acheson reaffirmed America's reliance on the shah as 'our best hope of providing firmness and leadership'. When the shah wanted tanks, the State Department – overriding military objections – decided he should have them, not because they would enhance security but because they would please him.[6]

The United States did not plan to encourage dictatorship, but its policies assisted a gradual move in that direction. Neither Washington nor the embassy believed that the shah-army group threatened the balance maintained since the abdication of Reza Shah. Allen and John Jernegan had praised the Majlis. A few years later officials no longer mentioned a balance between parliament and court; dispatches spoke of an excess of democracy. Wiley advised that Iranians must make haste slowly towards democracy. Loy Henderson, Grady's successor, admitted that it was impossible for any small country on the Soviet periphery to survive as a democracy. Diplomats could take comfort in increasing royal power by arguing that this was what the Iranian people wanted. 'The mass of Iranians would be ready today, to barter whatever liberty they possess for a strong rule which would promise order and growth', said Wiley.[7]

Ironically, by the end of these years the shah did not trust Washington. Americans had not given the arms he requested. Such stinginess disappointed him. He also took a jaundiced view of foreign meddling; he resented Schwarzkopf's ties with the opposition and was suspicious of Dooher's effort among the tribes.

All the while Iranian popular attitudes were turning towards hostility. At the end of 1946, American prestige had been high, but as the war years receded, Iranians became frustrated with a policy that aimed at strengthening court and army rather than the economy. They favoured a balance among the powers or, like Musaddiq, the ending of great power interference in Iran's affairs.

The embassy lost contact with opposition in Iran. In the diplomatic files one searches almost in vain for evidence of meetings between diplomats and the opposition, meetings that had been common earlier. In one of the few recorded there – between Grady's assistant, Leslie Rood, and General Hasan Arfa – the general, a National Front sympathiser with ties to the court, castigated the Americans for associating only with the aristocracy. Although Grady held frequent dinner meetings with court supporters he did not meet with Musaddiq until 2 May, 1951, ten months after arriving in Tehran. The embassy's isolation caused great concern in later years, but the trend was established even before Musaddiq became prime minister.[8]

Among issues of the time that caused this decline in confidence on the part of the Iranian public, none proved more important than American concern over communism. It prompted support for the shah. It influenced policy towards all nations. This fixation with containment especially affected US policy in the Middle East. When McGhee travelled through the region in early 1951 he made such a view abundantly clear. His speeches, redolent of the Cold War, warned that nations must choose sides. In Cairo he addressed the nations of the Middle East, saying, 'I am convinced that they are already in the camp of the free world'. In Damascus he warned that neutralism worked for the enemy. 'It is impossible', he declared, 'to have neutrality between the aggressors and defenders of liberty'. For his hosts it must have seemed ironic to identify Britain as a defender of liberty. One can imagine as well their hostility towards the pro-Israeli policy of the Truman administration.[9]

Events of the Musaddiq period, 1951–53, worked themselves out in almost predictable ways. Washington judged governments on the basis of the Cold War, and here the Musaddiq government was suspect. Not that anyone considered the prime minister a communist, but Americans worried that disorder might open the door. Prior to April 1951, if American diplomats mentioned the front, they considered it a pro-Soviet organisation inclining towards Tudeh policies or a misguided, anti-foreign group. The exception was Grady's assistant, Leslie Rood, who stressed the front's commitment to nationalism. To him the National Front championed the cause of the Iranian people, unconcerned with the struggle against communism. No one listened. The United States could not tolerate developments in Third World nations that promised advantage to communism.[10]

At first after Musaddiq came to power, the British ties seemed paramount. Long before Musaddiq, officials in the State Department had believed that whatever happened, the United States could not break with Britain. The United States needed co-operation in East Asia, and even if the Korean War had not developed, Secretary Acheson would not have jeopardised relations by twisting Britain's arm. Britain took priority over Iran or any other state in the region; America's task, the secretary said, was 'to pull the core of the free world together'. Without Britain the goal would be unreachable. This decision left Musaddiq less possibility than he suspected to exploit Anglo-American differences. He considered himself master of the oil situation, but factors beyond his control determined the policies of the United States and Britain.[11]

Belatedly the United States became intensely involved in the oil crisis during the summer of 1951. Musaddiq approached agreement through American effort, only to pull back, either pressed by supporters, pricked by statements from London, or troubled by a conscience that would not accept less than victory after years of opposition to the AIOC. Averell Harriman spent July-August trying to bridge the gap between the parties. The department avoided referring to him as a mediator, a designation unacceptable to the British, but he became one as negotiation dragged through the broiling heat of summer. Harriman introduced an early version of shuttle diplomacy, flying to Tehran, back to London, again to Tehran, down to the refinery at Abadan, back to London. He almost succeeded. But the British in mid-September, without consulting Washington, submitted the dispute to the United Nations Security Council, clumsily offering the Iranian leader an international forum. Musaddiq thereupon won the American public, especially the early television audience, with his performance at the UN, where members refused to condemn Iran or force it to arbitrate as the British proposed, and rejected a US-sponsored compromise resolution.

One thing followed another. Musaddiq visited Washington. McGhee spent days with him, bringing him again close to agreement. But the British rejected McGhee's scheme to allow Royal Dutch Shell to operate the AIOC concession under contract with the Iranian government. Musaddiq returned to Tehran, his popularity enhanced.[12]

For the Americans the Musaddiq visit was almost an enjoyable affair. Truman and Acheson met the prime minister during his stay, and the secretary was taken with the old gentleman, later describing the scene at Union Station when the prime minister, cane in hand, hobbled along the platform until he caught sight of the secretary, whereupon he tossed the stick aside and fairly skipped along. At Blair House, with serious demeanour, he presented a picture of his country to accentuate its poverty, lack of natural resources and social ills – nothing but camels, sand, barren spaces. Acheson wryly commented: 'Oh! Rather like Texas'. Musaddiq dissolved in laughter, his exaggeration unmasked.[13]

As the months passed there were times when even Acheson lost patience with the British. One expected Iranians to act emotionally, but that luxury he denied Western statesmen. At Paris in November 1951 he spoke frankly to the new foreign secretary, Anthony Eden, and again during Churchill's visit to Washington in January 1952. Eden seemed to minimise the danger of the crisis, and Acheson pulled him up sharply. But the secretary never forced the British, for he valued the special relationship. He could regret British policies and sympathise with McGhee and his successor, Henry Byroade. He proposed compromises. He refused all suggestion of an ultimatum.[14]

American military leaders several times in 1952 and early 1953 suggested a harder line. They were concerned that the Soviets might take advantage of instability in Iran, at a time when the United States was unprepared to defend that area. The military wanted purchases of Iran's oil to prop Musaddiq, regardless of the effect on Anglo-American relations. Their pleas failed to convince the secretary of state.[15]

Exasperated over continuing crisis in Iran, the United States and Britain recommended that the shah dismiss the prime minister. The shah showed more sense than the diplomats when he resisted, for he knew Musaddiq was popular. Eventually he yielded, appointing the aged Qavam on 17 July, 1952, after Musaddiq had resigned. Qavam failed, in part because the shah denied him emergency powers. Popular rejection of the appointee, which included violent street demonstrations, led to Musaddiq's reappointment.[16]

Gradually the Iranian scene began to clarify, in part because of internal Iranian developments. Musaddiq faced pressure not only from Britain and the United States but at home as well. The court served as a rallying point for disaffected National Front leaders like Ayatollah Kashani, who received a warm reception at the palace. Waiting for the British, Musaddiq allowed his opponents to determine the progress of the oil dispute, and this strategy contributed to his downfall. As the economy worsened, enemies convinced Iranians that the prime minister only wanted power. Musaddiq thus allowed himself to be boxed in. Perhaps he was, as many observers claimed, a one-issue leader. The prime minister looked to America and the Eisenhower administration. Alas, Eisenhower and Secretary of State John Foster Dulles offered the same package as the outgoing Truman administration. Musaddiq allowed the offer to lapse.

He, of course, fell because of a CIA-supported coup. There can be no doubt of American involvement in the coup of August 1953, the coup in which Kermit Roosevelt played such a prominent part. The CIA had channelled money to anti-Musaddiq leaders and tried to co-ordinate activities of the shah and General Fazlollah Zahedi who was in hiding. From the security of a seaside retreat on the Caspian, the shah replaced Musaddiq with Zahedi. At first everyone disregarded the royal order and army units arrested royalist officers. Fearing for his safety, the shah fled the country. He flew to Baghdad and then to Rome where the Iranian ambassador refused assistance. As news of the flight spread, anti-royalist crowds in Tehran and other Iranian cities toppled statues of the Pahlavis and demanded an end to monarchy. Within two days, however, events turned in favour of the conspirators. Musaddiq's police dealt harshly with leftist demonstrators. The prime minister wanted to assure Henderson that he still controlled the capital and could maintain order. The police welcomed the opportunity to use their truncheons on what they considered Tudeh demonstrators, whom they drove from the streets. When pro-shah mobs, financed by American money, appeared, the sullen leftists stayed home. Musaddiq, fearing civil war, refused to arm his supporters. Military units sided with the pro-shah demonstrators. To escape the mob, the prime minister fled over his garden wall. He surrendered himself next day. The monarch returned.[17]

With Musaddiq out of the way the Eisenhower administration rushed to support General Zahedi with military and economic grants. In a single year, 1953, it gave $60 million, twice as much as in the previous decade. Assistance doubled in 1954. Washington foresaw a return to stability, which would foil any Soviet plots.

For a while the British maintained their Iranian pretensions *vis-à-vis* the activist Americans, and then their influence simply disappeared. Foreign Secretary Eden won his point that restoration of relations, broken in October 1952, must precede oil talks. At first the British dragged their feet over a new oil agreement, AIOC directors still considered it possible to return to the *status quo ante*, and months were necessary to disabuse them. With the shah-Zahedi government in power, the State Department was less reticent to discuss Department of Defense suggestions to press London. In early 1954 a plan was afoot to set a time for an agreement, after which the US would act, taking off enough Iranian oil to meet minimum revenue requirements of the Zahedi government. An oil agreement favourable to the AIOC was concluded in July of that year.[18]

Relations between the shah and Zahedi deteriorated, and Americans reported Zahedi spending much time trying to maintain support. Like every other Iranian leader who tried to remain independent of the court – Qavam, Razmara, Musaddiq – he was unsuccessful. The shah had to dominate, surrounding himself with officeholders who would not threaten his control. When the shah made a second visit to the US at the end of 1954, he received praise from the Eisenhower administration. The American press sang paeans for his anticommunist leadership. Zahedi lost out in 1955.

Only occasionally over the next years did Americans question this arrangement. Doubt usually confined itself to lower levels of the State Department and other agencies.

During the Kennedy administration there was an attempt to push reform, including political participation, but little came of it. Attorney General Robert F. Kennedy discussed repression in Iran with his brother, the president. The administration set up a task force, and reported to the National Security Council that the United States must push the shah towards a more constitutional role. The group supported Prime Minister Ali Amini as the last hope of averting chaos. The recommendation seemed inspired, after Chairman Nikita Khrushchev warned Kennedy during the Vienna summit in June 1961 that a popular uprising would overthrow the shah. For a year the shah tolerated the liberal, independent-minded Amini and then appointed his own adviser, Asadollah Alam. In part to neutralise US reaction the shah introduced land reform. The so-called White Revolution received overwhelming endorsement in a national referendum in January 1963. Officials in the Agency for International Development and in the office of the president's national security advisor, McGeorge Bundy, pressed for broader political participation. Secretary of State Dean Rusk and Ambassador Julius Holmes supported the shah, warning that political change might destabilise the regime.[19]

When the Vietnam War heated up in the mid-1960s the shah became adept at getting what he wanted. All he had to do was raise the Russian bogey. Once he casually informed an American visitor, Edward A. Bayne, that he had decided to purchase ground-to-air missiles from the Soviet Union. Bayne reported this point to Ambassador Armin Meyer, who knew nothing of it. The American government suggested the superiority of American missiles. The shah allowed the US to supply the missiles.[20]

Wholehearted commitment to the shah came during the Nixon administration when the new president's national security adviser, Henry A. Kissinger, accepted the shah's drawing of Iran as policeman of the Persian Gulf.

American policy-makers for a quarter of a century thus believed that rising living standards would bring content, that Iran's armed forces using sophisticated weapons would bring stability, that the shah knew what was best. Even after the revolution began in 1978 an American official summed affairs up by saying, 'Well, the policy worked for us for twenty-five years, that's not bad!' Americans of the present generation would hardly agree.[21]

Notes

NOTES TO CHAPTER 1

1. Several studies detail US-Iranian relations, Iranian foreign policy, and Iran's internal politics for the period 1941–46, and especially helpful are: Bruce Kuniholm, *The Origins of the Cold War in the Near East: Great Power Conflict and Diplomacy in Iran, Turkey, and Greece* (Princeton: Princeton University Press, 1980); Mark Hamilton Lytle, *The Origins of the Iranian-American Alliance, 1941–1953* (New York: Holmes & Meier, 1987); George Lenczowski, *Russia and the West in Iran, 1918–1948* (Ithaca: Cornell University Press, 1949); Rouhollah K. Ramazani, *Iran's Foreign Policy, 1941–1973: A Study of Foreign Policy in Modernizing Nations* (Charlottesville: University Press of Virginia, 1975); Richard W. Cottam, *Nationalism in Iran* (Pittsburgh: University of Pittsburgh Press, 1964); Ervand Abrahamian, *Iran Between Two Revolutions* (Princeton: Princeton University Press, 1982); Barry Rubin, *Paved with Good Intentions: The American Experience and Iran* (New York: Oxford University Press, 1980).
2. Nikki R. Keddie, 'Iranian Revolutions in Comparative Perspective', *American Historical Review*, 88 (1983): esp. 586, Donald Wilber, *Riza Shah Pahlavi, 1878–1944: The Resurrection and Reconstruction of Iran* (Hicksville, NY: Exposition, 1975), Hasan Arfa, *Under Five Shahs* (London: John Murray, 1964), L. P. Elwell-Sutton, 'Reza Shah the Great: Founder of the Pahlavi Dynasty', in George Lenczowski (ed.), *Iran under the Pahlavis*, Hoover Institution, number 164 (Stanford, Calif.: Hoover Institution Press, 1978), and Joseph M. Upton, *The History of Modern Iran: An Interpretation*, Harvard Middle Eastern Monograph Series (Cambridge, Mass.: Harvard University Press, 1965) 36–80. Brian Lapping's anecdotal study, *End of Empire* (New York: St. Martin's, 1985), contains an interesting chapter on Iran.
3. Muhammad Reza Pahlavi, *Mission for My Country* (London: Hutchinson, 1960) 66–81, Ashraf Pahlavi, *Faces in the Mirror* (Englewood Cliffs, NJ: Prentice-Hall, 1980) 1–43. These memoirs are not generally reliable, but they reveal the relationship between Reza Shah and has children.
4. Peter Avery, *Modern Iran* (London: Ernest Benn, 1965) 350–67, Lenczowski, *Russia and the West in Iran*, 167–92; Ann K. S. Lambton, *Landlord and Peasant in Persia: A Study of Land Tenure and Land Revenue Administration* (New York: Oxford University Press, 1953) 274, Abrahamian, 375–82, Herbert H. Vreeland, *Iran, Country Survey* (New Haven: Human Relations Area Files, 1957) 3, 84–5, 128.
5. Upton, 108, Lambton, *Landlord and Peasant*, 263, idem., *Persian Land Reform, 1962–1966* (New York: Oxford University Press, 1969) 20, 35.
6. Abrahamian, 187, Cottam, 33–50, 101, Vreeland, 84–5.
7. Papers of Harry S. Truman, Box 569, Official File, Folder 134 (1945–49), 10 September 1945, Shah to President Truman, Harry S. Truman Library [hereafter HSTL], Independence, Missouri. The shah's observations find

support in a memorandum from Deputy Assistant Secretary of State Burton Y. Berry to Averell Harriman. Record Group [RG] 59, 888.401/18 April 1951. Julian Bharier, *Economic Development in Iran, 1900–1970* (New York: Oxford University Press, 1971) 49, 67, 170–8; Abrahamian, 347–71, Habib Ladjevardi, *Labor Unions and Autocracy in Iran*, Contemporary Issues in the Middle East (Syracuse: Syracuse University Press, 1985) 28–69.

8. Lambton, *Landlord and Peasant in Persia*, 383, Upton, 117–19.

9. For United States relations with the Middle East before World War II, see John A. De Novo, *American Interests and Politics in the Middle East, 1900–1939* (Minneapolis: University of Minnesota Press, 1963); for American missionary activity, Joseph L. Grabill's *Protestant Diplomacy and the Near East: Missionary Influence on American Policy, 1810–1927* (Minneapolis: University of Minnesota Press, 1971); for US relations with Iran, see Abraham Yeselson, *U.S.-Persian Diplomatic Relations, 1883–1921* (New Brunswick, NJ: Rutgers University Press, 1956). For a recent view of the impact of Palestine on Anglo-American relations, see Roy Jenkins, *Truman* (New York: Harper & Row, 1986) 115–17.

10. Alan Bullock, *Ernest Bevin: Foreign Secretary, 1945–51* (New York: W. W. Norton, 1983) 118, 241–6, 348–51.

11. Strobe Talbott (ed.), *Khrushchev Remembers* (Boston: Little, Brown, 1970) 329–39, Svetlana Alliluyeva, *Twenty Letters to a Friend* (New York: Harper & Row, 1967) 196–7.

NOTES TO CHAPTER 2

1. Cottam, *Nationalism in Iran*, 129; Record Group 59, 891.00/14 February 1947, Marshall to Allen, National Archives; William O. Douglas, *Strange Lands and Friendly People* (New York: Harper, 1951) 45–50; RG 891.00/21 August 1947, Spivack to Marshall; Foreign Office 371/Persia, 61978, File 13, Diary of Tabriz Consul, Public Record Office, London; Papers of Harry S. Truman, President's Secretary's Files (PSF), Intelligence File, Central Intelligence Group, 'Developments in the Azerbaijan Situation', 4 June 1947, Harry S. Truman Library.

2. British and American diplomats in 1947 questioned Razmara's honesty and raised the issue of his suspected dealings with the Soviets. Paradoxically, in later years the diplomats praised him as one of the few honest officials in Iran. F0 371/Persia, 61982, 19 January 1947, Military Attaché's Intelligence Summary no. 3. Prime Minister Musaddiq removed General Shahbakhti, but Prime Minister Zahedi returned him to command in Azerbaijan in 1953, RG 59, 891.00/15 April 1947, Allen to Marshall; RG 59, 891.00/9 May and 30 September 1947, Monthly Political Review.

3. RG 59, 891.00/26 April 1947; RG 59, 891.00/7 June 1947, Monthly Political Review; RG 59, 891.00/24 September 1947, Allen to Marshall.

4. RG 59, 891.00/7 November 1947, Allen to Marshall; RG 59, 891.00/24 December 1947, Allen to Marshall.
5. The ulama in the holy cities of Qum and Mashhad opposed the reinterment of Reza Shah at either of these two sites because of his harsh actions against them during his reign. See Wilber, *Riza Shah Pahlavi*, 127, 166–7. Qavam refused to press them, and the royal family decided to wait until a tomb could be built at Rey a short distance south of Tehran. F0371/Persia, 61976, 20 March 1947; RG 59, 891.00/9 May and 30 September 1947, Monthly Press Review.
6. RG 84, Tehran Post Files, Box 17, Confidential File: 1948, 800 Internal Political Affairs – General, 21 January 1948, Allen to Jernegan, Washington National Records Center Suitland, Md.; RG 59, 891.00 Mohammad Reza Pahlavi/7 June 1947; RG 59, 891.001/16 January 1947; Department of State, *Foreign Relations of the United States 1947* (Washington: Government Printing Office, 1971) 5: 938, 958, 960. (Hereafter *FR*); RG 59, 891.00/12 May 1948, Wiley to Marshall; F0 371/Persia, 61990, 24 July 1947, Pyman Minute; RG 59, 891.00/13 January 1947, Allen to Byrnes; RG 59, 891.00/17 January 1947, Allen to Byrnes; RG 59, 891.00/26 December 1947, Allen to Jernegan. For an interesting editorial linking Qavam and the United States, see *Sada-yi Mardum* [The Voice of the People] 2 Mehr, 1326 (1947).
7. RG 59, 891.00/26 March 1947; 3 and 22 February 1947; 5 February 1947; Papers of George V. Allen, Box 1, 'Mission to Iran', unpublished manuscript, chapter 2, HSTL. Dooher left Iran in autumn 1947. He was reassigned in March 1948 to the consulate at Tihwa in Sinkiang province, China. He returned to Tehran to wait for a Soviet visa to travel overland through Central Asia, and meanwhile offered to do political reporting for the embassy. Ambassador Wiley arrived in early April. The new ambassador had no experience in the region and thus urged the State Department to allow Dooher, the only Persian-speaking officer, to stay in Iran. In November the department cancelled his China assignment. RG 59, File 123, Gerald F. P. Dooher. For discussion of CIA activity in Iran from the late 1940s, see Mark Gasiorowski, 'The 1953 Coup D'état in Iran', *International Journal of Middle East Studies* 19 (1987) 261–86.
8. The British military attaché referred to Dr Musaddiq on this occasion as 'the hysterical and demented demagogue', a characterisation repeated by many British diplomats throughout the period. FO 371/Persia, 61982, 19 January 1947, Military Attaché's Intelligence Summary no. 3.
9. FO 371/Persia, 61970, 1 April 1947; *FR, 1947*, 5: 929–30, 934, 953.
10. *FR, 1947*, 5: 965, 968.
11. FO 371/Persia, 61971, 7 July and 11 August 1947, 61972, 14 August, 12 and 13 September 1947, and 61973, 13 October 1947. Ambassador Allen had assured Prime Minister Qavam that Bevin and Stalin could not discuss Iran at the foreign ministers' meeting in Moscow without Secretary of State Marshall's knowledge. Bevin did inform Marshall the day following his commitment to Stalin, but the Americans had not been consulted beforehand. RG 59, 891.00/10 April 1947, FO 371/Persia, 61973, 22 September 1947; FO 371/Persia, 61974, 31 October 1947; RG. 84, TPF, Box 13, Confidential File: 1947, 800 Iranian Political Affairs, 12 September 1947, Marshall to Allen.

12. FO 371/Persia, 61972, 12 September 1947, 61973, 29 September 1947; RG 84, TPF, Confidential File: 1948, 700 British-Iranian Relations, 15 March 1948, Dooher to Dunn; *FR, 1948*, 5: 97; RG 59, Records of the Military Advisor to the Office of Near Eastern, South Asian, and African Affairs, Box 3, State-War-Navy Co-ordinating Committee 360, Correlation Committee (FACC), 24 April 1947.

13. *FR, 1947*, 5: 951; Papers of George V. Allen, 'Mission to Iran', unpublished manuscript, chapter 8, 139. The nationalistic newspaper, *Khavar* [The East], appreciated Allen's 'reaffirmation of Iranian independence', 14 September 1947. Marshall and Lovett wired belated approval.

14. Robert A. Pollard, *Economic Security and the Origins of the Cold War, 1945–1950* (New York: Columbia University Press, 1985) 113. During the war years, 1943–44, Tehran witnessed Soviet-American competition for oil concessions, and the State Department wanted to avoid a recurrence in 1947. For more on Iranian oil in World War II, see Kuniholm, *Origins of the Cold War in the Near East*, 192–202, and Lytle, *Origins of the Iranian-American Alliance*, 82–99. FO 371/Persia, 61970, 12 and 31 March 1947; RG 84, TPF, Box 14, Confidential File: 1947, 863.6 Petroleum, 14 February 1947, Minor to Allen; RG 84, TPF, Box 109, General Records: 1947, 863.6 Petroleum, November 1946, January 1947. It is possible that the Soviets really did want Iranian oil, what is certain is that they would have exercised increased political influence in northern Iran had they obtained the concession–an influence similar to that of the British in the southwest.

15. RG 84, TPF, Confidential File: 1948, 800 Internal Political Affairs–General, 21 January 1948, Allen to Jernegan, Shahpour Bakhtiar, *Ma fidélité* (Paris: Albin Michel, 1982) 44–5, John R. Oneal, *Foreign Policy Making in Times of Crisis* (Columbus: Ohio State University Press, 1986) 108.

16. Irene W. Meister, 'Soviet Policy in Iran, 1917–1950: A Study in Technique' (M.A. Thesis, Fletcher School of Diplomacy, 1954). A typical Soviet attack appeared in the trade union paper, *Trud*, on 30 November 1947. Referring to the members of the Majlis, it asked whether they were 'Representatives of the Iranian People or American Lackeys?' *Soviet Press Translations* (November 1947) 84. *FR, 1948*, 5: 130.

17. RG 84, TPF, 863.6 Petroleum-Confidential, 3 May 1948, Wiley to Henderson; Box 16, Confidential File: 1948, 24 June 1948, Wiley to SS: *FR, 1948*, 5: 160–1; RG 84, TPF, Box 16, Confidential File: 1948, 15 July 1948, Marshall to Wiley; Confidential File 711: 1948, 21 October 1948, Lovett to Bohlen; Confidential File 710, 5 November 1948, Bohlen to Wiley; Relations of States, Treaties, Agreements, 1948, 29 October 1948, 'Memo of Discussion with the British Ambassador, Washington'. Signed originally to control White Russian exiles in Iran, the treaty had long since become an albatross around Iran's neck and a cause for concern in Washington and London. *FR, 1948*, 5: 173; FO 371/Persia, 68716, E5327/332/34/15 April 1948, and 75477, E10730/10338/34/4 September 1949; RG 84, TPF, Box 16, Confidential File 710, 6 November 1948, Wiley to Bohlen; Relations of States, Treaties, Agreements: 1948, 28 July 1948, Jernegan to Wiley. John D. Jernegan worked closely with Iranian affairs for nine years, 1941–50. He joined the Near Eastern division of the State Department in August 1941 and was the department's first desk officer for Iran. He served in Tehran

from June 1943–June 1946, and headed GTI from its formation in 1947 until his assignment as consul at Tunis in July 1950. Surprisingly, Jernegan, the department's most experienced officer on Iran, was unavailable during the oil nationalisation crisis, 1950–51. He returned to the department in May 1952. For more details of Jernegan's early career in the State Department, see Kuniholm, *The Origins of the Cold War in the Near East*, esp. 155–60.

18. Seyom Brown, *The Faces of Power: Constancy and Change in United States Foreign Policy from Truman to Reagan* (New York: Columbia University Press, 1983) 46–7.

19. *FR, 1948*, 5: 199–200; Abrahamian, 346–7.

20. Ibid., 155–6; RG 84, TPF, 320–Political Relations Between Iran and Other Countries: 1949, 2 March 1949, Dunn (Assistant Chief GTI) to Wiley; RG 59, 761.91/9 April 1949, Wiley to SS, RG 84, TPF, Box 21, Confidential File: 1949, 300 Political Relations Between Iran and Other Countries, 23 April 1949, SS to Wiley.

21. *FR, 1949*, 6: 492–4. Wiley was a member of that informal group of American diplomats made famous by Daniel Yergin's *Shattered Peace*, who served in the Baltic states and Moscow during the 1920s and 1930s. See chapter 1, 'The Riga Axioms'. *FR, 1949*, 6: 519–21; RG 84, TPF, 320, Political Relations Between Iran and Other Countries: 1949, 27 June 1949, Wiley to Jernegan.

22. RG 59, 891.00/12 November 1948, Weekly Press Airgram: 891.00/17 December 1948; 891.001 Pahlavi/ 12 July 1949, Wiley to Acheson; RG 84, TPF, 1949, 360–2 Government, Cabinet, Constitution, Governmental Agencies, 24 May 1949, Wiley to Jernegan.

23. RG 84, TPF, Confidential File: 1948, 800 Internal Political Affairs–General, 21 January 1948, Allen to Jernegan; RG 59, 891.00/12 May 1948; 891.00/14 January and 17 January 1949, Weekly Political Airgram. In December 1948 at the height of the shah's campaign for constitutional change, the BBC's Persian language broadcast presented a reading from a thirteenth-century Iranian classic, the *Siyasatnameh* ('Rules for Kings'), which advised the shah and ladies of his court not to interfere with day-to-day administration, nor to appoint favourites to office, and to accept the advice of elder statesmen. The government in Tehran protested at what seemed obvious interference in Iranian affairs. Colonel Pybus, an intelligence officer, informed the Foreign Office that he was certain Elwell-Sutton of the BBC, a British leftist and opponent of the shah, had selected the offending passages. (Laurence Paul Elwell-Sutton had worked for the AIOC and the British government in Iran and later became a distinguished professor in Edinburgh.) FO 371/Persia, 68709, E16371/25/34, 17 December 1948.

24. RG 84, TPF, Confidential File: 1948, 800 Internal Political Affairs–General, 22 December 1947, Jernegan to Allen, and 21 January 1948, Allen to Jernegan. Allen did momentarily support the ouster of Qavam in October 1946 when it seemed the prime minister had moved too far to the left. *Cahiers de l'orient contemporain* (Paris), 21 December 1947, RG 59, 891.00/26 February 1949, Somerville to Acheson, 'Memorandum of Conversation with the Shah'.

25. RG 59, 891.00/12 May, 4 July 1948, Wiley to Marshall; 891.00/9 July 1948, Weekly Political Airgram; Ashraf Pahlavi, *Faces in a Mirror*, 75–6, 110; Interviews with Edward A. Bayne (New Haven), December 1982 and Sir George Middleton (London) March 1983.
26. RG 59, 891.00/26 August 1948; 891.00/5 October 1948, Wiley to Marshall, and PSF, Intelligence File, CIA Reports, 8 October 1948, 'The Current Situation in Iran', HSTL; 891.00/11 October 1948, Weekly Political Airgram; 891.00/30 October 1948; 891.00/11 January 1949.
27. FO 371/Persia, 68728, E10084/1006/34, 8 July and 68729, E10349/1000/34, 30 July 1948. RG 84, TPF, Box 18, 801A Foreign Advisors-Miscellaneous, 1 October 1948, Wiley to Jernegan. RG 84, TPF, Box 123, General Records: 1948, 891 Iranian Press, 17 July 1948; RG 59, 891.001 Pahlavi, Reza Shah/ 14 July 1948, Wilson to Marshall; 891.00/4 July 1948, Wiley to Marshall, and 16 August 1948, Weekly Political Airgram.
28. RG 59, 891.00/5 August 1948, Lewis Douglas to Marshall. To restrain criticism of the shah in the left-wing French press, Iranian diplomats and representatives of the French foreign ministry suggested that editors go easy on the shah. This prompted the following from the satirical paper *Le Canard enchaîné*: 'The phone rings: an important personage warns us against any irreverence towards the imperial guest. When we protest against this infringement of speech he asks us whether we don't own cars and go away for weekends. Doesn't Persia remind you of anything? he asks. What about oil? [There was fuel rationing in France at the time.] Fatherlike he advises us to think how much petrol we need!' The visit passed without incident. Fereydoun Hoveyda, *The Fall of the Shah* (London: Weidenfeld & Nicolson, 1980) 90. RG 59, 891.00/3 September 1948, Weekly Political Airgram. Wiley noted the shah's enthusiasm. The ambassador believed that it lacked direction. The monarch seemed incapable of acting as an executive, and although he suggested ideas he had no plans.
29. RG 84, TPF, Box 17, Confidential File: 1948, 800 Internal Political Affairs, 10 January 1948; RG 59, 891.00/6 May 1948, Wiley to Marshall and *FR, 1948*, 5: 162–3. As for the British, Ambassador Le Rougetel cabled London that the shah was eager to serve his nation and impatient of constitutional restraints, but he did not realise, according to the ambassador, that even if he had the power of his father his inexperience and weakness of character would make success impossible. Lance Pyman, a Foreign Office expert on Iran added, 'Governmental institutions would work better if the shah did not intrigue against his prime minister'. FO 371/Persia, 61990, 24 July 1947.

Those opposed to the shah's plans for constitutional change could still speak openly in 1948, and one attack came from Qavam's group the Hizb-i Demokrat (Democrat party), which published a pamphlet entitled 'Can the Shah Intervene Directly in the Affairs of the State?' The answer, of course, was no! 'We cannot let the Constitution be trampled on', it said, 'We respect the position and person of the Shah but we cannot remain silent as a price of support . . . to remain silent and say nothing about violations of the law would be treason and would result in the destruction of Iran's independence and respect'. *Aya shah mitavanad mustaqiman dar umur-i mamlakat dakhalat konad?* (Tehran, 1948) 38–9, 46. *FR, 1947*, 5: 990; *FR, 1948*, 5: 92, *FR, 1949*, 6: 476. FO 371/Persia, 68705, E3823/25/34, 24 March 1948.

30. RG 59, 891.00/12 May 1948, Douglas (London) to Marshall; 891.011/26 February 1949, Somerville to Acheson; RG 84, TPF, 1949, 360–2 Government, Cabinet, Constitution, Governmental Agencies, Somerville to Acheson. RG 59, 891.00/21 December 1948, Wiley to Marshall; 891.001 Pahlavi/6 June 1949.
31. RG 84, TPF, Box 17, Confidential File: 1948, 800 Internal Political Affairs, 15 August 1948; RG 59, 891.00/27 October 1948, Wiley to Marshall; *FR, 1948*, 5: 191–2; RG 59, 891.001/1 February 1949, Somerville to Acheson. FO 371/Persia, 68706, E8537/25/34, 6 July 1948, 68708, E13821/25/34, 25 October 1948, and E14173/25/34, 27 October 1948. RG 59, 891.00/11 December 1948, Weekly Political Airgram; 891.00/23 December 1948.
32. See Muhammad Reza Pahlavi, *Mission for My Country* (London: Hutchinson, 1968) 54–8 for an interesting personal statement about his destiny. For reaction of Majlis members see *Muzakirat Majlis Showrayi Melli* [Parliamentary Proceedings], 15th Majlis, 9 February 1949.
33. RG 59, 891.011/5 December 1948; 891.00/7 December 1948.
34. *FR, 1949*, 6: 486; RG 59, Research and Analysis (R&A) Report no. 4801, 'Razmara', 6 January 1949; see also Ervand Abrahamian, *Iran Between Two Revolutions*, 246, n. 57. Tehran newspapers, important shapers of public opinion, accorded him increasing prominence.
35. RG 59, 891.00/6 May 1948, Wiley to Marshall; 891.00/21 December 1948, 'Summary of Conversation with Abbas Iskandari'.
36. RG 84, TPF, 1948, 801A Foreign Advisors: Miscellaneous, Wiley to Jernegan, 1 October 1948.

NOTES TO CHAPTER 3

1. None of the officers in the American missions had had experience in Iran, nor in any other part of the Middle East. John Waller Interview, December 1982, RG 59, 891.105A/2 July 1948, Wiley to Henderson. For the missions during World War II, see Lytle, chapter 7 and T. H. Vail Motter, *United States Army in World War II. The Middle East Theater. The Persian Corridor and Aid to Russia* (Washington: GPO, 1952).
2. RG 59, 891.24/1 December 1947, and 891.20/20 May 1949, RG 84, TPF, Box 18, Confidential File, 801A Advisors-Miscellaneous: 1948, 6 May 1948, Wiley to Henderson and RG 59, 891.105A/2 July 1948, Wiley to Henderson. According to the shah, Schwarzkopf expressed doubts about Razmara's trustworthiness to the State Department. The shah asked Ambassador Allen to prevent American officers from spreading such reports. RG 59, 891.20 Mission/18 July 1947, Allen to SS.
3. RG 319, Plans & Operations Division (P&O), 091 Iran, 'Letters', 17 February 1947, Schwarzkopf to Colonel Pottenger.

4. Ibid., Stephen Macfarland, 'The Crisis in Iran 1941–1947: A Society in Change and the Peripheral Origins of the Cold War' (PhD diss., University of Texas, 1981). 220.

5. RG 59, 891.105/22 January 1948, Allen to SS, 891.105A/9 February 1948, Allen to SS. FO 371/Persia, 68715, E1839/233/34/2 February 1948; RG 59, 891.105A/2 July 1948, Wiley to Henderson, 2 May 1948, Wiley to SS; 25 February 1948, Somerville to SS, and 23 March 1948, Somerville to SS; RG 84, TPF, Box 18, 801A Foreign Advisors-Miscellaneous: 1 June 1948, Wiley to Henderson.

6. Grow Diary, 10, 22 January, 14 February 1948; RG 319, P&O, 091 Iran, Decimal File 1946–48, 23 April 1948, Schwarzkopf to Colonel Mayo; TS(1948), F/W 15, Major Meguiar File, 31 May 1948, Schwarzkopf to Colonel Mayo.

7. RG 319, P&O, 091 Iran, Decimal File 1946–48, 23 April 1948, Schwarzkopf to Colonel Mayo; Grow Diary, 30 May 1948.

8. Husain Kayustuvan, *Siyasat-i Muvazinih-ye Manfi dar Majlis-i Chahardahom* [The Policy of Negative Equilibrium in the Fourteenth Majlis]. (Tehran: Ibn Sina, 1951) 233.

9. RG 319, P&O, 091 Iran, TS (Section I–A) (Case 6 only) Part 1, sub nos. I, 27 April 1948, Memorandum for General Wedemeyer.

10. RG 59, 891.105A/2 July 1948, Wiley to Henderson.

11. Grow Diary.

12. RG 59, 891.105A/29 May, 7 June, 16 July, 4 September 1948, Wiley to SS, and 7 July 1948, SS to Wiley; 891.00/6 November 1948, 6, 9 June 1949, and 891.105/18 June 1949, Wiley to SS.

13. RG 59, 891.105A/5, 18 May 1948, Wiley to SS; *FR, 1948*, 5: 184–5; RG 319, P&O, 091 Iran, Decimal File 1946–48, 6 March 1948.

14. RG 59, 891.20 Mission/1 October 1948, Wiley to SS; 891.24/10 November 1947, Allen to SS. The British did not consider that Article 24 applied to Iran's air force, only its army, and therefore they believed it did not restrict aircraft sales. FO 371/Persia, 68719, E10511/359/34/9 August 1948. William Stueck, *The Wedemeyer Mission: American Politics and Foreign Policy during the Cold War* (Athens: University of Georgia Press, 1984) 58; Wedemeyer papers, Wedemeyer to Brigadier General Francis G. Brink, 24 August 1947, Hoover Institution, Stanford University, Palo Alto.

15. RG 59, 891.20/Missions/21 October 1948, Wiley to Jernegan. The following quotation from a speech to army officers encapsulates one aspect of Razmara's nationalism, 'Every foreigner is a foreigner', he said, 'and no foreigner is better than any other foreigner.' FO 371/Persia, 75465. E4056/1015/34/23 March 1949.

16. RG 59, R&A, No. 4801, 'Razmara', 6 January 1949; 891.20/9 October 1947, Allen to SS; RG 84, TPF, 801A Foreign Advisors–Miscellaneous, Confidential File: 1948, 22 May 1948, Grow to Wiley.

17. Papers of Major General Robert W. Grow, Grow to General Omar Bradley, 13 September 1948.

18. Grow Diary, 26, 28 November, 6 December 1947.

19. RG 319, P&O 091 Iran, Decimal File 1946–48, 18 July 1948, Grow to General Maddocks; RG 59, 891.20 Mission/28 August 1948, Jernegan to Wiley; RG 319, P&O, 091 Iran, Decimal File 1946–48, 30 August 1948; RG

84, TPF, 801A Foreign Advisors – Miscellaneous, Confidential File: 1948, 8 September 1948, Wiley to Jernegan; RG 59, 891.00/19 September 1949, Wiley to SS. General Grow was convinced that Schwarzkopf had been instrumental in his untimely removal. Diary, 10 September 1948. There is no evidence of Schwarzkopf's involvement. The documents do not indicate the origin of the move to recall Grow, whether it began in the Pentagon or in the State Department. The general was outspoken but probably no more so than many other American officials of the time. There is no indication what 'highly classified information' he revealed, nor to whom. In any case the army must have had second thoughts, for General Grow went to Moscow as US military attaché in 1950.

20. Grow Diary, 6 January, 20 December 1947, 3, 5 January, 12 February, 30 May, 2 August 1948.

21. Upton, *History of Modern Iran*, 100; RG 59, 891.24FLC, 25 February 1947, Allen to SS, RG 165, American-British Conversations, 400.336 Iran, 20 March 1947.

22. RG 59, 891.24FLC, 25 February 1947, Allen to SS, *FR, 1947*, 5: 974–6, 984–5, *New York Times* 18 February 1948. During the early postwar period sentiment to maintain Iran's neutrality and avoid involvement with either of the two power blocs was strong. In a book entitled, 'Iran Must Become the Switzerland of Asia', one prominent author, Muhammad Husain Maymandi-Nizhad, summarised the advantages that would accrue if Iran remained neutral, and argued that with powerful neighbours north (Russia) and south (England), Iran had no choice. Facing serious economic and social problems Iran should not become involved in the march towards another war. Iran's military, he wrote, had availed little in 1941, and he considered rebuilding the army a useless expense. Ideas similar to these were expressed frequently up to 1953. Maymandi-Nizhad, *Iran Bayad Suvis-i Asia Gardad* (Tehran, 1949) 7. See also, Mehdi Davudi, *Qavam Al-Saltaneh* (Tehran: 1948) 200, 204, 205, 214, *Khavar* [The East], 10 February 1948.

23. *FR, 1947*, 5: 901–02, 914–16; RG 59, 891.00, 13 April 1949, Wiley to Jernegan, 16 June 1949, and 19 September 1949, Wiley to SS; *FR, 1949*, 6: 1668; RG 59, 891.00 Pahlavi, 12 July 1948, Evan Wilson (chargé d'affaires), Memorandum of Conversation with the Shah.

24. RG 319, Records of the Army Staff, P&O Division, Box 81, Decimal File: 1946–48, November 1947, 'Letters from General Grow'; P&O, 091 Iran, 14 January 1948; RG 84, TPF, Confidential File: 1948, 700 US-Iranian Relations, 16 January 1948, Jernegan to Allen; *FR, 1948*, 5: 88–90.

25. *FR, 1947*, 5: 905. RG 59, 891.24, 9 December 1947, Memorandum from Loy Henderson to the undersecretary of state.

26. RG 59, 891.24, 26 December 1947, Allen to SS; *New York Times*, 8 February 1948.

27. *FR, 1948*, 5: 99–101; RG 84, TPF, Box 123, General Records: 1948, 891 Iranian Press, 7 January and 5 February 1948. In his autobiography written at this time an elder statesman questioned the use to Iran of $10 million of US arms. Iran, he wrote, must be concerned with the problems of hunger, poverty and disorder. Furthermore, he considered maintenance of good

relations with the Soviet Union vital. Mukhbir al-Saltaneh Mahdi-Quli Khan Hidayat, *Khatirat va Khatarat*, [Memoirs and Perils] (Tehran: 1950) 595–7.

28. Meeting in Washington in July 1948, representatives of the US and British chiefs of staff decided that the surplus arms recently sold to Iran were all that country could absorb. They also agreed that the US missions would train the Iranian army. *FR, 1948*, 5: 166.

29. RG 165, Records of the War Department General and Special Staffs, ABC, 400.336 Iran, 24 June 1947. RG 319, P&O, 091 Iran, Major Meguiar File, 'topics for Discussion with Major General Hedayat'; RG 59, 891.105, 4 August 1948, Wiley to SS, Marshall to Wiley; RG 59 891.24, 26 December 1947, Allen to SS; 4 December 1947, Lovett to Royall; RG 330, Office of Secretary of Defense, CD 19–1–10, 18 March 1948, Memorandum for the Secretary (Forrestal), RG 319, P&O, 091 Iran, Decimal File: 1946–48, 18 March 1948, Forrestal to Royall; RG 59, 891.24, 6 March 1948, Marshall to Tehran, 10 March 1948, Somerville to SS, and 27 May 1948, Kitchen to Dunn. The department estimated the replacement value of the equipment at $60–$70 million. *Department of State Bulletin*, 15 August 1948.

30. RG 59, 891.24, 10 June 1948, Jernegan to Lovett, and Lovett to Bureau of the Budget.

31. RG 59, 711.91, 1 July 1948, Marshall to Wiley; *FR, 1949*, 6: 1–5.

32. RG 59, Policy Planning Staff, 17 March 1948; *FR, 1949*, 4: 60; RG 59, E393 General Records of the Office of the Executive Secretariat, Position Papers and Reports for the Undersecretary's Meeting, 21 February and 3 March 1949 Papers of Dean Acheson, 15 March 1949, Memorandum of Conversation (Franks and Acheson), HSTL; RG 59, E393 Ex. Sec., Summaries of Secretary's Daily Meetings, 1949–50, 17, 25 and 29 March 1949. For a British version of this incident, see Nicholas Henderson, *The British and NATO* (Boulder, Colo.: Westview, 1983) 106–07. *FR, 1949*, 6: 514, RG 84, TPF, Box 21, 320 International Political Relations: 1949, 7 April 1949, Wiley to Satterthwaite (Director, Office of Near Eastern and African Affairs).

33. RG 59, E393 Ex. Sec., UMD–20, March 1949, and UM 19/1, 14 March 1949.

34. RG 59, E396.3, Minutes and Memos, UM 15 April 1949, Lawrence S. Kaplan, *A Community of Interests: NATO and the Military Assistance Program, 1948–51* (Washington: Office of the Secretary of Defense, History Office, 1980) 11, 67; Acheson Papers, 19 April 1949, Memorandum of Conversation with the President, HSTL; RG 59, Records of the Military Advisor to the Office of Near Eastern, South Asian and African Affairs, Foreign Military Assistance Coordinating Committee (FMACC), 27 June 1949, Jernegan to Budget Director Bell; FO 371/Persia, 75491, E10262/11345/34, August 1949; *FR, 1949*, 6: 536–9, RG 59, 891.20, 12 September 1949, Memorandum of Meeting (Ebtehaj and McGhee); *FR, 1949*, 6: 545–51; 517–18, 528–9; RG 319, P&O, 091 Iran, Decimal File: 1949–50, 28 January 1949; RG 59, 891.20, 9 November 1949, Webb to Tehran.

NOTES TO CHAPTER 4

1. In early 1947 it seemed that Iran might recoup its losses from the Germans. Prince Muzzafar Firouz, friend of Qavam and Iran's ambassador in Moscow, got Marshall and Bevin to agree that Iran would have a part in drawing up the peace treaty with Germany. Firouz hoped for a liberal indemnity, but this scheme evaporated and Iran continued to seek American assistance. Freidoune Sahebjam, *L'Iran des Pahlavis* (Paris: Editions Berger-Levrault, 1966) 207, *Diplomat* [The Diplomat], 20, 28, Esfand, 1325 (1947); RG 165 (Records of the War Department General and Special Staffs), (American-British Conversations) ABC 400.336/Iran, State-War-Navy Coordinating Committee: Special Ad Hoc Committee, 7 April 1947; Alan W. Ford, *Anglo-Iranian Oil Dispute, 1951–52* (Berkeley and Los Angeles: University of California Press, 1954) 47–8; RG 59, 891.00/17 August 1949, Weekly Press Airgram; *New York Times*, 20 November 1949, *Ettela'at* (Tehran), 15, 21 Tir, 16 Azar 1329 (1950); *FR, 1949* 6: 523–5, RG 84, TPF, 1949; 500 Economic Matters–Seven-Year Plan, 25 May 1949, Somerville to Acheson.
2. *FR, 1946* 7: 520, 521, 523–5.
3. Robert A. Pastor, *Congress and the Politics of U.S. Foreign Economic Policy, 1929–1976* (Berkeley and Los Angeles: University of California Press, 1980) 258–9.
4. RG 59, 891.00, 27 March 1947; Loy Henderson, Oral Interview (1973), HSTL; RG 59, 891.00 28 June 1947, Allen to Marshall, *FR, 1947* 5: 924–7; RG 59, 761.91/11 July 1947, Allen to Marshall, *FR, 1947* 5: 974; *FR, 1947* 5: 992–3; *FR, 1948* 5: 88–90, 93–7, RG 84, TPF, Confidential File: 1948, 700 US-Iranian Relations, Jernegan to Allen, 16 January 1948; RG 59, 891.00/12 February 1948. Lovett cautioned against burning bridges to the USSR. Allen Papers, 'Mission to Iran', 158, HSTL.
5. Robert H. Ferrell, *George C. Marshall*, The American Secretaries of State and Their Diplomacy, 15 (New York: Cooper Square, 1966) 172–80.
6. See, *Iran and the USA* 2 (May 1947): 1–4 for a speech by Randall S. Williams, economic affairs officer at the US embassy, stressing the separation between the American government and the International Bank. Also, Edward A. Bayne, 'Crisis of Confidence in Iran', *Foreign Affairs* 29 (July 1951): 587, Bayne interview, December 1982, Ford, *Anglo-Iranian Oil Dispute*, 47–8. Frank A. Southard, Jr., a Truman administration official, has discussed the overwhelming American influence in the International Monetary Fund as well during this period. See his oral interview (1973). HSTL.
7. Pollard, *Economic Security and the Origins of the Cold War*, 204, Bayne Interview, Edward A. Bayne, *Persian Kingship in Transition* (New York: American Field Universities Staff, 1968) 146–8, International Bank for Reconstruction and Development, *Second Annual Report, 1946–47* (Washington: IBRD) 14–18. The Morrison-Knudsen report was well done but, initiated under ex-Prime Minister Qavam, it did not meet the requirements, political and otherwise, of his successors. A new, more costly

development report based on projects was contracted – the resulting plan differed little from its predecessor. Bayne interview. The prime minister did it without discussion either with his cabinet or the governor of the Bank-i-Melli, Abul Hasan Ebethaj. He, of course, sought popular support. But his action was precipitous. Not only did many Iranians oppose large-scale foreign borrowing, but overseas bankers, including the International Bank, would not lend money without proper accumulation of facts and details. RG 84, TPF, Box 13, Confidential File: 1947, 850-Secret, 22 April 1947, Somerville to Marshall. Bayne Interview, *Persian Kingship*, 147, *FR, 1947*, 5: 907.

8. RG 84, TPF, Box 19, Confidential File: 1948, 850 Economic Matters, 20 February 1948.

9. Bayne interview. Bayne knew Thornburg from Tehran where they had shared a house in this period. RG 84, TPF, 850 Economic Development (Max Thornburg – 1948, 12 November 1947, Thornburg to Ebtehaj.

10. Bayne Interview, *Persian Kingship*, 148, RG 84, TPF, Box 23, 500 Economic Matters, January 1949, Waggoner (Tabriz) to Wiley. Within Iran opposition to loans came from several sources. Men like the highly-respected Hasan Taghizadeh believed a corrupt government would misuse foreign loans. Others, with no opposition to loans in principle, wanted to wait until they were in office before loans were contracted. Nationalists remembered the ill-advised loans from Russia of the Qajar period and wanted to stay clear of foreign entanglements. Conservative landowners, the bulk of Majlis deputies, recalled the runaway inflation of the war years and hoped to avoid a repetition. FO 371/Persia, 68741, E2232/2232/34, 2 October 1948. See *Mard-i Imruz* [The Man of Today], 13 Bahman, 1326 (1947) for a spirited atta ck on the idea of foreign loans.

11. FO 371/Persia, 62001, 8 April 1947.

12. FO 371/Persia, 62001, 19 February 1947, 62003, File 247, 1947, 68712, E1166/100/34, 6 September 1948, 68713, E12133/100/34, 17 September 1948; 62002, November 1947; 68731, E12972/1223/34, 5 October 1948, 68714A E15518/100/34, 1 December 1948, E15695/100/34, 8 December 1948.

13. RG 84, TPF, Box 23, Confidential File: 1949, 500 Economic Development, 2 February 1949; Box 108, General Records: 1947, 851 Financial Conditions – Loans, 22 September 1947, Randall S. Williams to Behbehani; Box 19, Confidential File: 1948, 850 Economic Matters, 8 September 1948, 12 November 1948.

14. Bayne, *Persian Kingship*, 148–9, 'Crisis of Confidence', 588, 'U.S. Engineers in Iran', *Fortune* 41 (February 1950): 70–3, 131–4, *Time* 54 (24 October 1949): 93–4.

15. FO 371/Persia, 75482, E1048/1103/34, 21 January 1949; Papers of Robert L. Garner, Diary, 8–14 March 1949, and 'This is the Way it Was', unpublished manuscript, 282–4, HSTL. Ebtehaj's colleagues did not agree that a loan was unnecessary, but as usual he spurned their advice. Ebtehaj, who according to Stewart Alsop was the 'financial genius' of Iran, did business in a frank, Western manner, and easily gained the attention of

visiting bankers and financial experts. Muhammad Reza Vaghefi, *Enterpreneurs of Iran* (Palo Alto: Altoan, 1975) 31–3.

16. RG 59, 891.00/12 May 1948, Douglas (London) to Marshall, *FR, 1949* 6: 523–5; RG 84, TPF, Confidential File: 1948, 700 British·Iranian Relations, 15 March 1948, Dooher to Dunn; TPF, Box 23, Confidential File: 1949, 500 General, 20 July 1949, Wiley to Acheson.

17. See for example, *Atesh* [Fire] 16 Bahman 1325 (1947).

18. For background on the Iranian oil industry see: R. W. Ferrier, *The History of the British Petroleum Company: The Developing Years, 1901–1932* (Cambridge: Cambridge University Press, 1982) (Ferrier, who once worked for British Petroleum, was invited to write this company history and was given access to company archives.) Charles Hamilton, *Americans and Oil in the Middle East* (Houston: Gulf, 1962) 32–4, Elwell-Sutton, *Persian Oil*, 10–52, Sara Reguer, 'Persian Oil and the First Lord: A Chapter in the Career of Winston Churchill', *Military Affairs* 46 (October 1982): 134–8, Sahebjam, *L'Iran des Pahlavis*, 238.

19. Elwell-Sutton, 67–79. At this time the name was changed from the Anglo-Persian Oil Company to the Anglo-Iranian Oil Company.

20. International Labour Office, *Labour Conditions in the Oil Industry in Iran* (Studies and Reports; New Series, number 24, [1950]) 20–60, Jack Jones, 'My Visit to the Persian Oil Fields', *Royal Central Asian Journal* 34 (January 1947): 60, Interview with Sir Peter Ramsbotham, London, March 1983, Clement Attlee, *As It Happened* (London: Heineman, 1954) 175–6.

21. Lenczowski, *Russia and the West in Iran*, 216–34; *FR, 1947* 5: 891; M. A. Fitzsimons, *The Foreign Policy of the British Labour Government, 1945–51* (Notre Dame: Notre Dame University Press, 1953) 167.

22. Ladjevardi, *Labor Unions and Autocracy in Iran*, 120–1, 128, 132–3; Fitzsimons, *Foreign Policy of the British Labour Government*, 166, FO 371/Persia, 62044, Quarterly Reports on AIOC (January-March, July-September, 1947) submitted by V. W. D. Willoughby, H. M. Consul, Khorramshahr.

23. Wolfgang Lentz, *Iran, 1951/52* (Heidelberg: Kurt Vowinckel, 1952) 20, Ramesh Sanghvi, *Aryamehr: The Shah of Iran: A Political Biography* (London: Macmillan, 1968) 154–5.

24. Garner Papers, Diary, 14 May 1949, HSTL; Elwell-Sutton, *Persian Oil*, 155.

25. Zuhayr Mikdashi, *A Financial Analysis of Middle East Oil Concessions: 1901–65* (New York: Praeger, 1966) 111–14, Fitzsimons, *Foreign Policy of the British Labour Government*, 167–8, Anthony Eden, *Full Circle* (Boston: Houghton Mifflin, 1960) 214–15.

26. Jacob Colemans Hurewitz, *Middle East Dilemma: The Background of U.S. Policy* (New York: Harper, for the Council on Foreign Relations, 1953) 39–40. The following was the Foreign Office breakdown of proceeds from the Iranian oil industry for the years 1939–46:

Royalties and Taxes to Persia	£37 488 000
Taxes Paid to the British government	£75 000 000
Payments to Stockholders	£34 245 000
(50 per cent to British government)	

FO 371/Persia, 68707, E10496/25/34, 9 August 1948.

27. RG 84, TPF, Confidential File: 1948, 863.6, Petroleum, 3 May 1948, Wiley to Henderson, 820 Military Affairs–Arms Credit Agreement, 21 June 1948,

700 British-Iranian Relations, 16 August 1948, Wiley to Marshall, Confidential File: 1949, 350 Iran Internal Affairs, October 1949.

28. Of course, Labour usually brought under government control only ailing companies or industries, for instance, coal, railways, shipbuilding. The AIOC did not belong in that group. Anthony Sampson, *The Seven Sisters: The Great Oil Companies and the World They Made* (New York: Viking 1975) 113–14, RG 84, TPF, Confidential File: 1947, 863.6, Petroleum, 16 June 1947, Gallman (London) to Marshall. For a more sympathetic view of Fraser see Louis, *The British Empire in the Middle East*, esp. 643–4.

29. FO 800 (Bevin Papers)/489 Persia, 20 July 1946. FO 371/Persia, 62047, 22, 25 May 1947; W. A. Berthoud, petroleum specialist in the Foreign Office, claimed that in 1947 the AIOC paid a 30 per cent dividend when it could easily have paid 50 per cent; this would have meant £800 000 more for Iran. FO 371/Persia, 68713, E11589/100/34, 5 September 1948, Berthoud to Sir Orme Sargent.

30. Sir William Fraser was convinced that this paragraph did not apply to the AIOC concession but only to future oil concessions in the southeast. FO 371/Persia, 61974, 4 November 1947; 61975, E10505/1/34, 10 November 1947; Rose L. Greaves, *Relations with the Iranian Government, 1947–52* (London: British Petroleum, 1970) 2: 12. At British urging the State Department instructed Allen to counsel Qavam's successor not to make public attacks on the British government or oil concession. FO 371/Persia, 61992, [Allen] 8, 22 December 1947.

31. FO 371/Persia, 62044, 3 December 1947; Greaves, *Relations with the Iranian Government*, 2: 4, T236 (Treasury), 2817, 1, 25 March 1949, Greaves, 2: 8; FO 371/Persia, 68731, E11662/1223/34, 30 August 1948, Sargent to Cripps, E12132/1223/34, 13 September 1948, Cripps to Sargent, 68713, E11589/100/34, 5 September 1948, Berthoud to Sargent; 68731, E13209/1223/34, 20 September 1948, 68713, E11589/100/34, 5 September 1948, Greaves, 2: 11.

32. FO 371/Persia, 68732, E14542/1223/34, 12 November 1948, E13507/1223/34, 13 October 1948.

33. FO 371/Persia, 68714A, E13510/100/34, 13 October 1948, 68732, E14105/1223/34, 27 October, 1948.

34. FO 371/Persia, 68713, E12271/100/34, 20 September 1948.

35. On Bevin's health see Kenneth L. Younger Diary, 11, 29 May 1950. FO 248 (British Embassy, Tehran) 1489, G100/60/49, 29 March 1949; T236, 2817, 1, 25 March 1949, RG 59, 891.00/29 April 1949, Wiley to Acheson.

36. Sanghvi, *Aryamehr*, 169.

NOTES TO CHAPTER 5

1. *FR, 1948*, 5: 147–8, Truman Papers, PSF, Box 180, Office Memorandum, 13 January 1949, HSTL.

2. Warner R. Schilling *et al.*, *Strategy, Politics, and Defense Budgets* (New York: Columbia University Press, 1962) 288, David McLellan, *Dean Acheson: The State Department Years* (New York: Dodd, Mead, 1976) 406, Truman Papers, Post Presidential Files [hereafter, PPF], Memoirs: Dean Acheson, 18 February 1955, HSTL.

3. Interview with John H. Waller, Washington, DC, December 1982. Waller, a foreign service officer, served in Iran from 1947 to 1952. Dean Acheson was a close friend of the Waller family. William Whitney Stueck, Jr., *The Road to Confrontation: American Policy Toward China and Korea, 1947–50* (Chapel Hill: University of North Carolina Press, 1981) 123; McLellan, *Dean Acheson*, 398, see also 53, 172, 358, 406; Dean Acheson, *Present at the Creation: My Years in the State Department* (New York: W. W. Norton, 1969) 502.

4. Robert J. Donovan, 'Truman's Perspective', *Economics and the Truman Administration* (Lawrence: Regents, 1981) 18–19.

5. RG 59, 891.00, 13 April 1949, Wiley to John Jernegan, and 891.001 Pahlavi, 27 October 1949, Wiley to Stanley Woodward (Protocol). The shah alas was no reader.

6. Truman Papers, PSF, Subject File: Iran, 25 October 1949, Wiley to Truman, HSTL.

7. RG 59, 891.00 Pahlavi, Reza Shah, 1 November 1949, 'Department Brief for the President'.

8. The State Department did not analyse these developments and its favourable assessment proved premature. The shah had indeed augmented his power but also his responsibility; when political and economic conditions deteriorated after he and his supporters had promised improvement, the people blamed the court. And despite royal support, the development plan appeared doomed. Although its failure was only partly the result of court intrigue, the opposition charged that the plan provided sinecures for royalists and little else. People became disenchanted at the lack of progress. FO 371/Persia, 75468, E14184/11015/134, 18 November 1949. *Ettela'at*, 21 Deh, 15 Bahman, *Kayhan*, 12 Bahman 1328 (1950).

9. Not all press reaction was unfavourable, and according to one leading daily the visit could help Iran: 'The American people know little about monarchies especially one so far off as Iran, and this trip will acquaint them with our nation, which they still refer to as the land of a thousand-and-one nights . . . In America the whole people influences decisions and therefore it is important that all Americans come to know Iran'. *Ettela'at*, 13 November 1949. Nevertheless, the editor of *Kayhan* was relieved that the shah's broadcast from the United States showed no trace of despair or sycophancy. 11 Deh 1328 (1950).

10. RG 59, 891.00, 27 May 1948, 891.00, 11 July 1949; 891.105, 14 November 1949. General Zahedi had served as aide to General Schwarzkopf, former head of the American Military Mission to the Iranian Gendarmerie. Razmara was chiefly responsible for the American's departure in 1948, a further irritant in the relationship between the chief of staff and Zahedi. 891.00, 22 August 1949, Wiley to Jernegan.

11. RG 59, 891.00 Pahlavi, 10 November 1949, James E. Webb to Wiley, and 11 November 1949, Wiley to Secretary of State. British Ambassador John Le

Rougetel thought Wiley had agreed that the shah should postpone his visit, but when he heard nothing for several days and called on Wiley, the American ambassador insisted that the shah must go as planned. FO 371/Persia, 75467, E13612/1015/34, 10 November 1949; RG 59, 891.00, 22 August 1949, Wiley to Jernegan.

12. *Newsweek*, 28 November, 5, 19 December 1949, *Louisville Courier-Journal*, 29 November 1949, *Idaho Daily Statesman* (Boise) 8, 13 December 1949, *Detroit News*, 26 November 1949, *Life*, 5 December 1949. RG 59, 891.001 Pahlavi, 19 November 1949, Wiley to Secretary of State. Henry Suydam had held several government positions before he went to work temporarily for the shah in 1949. During World War I he served the Committee on Public Information in London and the Hague. In 1921 Secretary of State Charles Evans Hughes named him chief of current information in the department, and in 1934 he became press adviser to Attorney General Homer Cummings. In the years between he worked as a journalist and editorial writer for a succession of newspapers in New York and New Jersey. Secretary of State John Foster Dulles appointed him chief of the news division and spokesman for the State Department (1953–55), the post he held at his death. *New York Times*, 12 December 1955, 31.

13. *FR, 1949*, 6: 572–4. The department was only repeating the advice given Iran's ambassador, Husain Ala, in September by Assistant Secretary for Near Eastern Affairs George McGhee, who had spoken about Iran's lifting itself by its own bootstraps. RG 59, 891.20, 12 September 1949, Memorandum of Conversation. Officials assured the shah of help with the International Bank, where they predicted success. They could hardly do less for only a few days after the shah's arrival the American government with execrable timing announced an Export-Import Bank loan to Afghanistan. To be sure, this loan had been under negotiation for months, but as Ambassador Ala pointed out almost plaintively, it would make the shah's position even more awkward if he returned home empty-handed. RG 59, 891.00, 29 November 1949.

14. RG 59, 891.00, 2 June 1949, Wiley to Secretary of State; RG 319 (Records of the Army Staff), Box 159, P&O (Plans and Operations Division), 091 Iran, TS, Evans to General Bolte. RG 59, Records of the Military Advisor to the Office of Near Eastern, South Asian, and African Affairs, Box no. 1, 18 November 1949, 'Shah's Strategic Plan', 891.001 Pahlavi, 19 November 1949.

15. *FR, 1949*, 6: 579–80. An interesting contrast to these meetings were the amiable sessions in Washington from November 14 to 20 between Assistant Secretary McGhee and his British counterpart, Undersecretary of State Sir Michael Wright, an expert on the Middle East. The talks had evolved out of a suggestion by Foreign Secretary Ernest Bevin to Acheson at Paris in June. Covering Middle Eastern topics from Palestine to the former Italian colonies, the two men were silent on Iran, a recognition perhaps of agreement, certainly of absence of concern. McGhee left immediately afterwards for a meeting in Istanbul of heads of American missions in the Middle East. For details of the talks, see *FR, 1949*, 6: 54–89.

16. *FR, 1949*, 6: 585–8; Papers of Robert B. Landry, Shah of Iran Folder, 24 December 1949, Ala to Chief of Protocol, HSTL, RG 59, 891.001 Pahlavi,

28 December 1949, Acheson to Wiley. An eminent elder statesman, Gozam al-Mulk, visited Wiley when reports of the KLM charter reached Tehran and warned of the unfortunate impression this would make. Wiley told him the United States did not have the physical facilities to transport the shah and his enlarged party, but the visitor persisted, 'referring querulously to our ability to maintain air lift to Berlin'. He claimed the State Department had bungled the return. This was too much for Wiley who 'repudiated this suggestion indignantly and in no uncertain terms'. Still, it seems the elderly gentleman got the better of the usually glib ambassador. Papers of John Cooper Wiley, Box 5, Iran file, n.d., Draft Telegram to Secretary of State, Franklin D. Roosevelt Library, Hyde Park, NY.

17. Acheson, *Present at the Creation*, 502; *FR, 1949*, 6: 172; RG 84, Tehran Post Files, 1949: 500 Economic Matters, Seven-Year Plan, 13 December 1949, Wiley to Jernegan; Interview with George McGhee, Washington DC, January 1982.

18. *FR, 1949*, 6: 590–2, RG 59, Records of MILADV, Box 4, Minutes FMACC, M–8, 16 March 1950, M–9, 22 March 1950; *FR, 1950*, 5: 475–8; 483–5. Ambassador Wiley wrote the State Department on 18 November 1949, supporting tanks for Iran on political grounds–humouring the shah. *FR, 1949*, 6: 582–3. Even earlier, on 21 October, McGhee had admitted that the political repercussions of omitting them would be unfortunate, 'to put it mildly'. *FR, 1949*, 6: 565.

19. *Newsweek*, 28 November, 5, 19 December 1949.

20. The effect on the shah of his exposure to America was less than the ambitious and ebullient Wiley had expected, but the visit drew attention to the gap in living standards between the two nations and increased the shah's impatience with the glacial pace of reform in Iran, enhancing the attractiveness of ruling as well as reigning. Such also was the shah's reaction after visiting Europe in 1948. See, 'Safar shahanshah beh Amrika' [The Shah's Visit to America], *Danesh* [Knowledge] 1 (1949) 396.

21. *FR, 1950*, 5: 447.

22. Cottam, *Nationalism in Iran*, 261.

23. Abrahamian, *Iran Between Two Revolutions*, 252–63.

24. Muhammad Reza Shah Pahlavi, *Mission for My Country* (London: Hutchinson, 1968) 89. For Iranian interpretations of the election, see Abdul Husain Bihniya, *Pardih-hay-i Siyasat: Naft, Nihzat, Musaddiq, Zahedi*, [Behind the Scenes: Oil, Resurgence, Musaddiq, Zahedi] (Tehran: Chap-i Rangin, n.d.) 26, 48–9, and *Kayhan*, 10 Esfand, 1328 (1950).

NOTES TO CHAPTER 6

1. For an interesting article recommending American aid to Iran, see, T. Cuyler Young, 'Russia and Reform in Iran', *Foreign Affairs* 28 (1950): 282–3. *FR, 1950*, 5: 470–1, 482–3, 506–7.

2. Interview with William Rountree, Gainesville, Florida, March 1982.

3. *FR, 1950*, 5: 491–9, *New York Times*, 4 April 1950; M. A. Hedayati, *Situation politique et sociale de l'Iran en 1950–1951: Année de la nationalization du pétrole* (Neuchâtel: H. Messeiller, 1951) 55, 57; Bayne Interview.

4. Rountree Interview; *FR, 1950*, 5: 509–18.

5. *FR, 1950*, 5: 519.

6. Ibid., 519–20.

7. Papers of Henry F. Grady, Box 2, 1 August 1953, 'Biographical Sketch', HSTL; RG 59, E 393 General Records of the Office of the Executive Secretariat, Box 6, Memoranda of Conversations with the President, 1949–50, 15 April 1949, Box 4, Summaries of the Secretary's Daily Meetings, 1949–50, 16, 17 August 1949. President Truman appointed Gordon R. Clapp head of the UN Survey Mission to the Near East in September 1949. Interview with Herman B. Wells, Bloomington, Indiana, 1981. Rountree Interview, Personal Letter from Leslie L. Rood, 26 May 1982. [Rood worked with Grady on the Palestine problem in 1946 and served as his assistant in Athens and Tehran].

8. Rood Letter, Grady Papers, Box 5, 'Adventures in Diplomacy', Unpublished Manuscript, Chapter 1: 4–5, HSTL.

9. Rood Letter; Grady Papers, Box 1, Folder 7, 26 August 1950, Grady to SS; Folder 12, 27 October 1950, Grady to Rountree, HSTL.

10. Grady Papers, Box 1, Folder 2, 20 January 1950, Grady to McGhee, HSTL; Acheson Papers, Princeton Seminars, 15 May 1954, HSTL; *FR, 1950*, 5: 521–2, n.1; Grady Papers, Box 1, Folder 10, 3 August 1951, Grady to Willard M. Kiplinger; General Correspondence: 1952, 22 November 1952, Grady to President Truman, HSTL.

11. RG 84, TPF, 350 Iran Internal Political Affairs: 1949, 15 December 1949, Wiley to Jernegan.

12. FR, 1950, 5: 503; Abrahamian, *Iran Between Two Revolutions*, 262. Mansur impressed the British, who considered him intelligent, shrewd and capable. Actually the British preferred Seyed Zia ed-Din Tabataba'i and Mansur was their second choice, while the United States supported General Razmara. FO 371/Persia, 68705, E5639/25/34, 4 May 1948, 68709, E14939/25/34, 10 November 1948, and 75468, E15365/1015/34, 16 December 1949. E. A. Bayne told Ambassador Shepherd that the shah had appointed Mansur for two reasons: he was the only one who could handle Ebtehaj, and he was willing and best able to put through the supplementary oil agreement. FO 248/Persia, 1493, G101/2/57/50, 28 March 1950. *FR, 1950*, 5: 504–5.

13. *FR, 1950*, 5: 549–50. The British were moving in the same direction as the Americans. They would support the nomination of a strong candidate for prime minister but would not force the shah to accept their choice. They did advise the shah, however, that he must be loyal to his prime minister if any progress was to be made. FO 371/Persia, 75468, E15087/1015/34, 29 November 1949, and 82310, EP1016/2/34, 19 January 1950.

14. FO 371/Persia, 82308, EP1013/23/34, 5 May 1950, 82311, EP1016/51/34, 16 June 1950.

15. According to the British embassy, the election for members to the constitutional convention was so corrupt that the elder statesman Hasan Taghizadeh and several other delegates refused to take their seats, pleading illness. FO 371/Persia, 75465, E5495/1015/34, 27 April 1949. For reaction to

the Majlis election in November 1949 see, FO 371/Persia, 75468, E14184/
1015/34, 18 November 1949. Qavam's letter read in part: 'The shah should
realize his sovereign powers are on loan from the nation, they are not
God-given. Even Reza Shah did not think of asking for veto rights. Nor did
the greatest enemy of the constitution, Muhammad Ali Shah Qajar, look for
such powers . . . The Shah will reap a harvest of popular anger and
resistance. At that time neither force nor bayonets, persecution nor
imprisonment will be remedy for the chaos which will ensue'. RG 59,
788.00/6 April 1950, Wiley to SS. The shah stripped Qavam of his title,
'Highness', in retaliation for the letter. Wiley papers, Box 5, Iran File,
788.00/29 May 1950, Wiley to SS, FDR Library. See also Sahebjam, *L'Iran
des Pahlavis*, 226, 228, Abrahamian, 262.

16. *FR, 1950*, 558–62, Interview with John Waller, December 1982. Dooher did
not improve his standing with the British after his return to Iran in spring
1948. He reportedly told General Yazdanpanah, a close friend of the shah,
that the US had pressed the British to change the supplementary oil
agreement in Iran's favour. FO 248/Persia, 1512, G153/2/141/50, 16 August
1950. Ambassador Le Rougetel considered Dooher an intriguer and
charged that he had influenced Wiley. FO 371/Persia, 68708, E14428/25/34,
1 November 1948, and FO 248/Persia, 1486. G21/183/49, 26 August 1949.
The shah referred to Dooher as the 'tribal attache at the US Embassy', and
deprecated his influence on the ambassador and his undiplomatic comments
about Iranian leaders. FO 371/Persia, 82310, EP1016/28/34, 8 April 1950.
Dooher returned to the United States in September 1950 to take charge of
Persian language programming at the Voice of America. Wiley Papers, Box
5, Iran File, 8 March 1951, Wiley to H. Freeman Matthews, FDRL. Cottam,
209. To anyone researching State Department files on Iran, the changing
composition of interviews and contacts becomes apparent. Until early 1949
alternative views abound; after that date few appear. James Bill has written
that during the mid-1960s when he was conducting research in Tehran the
invitation lists for embassy functions contained the same names over and
over again. *The Eagle and the Lion: The Tragedy of American-Iranian
Relations* (New Haven: Yale University Press, 1988) esp. 386–92.

In Washington State Department officials who earlier had expressed
concern over the shah's ineptitude now put aside their reservations and
made clear their support for greater personal rule. Acheson praised the shah
as the only source of leadership. *FR, 1950*, 5: 505; RG 330, JCS 1948–50,
Report by Joint Strategic Survey Committee, CCS337 (2–20–50) Section 1,
9.

17. RG 59, Records of the Military Advisor to the Office of Near Eastern, South
Asian and African Affairs, Box 1, 10 February 1950. McGhee to Bruce; *FR,
1950*, 5: 473–5; Interview with General Collins, January 1982; *Ettela'at*,
Farvardin 23 1329 (March, 1950); *FR, 1950*, 5: 523, RG 330, Secretary of
Defense, CD 9–4–27, JCS, 2 May 1950, Omar N. Bradley to Secretary of
Defense.

18. Truman Papers, Official File 134 (1950–53) 1 May 1950, Memorandum for
the president, HSTL; *FR, 1950*, 5: 552–5.

19. RG 59, 788.00/27 May 1950, Richards to SS; RG 84, TPF, Box 29, 350 Iran:
Internal Political Affairs, 1951, 15 May 1951.

20. *FR*, *1950*, 5: 574; FO 371/Persia, 82353, EP1192/7/34, 13 June 1950, *FR*, *1950*, 5: 622, RG 59, 788.5 MAP, 29 December 1950, Grady to SS.
21. *FR*, *1950*, 5: 551; Ibid., 485–7.
22. For interesting parallels between US policy in Korea and Iran prior to June 1950, see Stueck, *Road to Confrontation*, 67, 165, 168–9; Kaplan, *A Community of Interests*, 95–6; RG 59, Military Advisor NE, SA, AA, Box 2, 15 July 1950, MDAP Newsletter no.7.
23. *FR*, *1950*, 5: 556, 560.
24. Ambassador Allen was more suspicious of General Razmara than either Wiley or Grady. See, RG 59, 891.24, 6 May 1947, Allen to SS, and 891.00, 12 July 1947, Allen to SS. Research and Analysis Report, no. 4801.1, 8 June 1950, 'Razmara'. Razmara presents something of an enigma. He came from a modest middle-class background, and experienced a meteoric rise after the events of December 1946 in which he took a lead and gained the shah's confidence. British and American embassy cables in 1947 and 1948 linked his name with graft and a pro-Soviet attitude, and yet by early 1950 he had become a favourite of the American embassy and reports spoke of his honesty and simplicity. Rumours abounded of supposed plots to unseat the shah; the truth may have been far less titillating. Some of those who worked with him in 1950–51 have claimed that the general was idealistic and patriotic, a simple, uncomplicated man, devoid of ulterior motives. Certainly his performance as prime minister does not lend credence to the strongman image; rather he seemed overwhelmed by the complexities of governing. Interviews with E. A. Bayne, 27 December 1982, and Mehdi Sami'i, London, March 1983, Hedayati, *Situation politique et sociale*, 94, *FR*, *1950*, 5: 548.
25. Bihniya, *Pardih-hay-i Siyasat*, 29, 33.
26. Acheson Papers, Princeton Seminars, 15 May 1954, HSTL, FO 371/Persia, 91613, EP1531/2188, Memorandum by Thornburg to British government, 15 November 1951.
27. The British considered Seyed Zia ed-Din Tabataba'i the best candidate to lead a reform party, but in the face of the shah's reluctance and American coolness, the Foreign Office decided to wait for a more propitious time to advance his candidacy. FO 371/Persia, 82310, EP1016/2/34, 19 January 1950.
28. FO 248/Persia, 1493, G101/2/113/50, 5 June 1950, FO 371/Persia, 82311, EP1016/44/34, 29 May 1950, EP1016/48/34, 10 June 1950, 51/34, 16 June 1950, and 52/34, 19 June 1950. Louis provides a different interpretation of Razmara's appointment in his *British Empire in the Middle East*, 636.
29. *Ettela'at*, 2 Tir 1329 (June 1950), Abrahamian, 263–4.
30. *Ettela'at*, 15, 20, 24 Tir 1329 (July 1950); 10 Khordad 1329 (May 1950). Many Iranians assumed that Grady's role in Iran would be the same as in Greece: watchdog over American aid. See, RG 59, 611.88, 1 December 1950, Memorandum of Conversation with Razmara, Richards (Chargé d'Affaires) to SS.

NOTES TO CHAPTER 7

1. Papers of Dean Acheson, Princeton Seminars, 15 May 1954, HSTL; *FR, 1950*, 5, 180–4, 576.
2. *FR, 1950*, 1: 324, 329, 5: 572–3, 7: 181, 314, 369. President Truman confided to his diary on 30 June 1950 that, 'Russia is figuring on an attack in the Black Sea and toward the Persian Gulf. Both prizes Moscow has wanted since Ivan the Terrible'. Robert H. Ferrell, editor, *Off the Record: The Private Papers of Harry S. Truman* (New York: Harper & Row, 1980) 185.
3. *FR, 1950*, 1: 333, 380.
4. Ibid., 5: 519; Princeton Seminars, 15 May 1954, HSTL. Deputy Assistant Secretary of State Raymond Hare echoed Acheson in testimony before the House Committee on Foreign Affairs on 17 June 1950. He played down any notion that the Iranian economy was in desperate straits, stressing instead the poor morale. The department's solution, he said, was to send Grady, 'a man who inspires confidence . . . That one thing alone can do a great deal'. The Iranians were already receiving *matériel* under the MDAP, and in addition, he said, 'They are going to get a rather tangible ambassador, if you know Ambassador Grady, but something tangible means a lot to them'. US Congress, House Committee on International Relations, *Selected Executive Session Hearings of the Committee, 1943–50*. Part 2, *Military Assistance Programs*, Historical Series (Washington: Government Printing Office, 1976) 6: 103.
5. *Department of State Bulletin*, 10 July 1950, *Ettela'at* (Tehran), 15 Tir 1329 (1950); *Ettela'at*, 24 Tir 1329; *FR, 1950*, 5: 590–1, Princeton Seminars, 15 May 1954, HSTL.
6. Henry F. Grady, 'What Went Wrong in Iran', *Saturday Evening Post*, (5 January 1952) 30, Acheson, *Present at the Creation*, 502.
7. *FR, 1950*, 5: 546–8, 550–1; RG 59, E396.3, General Records of the Office of the Executive Secretariat, Minutes of the Undersecretary's Meetings (UM), Box 13, UM/19 April 1950.
8. A political lull had enveloped Britain after the February election that returned the Attlee government; no issues divided the cabinet. Labour might have proceeded if the US had given the lead. But Acheson tred softly. One British official, commenting on Acheson's ineffectiveness in London, attributed it to recent right-wing criticism at home. Kenneth O. Morgan, *Labour in Power, 1945–51* (Oxford: Clarendon Press, 1984) 399, 415. Kenneth Younger Diary, 11 May 1950. Younger was Minister of State at the Foreign Office, 1950–51 and often substituted for the ailing Bevin.
9. McGhee Interview, *FR, 1950*, 5: 591–600; FO 371/Persia, EP1119/23/34, 19 September 1950; EP1119/28/34, 18 September 1950; T236 (Treasury), 2822, 22 September 1950; FO 371/Persia, 82348, EP11345/24/3, 23 September 1950; T236, 27 September 1950; FO 371/Persia, 82343, EP1119/3634, 28 September 1950.
10. FO 371/Persia, 82343, EP1119/29/34, 29 September, 24 October 1950, and EP1119/57/34, 10 November 1950.
11. Princeton Seminars, 15 May 1954, HSTL; RG 59, 888.10/22 September 1950, Papers of Burton Y. Berry, Diary, 28, 29 September and 5 October

1950, Lilly Library (LL), Indiana University, Bloomington; Export-Import Bank, Minutes of Special Meeting of Board of Directors, 6 October 1950, *FR, 1950,* 5:613–15.

12. Ex-Im Bank Minutes, 6 October 1950. The State Department and the bank were disturbed at what they considered Grady's precipitous announcement of the loan. They argued that the British had been on the point of allowing Iran to convert sterling to dollars but that once London learned of Washington's decision the leverage disappeared. Berry papers, Diary, 10 October 1950. Foreign Office records show, however, that the British government had no intention of allowing full convertibility to finance the loan. Princeton Seminars, 15 May 1954, HSTL; Grady papers, Box 1, Folder 5-Misc., Dooher to Grady, 18 October 1950, Folder 10, Grady to Rountree, 27 October 1950, Folder 7-Misc., Grady to Adrian Fisher, 3 November 1950, Folder 3, Grady to Stephen Bechtel, 4 November 1950. Acheson, *Present at the Creation,* 502.

13. Ex-Im Bank Minutes, 6 October 1950, Grady papers, Box 1, Folder 10, Rountree to Grady, 9 October 1950, RG 59, 888.10/CS/RA/10 November 1950, Woodbridge to Dorsz, 'Memo. Regarding Ex-Im Bank and Iranian Loan': Grady papers, Box 1, Folder 10, Grady to Rountree, 27 October 1950, Folder 3, Grady to Stephen D. Bechtel, 16 March 1951, RG 59, 888.10/14, 17 November and 4 December 1950, Grady to SS; Grady papers, unpublished manuscript, 'Adventures in Diplomacy', 59.

14. RG 59, 611.88/30 November 1950, Richards to SS; *New York Times,* 27 September 1950; RG 59, 611.88/30 November 1950, Acheson to Grady, 1, 4 December 1950, Richards to SS.

15. Grady papers, Box 1, Folder 10, 27 October 1950, Grady to Rountree, RG 59, Grady to SS, 888.10/19 November 1950, *FR, 1950,* 5: 612–13, 624–30, Grady Papers, unpublished manuscript, 'Adventures in Diplomacy', 58–60, Grady to Harry Eaton, 1 February 1951 (*Declassified Documents, Retrospective Collection: Catalog of Abstracts,* Washington: Carrollton Press, 1976. 617 C); Grady Papers, Box 1, Folder 6, Grady to Herbert Elliston (*Washington Post* editor), 30 December 1949, Folder 12, Grady to Rountree, 6 March 1951, *FR, 1950,* 5: 174–6, 606, 625–6.

16. FO 371/Persia, 82343, EP1119/57/34/10 November 1950, 82348, EP11345/ 34/34/10 November 1950, EP11345/35/34/2 December 1950, EP11345/40/ 34; FO 371/Persia, 82342, EP1119/2/34/30 August 1950, 82343, EP1119/41/ 34/6 October 1950, 82313, EP1016/93/34/17 December 1950.

17. Grady papers Box 1, Folder 10, 27 October 1950, Grady to Rountree, RG 59, 888.10/22 November 1950, Grady to SS; *FR, 1950,* 5; 620–30; HST papers, PSF, Iran: Subject File, 22 December 1950, Herbet E. Gaston to Truman, HSTL.

18. RG 59, 888.10/13 January 1951, Grady to SS, Telegram 1577, 16 January 1951, Grady to SS; 888.10/19 January 1951, McGhee to SS, 22 January 1951, SS to Grady, 26 January 1951, Grady to SS; 888.10/8,12 January 1951, Grady to SS, 19 January 1951, Dorsz to Rountree, 26 January 1951, Grady to SS, 31 January 1951, Grady to SS, 21 February 1951, Berry to Fisher; 12 February 1951, Lucius D. Battle to SS, 14 February 1951, President to SS, 'Memo on the Iranian Situation', 15 February 1951, SS, 'Memo of

Conversation with the President', 16 February 1951, State Department to Grady. Acheson sent Grady's proposal to the White House and President Truman decided against a $100 million loan on 14 February. 13 January 1951, Grady to SS, 16 January 1951, McGhee to Assistant Secretary Thorp, Minutes of the Undersecretary's Meetings, Box 14, UM/M-301, 2 February 1951.

19. The Ex-Im Bank loan issue, overtaken by the oil crisis in spring 1951, remained unresolved until August when the Musaddiq government received authority from parliament to sign the loan agreement worked out in January. But the British pressed the State Department not to make the loan, and Acheson agreed. Ironically one of Grady's last official acts in Iran was to inform the prime minister that the loan would not be made. FO 371/Persia, 91494, EP11345/22/12 September 1951. Until the early 1950s the State Department tried repeatedly to use the Export-Import Bank as a political instrument, but the bankers resisted. The bank's inadequacies for this role were evident. The Iranian case was only an extreme example of similar situations that had developed earlier in Greece (1946), China (1947), Yugoslavia (1948), Argentina (1949), and Indonesia (1950). In each of these cases the bank acted slowly because of doubts concerning repayment and the political nature of the proposed loans. With the commencement of the Mutual Security Program in 1951, pressure on the bank lessened considerably. See, Terry H. Anderson *The United States, Great Britain and the Cold War, 1944–47* (Columbia: University of Missouri Press, 1981) 156, Oral Interview, Willard J. Thorp (1971) 49, 143, HSTL, and Stueck, 41; Acheson, *Present at the Creation*, 502.

20. International Bank for Reconstruction and Development, *Fifth Annual Report*, 1949–50 (Washington: IBRD, 1950) 30–1, *Sixth Annual Report*, *1950–51*, 21–2, Grady papers, Box 5, unpublished manuscript, 'Adventures in Diplomacy', 31; FO 371/Persia, 91485, EP1112/5/8 January 1951, RG 59, 888.10/29 January 1951, Grady to SS, Interview with Bayne, 26 December 1982, Hidayati, *Situation politique et sociale*, 53–4, *Ettela'at*, 13, 29 Shahrivar, 8 Mehr 1329 (1950), *Tulu* [The Sunrise], 12 Mehr 1329 (1950).

21. Bihniya, *Pardih-hay-i Siyasat*, 33–4, Abrahamian, *Iran Between Two Revolutions*, 264; *Tulu*, 17 Mehr 1329.

22. Interview with Mehdi Sami'i, London, 19 March 1983, FO 371/Persia, 75486, E12185/1103/34/4 October 1949, 82309, EP1013/40/34/5 August 1950. For an attack on Ebtehaj and his policies see, Danishpur, *Ebtehaj va nirkh-i as'ar* [Ebtehaj and the Foreign Exchange Rate] (Tehran, n.d.).

23. Bayne Interview; FO 371/Persia, 82312, EP1016/66/34/14 July 1950; RG 59, 888.10/14 December 1950, Telegram 1339, Richards to SS; Grady papers, Box 1, Richards to Rountree, 11 September 1950. But failure to co-operate undermined the government. Razmara's enemies, including the exiled Ebtehaj, Husain Ala, and the shah's brother, Prince Abdul Reza, seized on any success, no matter how small, as proof that the shah should beware. They did not limit themselves to sniping at the prime minister, for when Ala, now court minister, visited Grady in September, he concluded with a 15-minute tirade against Dooher and Wiley, who, he said, had brought Razmara to power. Grady papers, Box 1, Grady to Rountree, 13 September 1950, and Folder 5, Dooher to Grady, 18 October 1950.

24. *Ettela'at*, 16 Shahrivar 1329 (1950).
25. *Nation* (29 July 1950) 107–10, and the *New York Times*, 23 September 1950.
26. Frye, *The United States and Iran*, 252–3; RG 59, 788.5-MAP/15 December 1950, 15 January and 9 February 1951, Mutual Defense Assistance Program (MDAP) General Reports, *Ettela'at*, 22 Tir 1329, 9, 12. Many Iranians concluded that if the United States had difficulty overcoming the North Koreans from its nearby bases in Japan, what assistance could they expect when there were no American bases in the region. They had to get along with their northern neighbour. The Soviets took advantage of this psychological change, 'replacing the big club with the olive branch'. RG 59, 788.00/25 September 1950, Wagner to SS. When NATO announced the future adherence of Greece and Turkey to the alliance, there was barely a ripple of protest in Tehran; this surprised American diplomats who had expected Iranians to complain loudly. On Grady's advice the United States dropped plans to reassure the Iranian government. *FR*, *1950*, 5: 586, FO 371/Persia, 82322, EP1023/5/34/20 September 1950, EP 1023/12/14 October 1950, RG 59 788.00/9–2550, 888.10/12–1450.
27. RG84, TPF, Box 34, 400.1 Soviet, 31 August 1950, Acheson to Grady, William Stueck, 'The Korean War: An International History' (unpublished manuscript), 103–5. See *Current Digest of the Soviet Press* 2, no. 47 (1950): 20–1.
28. *FR*, *1950*, 1: 324, 380, 387, 437, 447, *FR*, *1951*, 1: 6–7, 68, 1018–19, 1039. Joint US UK military discussions in Washington in October 1950 considered sending American and British troops into Khuzistan in south-western Iran if the Soviets invaded or local communists seized power in Azarbaijan. The shah hoped that Britain would protect the oil fields in such an eventuality and not just blow everything up. His view fitted nicely with London's, unless of course there was a full-scale war. American military men, however, were cautious. Not only did they refuse to commit the United States to sending troops – for fear of being caught off-guard somewhere else – but they advised the British that dispatching troops to Khuzistan might exacerbate any crisis and call forth a dramatic Soviet counterthrust. The two allies had not settled the issue by the end of 1950, although the British chiefs of staff had begun to consider using commonwealth forces from Pakistan or India, who would appear, they thought, less threatening to the Russians. FO 371/Persia, 82353, EP1192/15/34/26 October 1950, and 82322, EP1023/14a/34/24 November 1950.
29. HST papers, PSF, Intelligence File, 'CIA Situation Reports', 25 August, 1, 8 September 1950, HSTL; Ibid., 'Memo. for the President', 27 July, 1950; *FR*, *1950*, 5: 608, RG 330, Records of the Secretary of Defense, 091.31 Iran 1950/28 November 1950, Matthews to General Burns.
30. Bihniya, 36; RG 59, 788.5-MAP/15 January, 9 February 1951, MDAP General Reports, 7 November 1950, 26 January 1951, Grady to SS. This was not the first time Razmara had denied travel permission to Americans. In September 1949 Razmara, then chief of staff, refused an embassy request to allow the US agricultural attaché to make a quick survey in Azarbaijan. The general replied that too many surveys had already been made and the United States would lose prestige if people knew America was aware of their plight and did nothing. RG 59, 891.20 Mission/16 September 1949, Wiley to SS;

Bayne Interview.
31. *Muzakirat-i Majlis* [Parliamentary Proceedings], 16th Majlis, 13 July 1950.
32. RG 59, 788.5-MAP/15 January 1951; 13, 20 December 1950, Ohly to General Scott; 15 December 1950, SS to Embassy Tehran.
33. Bayne Interview, *Persian Kingship in Transition*, 146–7, RG 59, 888.10/15 December 1950, 'Financial Reports of Seven Year Plan Organization', *Tulu*, 12 Mehr 1329.
34. FO 371/Persia, 75482, E1048/1103/34/21 January 1949, 75484, E4662/1103/34/8 April 1949, E6103/1103/34/25 April 1949; Max Thornburg, 'The Seven Year Plan', *Iran and the USA* (February, 1950) 27–38; Bayne Interview; RG 166, Department of Agriculture, Box 232, Agricultural Policy, 'Annual Economic Report for Iran, 1950', 15 March 1951; RG 59, 891.00/28 December 1949, Wiley to SS; RG 84, TPF, 500 Economic Matters: Seven Year Plan, 1949, 11 September 1949, Wiley to Jernegan; RG 166, Box 234, Iran-Economic Conditions, 1940–50, translation from *Kayhan*, 10 October 1950.
35. Grady papers, Box 1, Folder 10, 22 September 1951, 'Memo: Overseas Consultants Inc'. 1 November 1950, Woodbridge to McGhee, 3 November 1950, Grady to Rountree, HSTL.

NOTES TO CHAPTER 8

1. RG 59, 891.6363/21 July 1949, Wiley to SS, Ford, *Anglo-Iranian Oil Dispute, 1951–52*, 48–50, Mahdi Quli Hidayat, *Khatirat va Khatarat* [Memoirs and Perils] (Tehran, 1950) 589. Ford, 48–50, Ramazani, *Iran's Foreign Policy, 1941–1973*, 189–92; *FR, 1949*, 6: 149–50, 162; RG 84, TPF, Box 28, 350: Iran 1950, 16 November 1950; Fuad Ruhani, *Tarikh-i milli shudan-i san'at-i naft-i Iran* [History of the Nationalisation of the Iranian Oil Industry] (Tehran, 1973) 83–5.
2. RG 84, TPF, 350 Iran Internal Political Affairs, 1949, 12 October 1949, Wiley to Jernegan; Ralph Hewins, *Mr. Five Percent: The Story of Calouste Gulbenkian* (New York: Rinehart, 1958) 3–11, 54, 154, 219–22, 233–4, John Lodwick and D. H. Young, *Gulbenkian: An Interpretation of Calouste Sarkis Gulbenkian* (London: Heinemann, 1958) 1–13.
3. *FR, 1950*, 5: 579.
4. RG 84, TPF, 350 Iran Internal Political Affairs, 1949, 12 October 1949, Wiley to Jernegan, RG 59, 891.002/14 October 1949, Wiley to SS, FO 371/Persia, 75480, E12712/1055/34/18 October 1949, RG 59, 891.00/4

November 1949, and 19 December 1949, WPA. Sa'ed gained no concessions and on return told Wiley that the next prime minister in Tehran would have a difficult time.

5. FO 371/Persia, 82343, EP1119/33/34/2 October 1950; 82347, EP11345/7/ 34/1 June 1950; 82311, EP1016/44/34/29 May 1950, EP1016/20/34/3 March 1950; FO 248/Persia, 1512, G153/111/50/29 June 1950, G153/2/126/50/19 July 1950, and PG169/2/21/50/19 September 1950; 82310, EP1016/18/34/21 February 1950, 82330, EP1052/2/23 May 1950, and FO 248, 1512, G153/2/ 155/50/28 August 1950. The shah's proposals included requests for adjustment to the method of calculating royalties, speedier Iranisation, and Iranian government auditing of AIOC accounts. FO 371/Persia, 82312, EP1016/72/34/21 August 1950; 82342, EP1119/25/34/14 September 1950, Bevin Minute.

6. As an example of the company's callousness, a few days before the Iranian New Year in March 1950, the AIOC dismissed 500 redundant workers, without conferring with the British government or its representative in Tehran. Analogous to a Christmas Eve layoff, the action caused a stir in the country. By the time reports reached the Tehran press, the numbers laid off had swelled to 4000. George McGhee used this example to stress to the Foreign Office the company's irresponsibility. See, Hidayati, 44. *FR, 1950*, 5: 86–9, 97. As early as 1948 a leading American journal of the petroleum industry, *Oil Forum*, published a series of articles citing the danger to concessions in the Middle East, especially those controlled by the British in Iran and Iraq, unless the companies compromised over local government demands. 'Mid-East Concession Grievances Are Serious', *Oil Forum* (November 1948, February 1949).

7. *FR, 1950*, 5: 14, 529.

8. *FR, 1950*, 5: 576–7, n. 2; *BP History*, 2: 74–5. The British government was concerned at loaning money to balance the Iranian budget. London also worried that concessions made before ratification of the supplementary oil agreement would not prevent more requests later.

9. *FR, 1950*, 5: 581, n. 1, McGhee Interview, 13 January 1982, *FR, 1950*, 5: 591–602, *BP History*, 2: 77–8.

10. FO 371/Persia, 82343, EP1119/64/18 December 1950, EP1119/62/34/15 December 1950, and 91481, EP1102/1/9 January 1951; RG 84, TPF, Box 38, 523.1 Petroleum, 3 January 1951, Grady to SS. Acrimony developed among the Americans, with suggestion that Ambassador Grady was encouraging Iranian resistance. Ambassador Lewis W. Douglas reported from London that the British thought American diplomacy one-sided. This brought a sharp denial from Grady, but no progress towards a solution.

11. FO 371/Persia, 82342, EP1119/21/34/18 September 1950.

12. FO 371/Persia, 91521, EP1531/16/3 January 1951, 91522, EP1531/47/6 February 1951.

13. FO 371/Persia, 91485, EP1112/4/8 January 1951; T 236/Persia, 2824, 18 January 1951, 12 January 1951, 2820, 20 January 1951, FO 371/Persia, 91522, EP1531/31/13 January 1951, EP1531/35/24 January 1951, 91485, EP1112/10/24 January 1951.

14. *BP History*, 2: 83.

15. Ibid., Ruhani, 90.
16. For details of Musaddiq's life see Farhad Diba, *Mossadegh: A Political Biography* (London: Croom Helm, 1986).
17. A State Department research and analysis report of June 1950 listed several elements in Musaddiq's programme but not nationalisation. More perceptively it concluded that Musaddiq was unrealistic and that he would be frustrated in office. This was one of the few studies of Musaddiq and the National Front before spring 1951. RG 59, Reseach and Analysis Report (R&A) No. 5272, 9 June 1950. In February 1951 the move towards nationalisation gained religious support when the leading mujtahid, Ayatollah Khonsari, condemned any government that gave away the public inheritance to foreigners and turned its own people into beggars. Elwell-Sutton, 204. FO 371/Persia, 82343, EP1119/61/34/29 November 1950. Acheson warned the British of probable new financial arrangements in Saudi Arabia that would make the position of the AIOC more difficult. Ambassador Shepherd in Tehran suggested asking the secretary of state to slow down ARAMCO's negotiations with Saudi Arabia until the Majlis had accepted the supplementary oil agreement, but the Foreign Office rejected his proposal. FO 371/Persia, 91521, EP1531/13/21 December 1950. A. F. Lager, American petroleum attaché in Cairo, visited Tehran on 17 December 1950 and confirmed that the ARAMCO-Saudi Arabian negotiations would probably lead to a fundamental revision of concession terms. *BP History*, 2: 81. According to Fuad Ruhani, an AIOC official at the time, the oil company told Razmara that no agreement had been signed in Saudi Arabia. Ruhani, 88.
18. FO 371/Persia, 91522, EP1531/41/10 February 1951; 91452, EP1015/13/34/23 January 1951; *BP History*, 2: 85–6.
19. FO 371/Persia, 91523, EP1531/69–86/26 February–6 March 1951. Razmara had made the same argument in a secret speech to the Majlis in December, saying: 'I declare here openly that he who puts in danger the nation's capital and mineral resources constitutes the greatest treason', Hidayati, 169. Ruhani, 91–2.
20. FO 371/Persia, 91522, EP1531/50/14 February 1951, 91452, EP1015/9/34/19 January 1951, EP1015/13/34/23 January 1951.
21. FO 371/Persia, 91449, EP1013/10/34/5 February 1951, 91522, EP1531/49/7 February 1951, T232, 2821, 9 February 1951, pp. 58–9. Rumours of Anglo-American rivalry abounded in Tehran. See, for example, RG 59, 891.00/12 August 1949, WPA.
22. Although it seems clear the assassination was the work of the fidayan-i Islam, it was rumoured that the court and the United States were responsible. See, for example, Fereidun Keshavarz, *Man motaham mikonam* [I Confess] (Tehran, 1977) 146–8. The Soviet newspaper *Pravda* ran a front-page editorial on 18 March, accusing the Americans because, it said, Razmara had rejected them. *Current Digest of the Soviet Press*, 3, no. 11 (1951): 7.
23. The British believed that their note would discourage nationalisation and they were upset when the speaker of the Majlis failed to publicise it before the deputies voted. FO 371/Persia, 91524, EP 1531/1114/16 March 1951.
24. FO 371/Persia, 91525, EP1531/136/24 March 1951, 91453, EP1015/36/34/16 March 1951.

25. Truman papers, PSF, Intelligence File, CIA, 'The Current Crisis in Iran', 16 March 1951, HSTL. The former British ambassador in Tehran, John Le Rougetel, told Harold Macmillan that the Soviets were behind the whole problem in Iran and were using the nationalists. Harold Macmillan, *Tides of Fortune, 1945–1955* (London, 1969) 343–4; FO 371/Persia, 91524, EP 1531/133/27 March 1951, 91470, E1024/10/2 April 1951, and 91456, EP1015/146/34/20 April 1951.
26. Attlee, *As It Happened*, 196–7, 202; FO 371/Persia, 91470, EP1023/11/34/ 6 April 1951; 91454, EP1015//46/34/12 March 1951; *Clem Attlee*, Granada Historical Records Interview, No. 5: 55.
27. Morgan, *Labour in Power*, 472, *Daily Telegraph*, 6, 9 October 1951.
28. The French government consulted London as the crisis developed. The French, concerned about their interests in Iraqi oil, told the Foreign Office that they thought the US was too ready to give way on Middle East oil. FO 371/Persia, 91471, EP1023/53/30 April 1951. Morgan, 235, 250–1. 278, 466.
29. Attlee, *As It Happened*, 175–6; FO 371/Persia, 91455, EP1015/91/34/13 April 1951; EP1015/101/34/15 April 1951; EP1015/104/34/15 April 1951/ 91456, EP1015/118/34/23 April 1951.
30. Shinwell, *I've Lived Through It All* (London, 1973) 211, Bernard Donoughue and G. W. Jones, *Herbert Morrison: Portrait of a Politician* (London: Wiedenfeld & Nicolson, 1973) 506.
31. RG 59, 788.00/7 March 1951, Webb to Grady; McGhee Interview, 13 January 1982.
32. Berry papers, Schedule, 12–13, 15–17, 20–21, 27, and 29 March, LL.
33. Ibid., 22–23 and 27 March.
34. RG 218, Records of the US Joint Chiefs of Staff, NSC 107, 14 March. The Joint Chiefs argued that if the president approved NSC 107, despite their opposition, then the State Department should report monthly on its implementation, and a general review should take place not later than 1 July 1951. This is indeed what happened. NSC Action: 454. 'The Position of the US with regard to Iran', 20 March 1951, NA. See also, *FR, 1951*, 1: 818, 840.
35. McGhee Interview, 13 January 1982, Muhammad Reza Shah, *Mission for My Country*, 89–90, Bayne, *Persian Kingship in Transition*, 153, Ashraf Pahlavi, *Jamais Résignée* (Paris: La Table Ronde, 1983) 102.
36. McGhee Interview; US House of Representatives, Committee on Foreign Affairs, *Selected Executive Session Hearings of the Committee, 1951–56: The Middle East, Africa, and Inter-American Affairs*, History Series, number 16 (Washington: Government Printing Office, 1980) 28–9.
37. FO 371/Persia, 91524, EP1531/116/18 March 1951, and 91525, EP 1531/ 149/20 March 1951. In his autobiography, McGhee explains how the British concluded (mistakenly) that he had spoken against their interests to Iranian officials in Tehran. See, *Envoy to the Middle World*, 339–41.
38. Grady, 'What Went Wrong in Iran', *Saturday Evening Post*, 5 January 1952; Grady papers, Box 1, Folder 3, Grady to Stephen Bechtel, 16 March 1951, and Herbert Elliston, 25 April 1951, HSTL. Ambassador Grady claimed that Shepherd had the 'colonial' frame of mind and resented Grady's attempts to bring about a solution. Grady papers, Box 5, 'Adventures in Diplomacy', 20. Ambassador Shepherd reported similar views about his American counterpart. FO 371/Persia, 91530, EP1531/260/1 May 1951. Grady's departure disturbed NEA, and on the 29th Berry discussed the

Grady's departure disturbed NEA, and on the 29th Berry discussed the ambassador's absence with Lucius Battle, Acheson's assistant, who favoured asking Grady to return to Tehran immediately. Berry convinced him it would be unwise, for the message would take time and the ambassador might return in an angry mood. If Grady's absence upset Berry, a close friend, what must Acheson have thought? Berry papers, Schedule, 28–29 March, 1 April 1951.

39. Grady papers, Box 1, Folder 10, Grady to State Department, 'Memo.: Overseas Consultants, Inc.', 22 September 1951; FO 371/Persia, 91524, EP1531/125/19 March 1951, EP1531/130/27 March 1951, 91525, EP1531/139/29 March 1951. From Panama, Ambassador Wiley wrote Deputy Undersecretary H. Freeman Matthews, warning him to watch Thornburg, who, said Wiley, might use the current situation in Iran to his own advantage. This was no time for 'free-wheeling'. Wiley papers Box 5, Iran File, 19 March 1951, FDRL. Acheson wrote Grady, saying he doubted Thornburg could stay out of the oil issue. RG 84, TPF, Box 28, 523.1 Petroleum, 23 March 1951.
40. *FR, 1951*, 5: 289–97.
41. Ibid.
42. FO 371/Persia, 91525, EP1531/178/9 April 1951, 91621, EP1531/1/2/23 March 1951, and 91470, EP1023/6/27 March 1951.
43. McGhee Interview 1982; FO 371/Persia, 91470, EP1024/10/34/5 April 1951. US Ambassador Walter S. Gifford noted division in the British government over how to respond to Iran. One faction led by lower-level officers at the Foreign Office favoured concessions and greater government control over the AIOC; the other, including most Treasury officials and some key officers at the Foreign Office, hoped to salvage as much as possible, using familiar pressure tactics in Tehran. The latter group gained control over policy after passage of the nine-point law implementing nationalisation and the coming to power of Musaddiq. The 'hard-liners' became even more influential after the Conservative victory in October 1951. See, *FR, 1951*, 5: 295.
44. FO 371/Persia, 91525, EP1531/156/3 April 1951, 91470, EP1023/10/34/6 April and 28 April 1951. McGhee laboured under an additional handicap – suspicion of his motives as a Texas oilman. Two left-wing MPs accused him of encouraging the Iranians to take away the concession. Newspapers drew similar conclusions, and even politicians found it difficult to dismiss this notion of 'conspiracy'. McGhee Interview, Selwyn Lloyd, *Suez: 1956* (New York: Mayflower, 1978) 6, *FR, 1951*, 5: 309–15. Ambassador Franks reported that the AIOC had a poor reputation in the United States and should do something to spruce up its image. FO 371/Persia, 91528, EP1531/241/21 April 1951. McGhee had worked hard to preserve the AIOC concession, while warning American companies to stay out. This was unnecessary, for the American companies had no intention of interfering. They were so concerned about a domino effect should Iran succeed that they told the secretary of state they preferred to lose Iran to the Soviets than let it take over the AIOC concession on its own terms. Acheson papers, Princeton Seminars, 15 May 1954, HSTL.

45. FO 371/Persia, 91525, EP1531/168/3 April 1951, and 91621, EP1537/3 + /5/ 4, 5 April 1951.
46. Committee on Foreign Affairs, *Selected Executive Session Hearings of the Committee, 1951–56*, 16: 27–31, 41–3.
47. FO 371/Persia, 91470, EP1023/11/34/6 April 1951.
48. FO 371/Persia, 91471, EP1023/29/34/7 April 1951. The British criticised the Americans for discussing in public what should be secret, thereby undermining British attempts to negotiate. At times exasperated British diplomats concluded that they paid too much for American support. 91470, EP1023/16/34/12 April 1951.
49. *Declassified Documents*, DD 771E, 11 April 1951 [Meeting of McGhee, Harriman and Acheson on Iran], RG 59, Undersecretary's Meetings, N–330/11 April 1951, FO 371/Persia, 91470, EP1023/16/10 April 1951; FO 371/Persia, 91470, EP1023/4/34/20 March 1951; EP1023/17/34/10 April 1951; EP1023/118/34/10 April 1951; EP1023/118/34/10 April 1951; EP1023/20/34/11 April 1951; EP1023/21/34/14 April 1951; 91471, EP1023/34/16 April 1951; EP1023/39/18 April 1951; EP1023/43/19 April 1951; EP1023/51/20 April 1951. While the talks were continuing in Washington, Ambassador Shepherd cautioned against any major change in AIOC policy for the nationalist furor seemed to be subsiding. This inaccurate assessment no doubt stiffened London's determination in Washington. FO 371/Persia, 91470. EP1023/22/12 April 1951.
50. Matthew J. Connelly papers, Post-Presidential File (PPF), Set 2, 'Notes of Cabinet Meetings', HSTL.
51. The American position was somewhat ironic given its pressure on the British at the same time for air retaliation against Manchuria without prior consultation. See, *FR, 1951*, 7: 338–42, 343–4. British General Headquarters Middle East Land Forces advised the minister of defence that any plan requiring large military units to hold the Iranian oil fields or refineries would be unrealistic because of the strain this would put on British forces already committed in other parts of the Middle East. FO 371/Persia, 91456, EP1015/169/34/1 May 1951.
52. RG 59, 788.00/9 April 1951, Grady to SS; *Foreign Broadcast Information Service*, 10–12 April 1951, RR1; *Journal de Tehran*, 17 April 1951.
53. *FBIS*, 16 April 1951, RR2, 23 April 1951, RR1; Sahebjam, 232; Arfa, *Under Five Shahs*, 395; FO 371/Persia, 91527, EP1531/209/24 April 1951, EP1531/212/23 April 1951, and 91528, EP1531/220/26 April 1951, Ruhani, 118.
54. Elwell-Sutton, *Persian Oil*, 215–16; Connelly papers, PPF, 'Notes of Cabinet Meetings', HSTL; FO 371/Persia, 91529, EP1531/237/29 April 1951. McGhee reacted more intemperately, claiming that Shepherd's statement went against the Washington decision not to provoke the Iranians and introducing the possibility that the United States might reconsider its whole attitude. Sir William Strang told Franks to assure Acheson of Britain's co-operation but to deprecate McGhee's tone. This time the embassy talked the Foreign Office out of a formal complaint, but Morrison spoke off the record to Ambassador Gifford in London (who shared the British view of McGhee). 91531, EP1531/291/30 April 1951, and EP1531/294/8 May 1951.

55. RG 59, Undersecretary's Meeting, N–336/25 April 1951, Notes. The State Department asked for British comment on the grant proposal. London urged the Americans not to propose economic assistance while the oil question was unsettled. Ambassador Franks did not present the Foreign Office reply, fearing the US would interpret this as another British 'plot'. He predicted accurately that the State Department would reconsider extending economic aid to Iran now that Musaddiq had replaced Ala. Thus the Foreign Office response was not delivered. FO 371/Persia, 91493, EP11345/7/19 April 1951, and EP11345/10/8 May 1951.
56. From the Soviet Union came a different interpretation. On 26 April *Izvestia* explained events in Southern Iran. It cited rivalry between the capitalist powers as reason for the British threat of force at Abadan. The Americans wanted to take Britain's place in Iran, therefore the British had to use force to maintain themselves. Although the Soviets could analyse these developments, they were less certain about the new Musaddiq government. Not until 10 May did the Soviet press acknowledge the change in Tehran, and it did so in terms that reflected mistrust and antagonism. In 1951–53 Stalin saw the world sharply divided between socialists and imperialists with no room for neutrals like Musaddiq. Abrahamian, 322; Cottam, 222–3.
57. FO 371/Persia, 91453, EP1015/30/34/9 March 1951; EP1015/31/10 March 1951; EP1015/35/14 March 1951; 91485, EP1112/19/20 March 1951, 91470, EP1023/5/34/24 March 1951; FO 248/Persia, 1514, G10101/126/51/28 March 1951, G10101/132/51/31 March 1951, FO 371/Persia, 91454, EP1015/105/34/16 April 1951, 91456, EP1015/139/34/20 April 1951, 91457, EP1015/162/34/28 April 1951, EP1015/164/34/29 April 1951, Grady papers, Box 5, 'Adventures in Diplomacy', 32–3, HSTL.
58. The shah tried to influence the senate against the nine-point law, but suffered another rebuff. FO 371/Persia, 91459, EP1015/207/21 May 1951.
59. RG 84, TPF, Box 29, 350 Iran: Internal Affairs, 1951, 7 May 1951. During April the shah was suffering from chronic appendicitis and what his doctors feared was a blocked intestine. Arthur L. Richards, American chargé d'affaires, reported that the shah as usual was obsessed with his health. This could have affected his judgement during the hectic weeks leading up to nationalisation and Musaddiq's appointment. RG 84, TPF, Box 32, 361.1 Shah, 1950–52, 5, 27 April 1951.

NOTES TO CHAPTER 9

1. Sanghvi, *Aryamehr*, 184.
2. *FBIS*, 1 May 1951, RR 1–2. Musaddiq argued that during the first year of nationalisation oil sales would expand and living standards rise. Ruhani, 95.
3. Rumour and misunderstanding blurred Iranian perception of foreign attitudes towards nationalisation. It was said, for example, that the British wanted Iran to take over the Abadan refinery because it was old and obsolete and this was the only way the AIOC could get a lot of money for it.

Interview with Sir Peter Ramsbotham, London, March 1983. Others claimed that Britain favoured nationalisation because it saw the justice of Iran's case and also wanted to thwart the Russians. FO 371/Persia, 91457, EP1015/164/34, 29 April 1951. Husain Makki of the National Front claimed that petroleum importing countries depended on Iran's oil so much that they would freely place oil technicians at Iran's disposal. Ruhani, 96. For an example of the widely-held view that Britain and the United States competed in the Middle East, see *Kayhan*, 17 Deh 1328 (1950).

4. FO 371/Persia, 91457, EP1015/162/34, 28 April 1951; 91458, EP1015/197/ 34, 14 May 1951; 91529, EP1531/256, 29 April 1951.

5. FO 371/Persia, 91531, EP1531/284, 2 May 1951. By not formally submitting Seyed Zia's name, the shah had allowed the Majlis to ignore the speaker's suggestion and nominate its own candidate. FO 371/Persia, 91450, EP1013/21/34, 5 May 1951. The chief AIOC representative in Iran, Richard Seddon, wrote Britannic House early in May that all the trouble had come because the company and London had been soft. He praised the tougher attitude that, he said, had a salutary effect in Tehran. *British Petroleum History*, 2: 109.

6. Wiley papers, Box 5, Iran file, 11 August 1951, Wiley to Henderson, FDRL; RG 59, 788.00/7 March 1951, Webb to Grady, 611.88/7 May 1951, SS to Grady.

7. Papers of Loy Henderson, Box 10, Iran-Miscellaneous, 28 January 1978, Henderson to Ron Cockrell, Library of Congress; Wiley papers, Box 5, Iran file, 29 June 1950, FDRL.

8. RG 59, 611.88/27 April 1951; RG 84, TPF, Box 560, 19 April 1951.

9. *Cahiers de l'orient contemporain*, February-March 1951, 44.

10. RG 84, TPF, Box 31, 350.1, Tudeh party.

11. Acheson papers, Post-Presidential Files: Memoirs File, 31, HSTL.

12. For details of negotiation with Musaddiq, October-November 1951, see RG 59, 888.2553, Box 5507, NA.

13. Acheson, *Present at the Creation*, 510–11.

14. RG 59, 888.2553, 14 November 1951, SS to Acting SS; Acheson papers, Memorandum of Conversation at Dinner at British Embassy, 7 January 1952, HSTL, *Present at the Creation*, 600.

15. RG 330, Office of the Secretary of Defense, CD 092.3 NATO (General) 1951, Joint Chiefs of Staff, 7 November 1951, CD 092 (Iran) 1952, 16 August 1952, Lovett to Bruce, CD 092 (Iran), Lovett to Acheson, 24 October 1952, 12 November 1952, National Security Council, Official Meeting Minutes, Meeting 178, 23 December 1953.

16. RG 59, 788.00/21 July 1952, Acheson Memorandum of Meeting with the President, FO 371/Persia, EP1015/173, 22 July 1952, EP1015/179, 21 July 1952.

17. Kermit Roosevelt, *Countercoup: The Struggle for the Control of Iran* (New York: McGraw Hill, 1979). What remains is the importance of the CIA intervention. Organisers boasted, but may have exaggerated. Musaddiq had lost popular support by mid-1953; the populace had become apathetic – unwilling to raise a hand, even to come into the streets. CIA money acted as a catalyst for the disatisfied and ambitious. An article by Mark J. Gasiorowski provides the most detailed discussion of the US plan to topple

Musaddiq. 'The 1953 Coup d'état in Iran', *International Journal of Middle East Studies* 19 (1987) 261–86.

18. Interview with Sir Denis Wright, London, March 1983, *BP History* 3: 92, NSC, Official Meeting Minutes, 178, 23 December 1953.

19. Rubin, *Paved with Good Intentions*, 106–14, National Security Files, Country Series, Iran, 16 May 1961, Bowles to NSC, 20 March 1961, David Bell to McGeorge Bundy, JFK Library, Boston. See also James Bill's informative chapter on Kennedy and Iran in *The Eagle and the Lion: The Tragedy of American-Iranian Relations*. National Security Files, Meetings and Memoranda, NS Action Memoranda 228, May 1963, JFKL.

20. Papers of Edward A. Bayne, Interview with Shah (taped) 9 July 1966, Lilly Library, Indiana University, Bloomington, Indiana.

21. Letter from Bruce Laingen (then a hostage in Tehran) to Henderson, quoting Undersecretary of State Joseph Sisco. Henderson papers, Box 9, Iran-misc., April 1980, LC.

Bibliographical Essay

MANUSCRIPTS

Most documents of the Department of State on United States-Iranian relations dated through 1949 were open for research prior to the revolution of 1978. Since that time restrictions have applied, and declassifying of post-1949 materials has lagged. Technically, State Department and central files through 1954, and so-called post files (for the embassy and consulates), have been declassified, but it is not unusual to find only a score of documents in a box that should contain hundreds, the others withheld at the request of the department or the Central Intelligence Agency. Many of the available documents have been so censored that only a few lines remain.

The State Department has not adhered to its own recently announced 30-year rule respecting these documents. Others have discussed the issue of restricted access, and I would direct the reader to the *Newsletter* of The Society for Historians of American Foreign Relations, especially the June 1985 and June 1986 issues.

Of materials available, the decimal files in Record Group 59 are indispensable for reports of diplomats in Tehran and discussions within the department, and less frequently between the State Department and other agencies of the executive branch. Research and Analysis Reports – there were only a few on Iran prior to summer 1951 – provide information not easily obtained on Iran's political leaders and Washington's assessment of their abilities. Records of the Military Advisor to the Office of Near Eastern, South Asian, and African Affairs are useful. See also Record Group 59, the General Records of the Executive Secretariat, summaries of the daily meetings of the undersecretary with division heads, which Secretary Acheson attended, as well as summaries of reports from abroad and information on the secretary of state's schedule when in Washington.

The Modern Military Branch of the National Archives holds three important record groups bearing on the subject. Most important is RG 319, Records of the Plans and Operations Division, US Army, Decimal File, providing details of military missions in Iran. RG 218, Records of the Joint Chiefs of Staff, and RG 330, Records of the Office of the Secretary of Defense, deal largely with policy within the executive branch.

The Washington National Records Center, at Suitland, Md., houses RG 84, which includes the Tehran post files. These are voluminous, and essential for perspective on bilateral relations. They contain information on movements and events in Iran summarised or omitted in the decimal files. The many translations from the Iranian press are rewarding, especially for non-Persian readers. Two points should be noted: many documents from the Tehran post files, 1951–54, housed in the National Archives rather than at Suitland, have been withheld. The files from the consulates are less useful than those from the embassy, although occasionally they reveal interesting provincial sentiment.

Elsewhere in Washington, the Export-Import Bank has destroyed almost all

145

records relating to the proposed loan of 1950–51, 'according to standard procedure', The Naval Archives at the Washington Naval Yard contain little on Iran prior to the end of 1951. The only pertinent collection at the Library of Congress is that of Loy Henderson, ambassador to Iran, 1951–55. It relates primarily to the period after September 1951 when Henderson took up his post. There are interesting letters from later years, observations by Henderson, by other diplomats, and by policy specialists, on Iran.

At the Harry S. Truman Library in Independence, Missouri, important collections await the researcher. Of President Truman's papers, the most helpful are those in the President's Secretary's Files, Subject File: Iran. The Official File and Post-presidential Files are well worth examining. The Henry F. Grady papers are crucial for understanding the mission in 1950–51. They provide instruction on misunderstanding and frustration within the foreign service. The papers of Dean Acheson often duplicate material at the National Archives, but his Princeton seminars (available on microfilm), on which he based his autobiography of the State Department years, *Present at the Creation* (New York: W. W. Norton, 1969), are valuable. The seminar meetings took place in 1953–54 when events were still fresh in the minds of former officials of the Truman administration. Much of the discussion revolved around policy in the Middle East, especially Iran. Views by Acheson, George McGhee, Paul Nitze and Averell Harriman are enlightening. Acheson's Memoirs File contains interesting comments on the special relationship with Britain. Robert L. Garner's papers, including a diary of a visit to Iran in 1949, and an unpublished manuscript, reveal more perhaps about American prejudice than about contemporary Iran. But Garner makes useful observations on Iranian, British and American officials in Tehran. The papers of George Allen add little to what we know of that ambassador's relationship with the shah, discussed so ably in Bruce Kuniholm's *Origins of the Cold War in the Near East* (Princeton: Princeton University Press, 1980).

Ambassador John C. Wiley's papers are at the Franklin D. Roosevelt Library, Hyde Park, New York. They include an interesting file on Iran, which reveals among other things that the ambassador did not lose interest in the country after he left in 1950.

The Lilly Library at Indiana University, Bloomington, houses two small collections worth a brief visit. The papers of Burton Y. Berry, an Indiana alumnus, present details of a long career in the Near East. Of special interest is a diary for February-April 1951 kept while his chief, McGhee, travelled in the Middle East. Berry used this diary to bring the assistant secretary up to date when he returned. Also at the Lilly Library are tape recordings of Edward A. Bayne's interviews with the shah and Asadollah Alam in 1966. Bayne based his *Persian Kingship in Transition* (New York: American Field Universities Staff, 1968) on these recordings. Some material on the tapes is not in the book.

Finally there is the diary and papers of General Robert W. Grow. The late general's family has retained these materials. The diary is especially interesting. It reveals the general's frustration as he tried to maintain a US presence, without much support from Washington, and to convince Iranian leaders to accept American advice. The papers on Iran concern Grow's attempt to discover why the army precipitously removed him as mission head in 1948.

Scholars can be thankful that the British government was involved in Iran. Its records provide information on policy-making – in Washington and London – during the 1940s and 1950s, a period yet to be fully revealed in the American archives. The British government has adhered scrupulously to the 30-year rule, and files at the Public Record Office, at Kew, near London, are open (1989) through 1958. Foreign Office files are indispensable, rich in detail and personal observation. FO 371 (Iran) consists of 200 files for the years 1947–51, and FO 248 (British Embassy, Tehran) has perhaps 20 files for the same period. FO 800, the papers of Ernest Bevin, contain little on Iran, indication that up to 1951 decisions came at lower levels in the Foreign Office. Bevin retired in March 1951, at the time of Razmara's assassination. Records of the British embassy in Tehran show close contact with a variety of Iranian opinion. Treasury files, T 236 (Overseas Relations), are crucial for understanding financial questions; they also reveal division between the Foreign Office and the Treasury. The ten files of the Ministry of Fuel and Power (POWE 33) detail the ministry's concern over fuel supplies, but also its subordinate position *vis-à-vis* the two other ministries. Cabinet (CAB 130), Prime Minister's Office (PREM 8), and the Ministry of Defence (DEFE 4, 5 and 6) contain only scattered references to Iran prior to May 1951, but are useful thereafter.

Outside the Public Record Office, two diarists provided pungent comment on developments within the Attlee government, including occasional reference to the deepening crisis in Iran. The diary of Hugh Dalton, Minister of Town and Country Planning (1950–51), available at the London School of Economics, presents a critical assessment of Herbert Morrison as Foreign Minister. The diary of Kenneth Younger, Minister of State (1950–51), in the possession of Professor Geoffrey Warner at the Open University, chronicles the sad tale of Bevin's failing health, which rendered him ever less able to cope – according to Younger – with any but the most urgent issues. Attlee's papers at the Bodleian Library, Oxford University, contain little on Iran for this period. The papers of Minister of Defence Emmanuel Shinwell, the last survivor of Attlee's cabinet (who died in July 1986 at the age of 101), will soon be catalogued at the London School of Economics.

Of special interest is a three-volume *History of British Petroleum in Iran* (1970) based on documents in the company archives. Rose L. Greaves compiled these volumes, which were restricted to the hierarchy of the company. On a visit to London in 1983, I had opportunity to take notes from a set that had found its way outside the company. Volume 2 covers 1947–52, and volume 3, 1952–54. These documents show ties between the company and Whitehall, disparage US diplomacy, and detail a supercilious attitude towards Iranian officials. Ronald Ferrier's second volume on the history of British Petroleum will no doubt incorporate much of the information in these privately published volumes.

ORAL HISTORIES

Out of the large collection at the Truman Library only Loy Henderson's oral history contributed significantly to my work. Of my own interviews several were extremely helpful, including those with Edward A. Bayne, George McGhee and Sir Peter Ramsbotham. An important oral history project, funded by the Federal government, has recently been opened to researchers at the Middle East

Studies Center, Harvard University. This project includes hundreds of interviews (in Persian) with Iranian exiles, former military and civilian officials. Many of the transcripts are available at the centre which is seeking another grant for translation into English.

PUBLISHED PRIMARY SOURCES

Foreign Relations of the United States, the State Department's grand series is, of course, the most valuable collection of published documents on United States-Iranian relations. After the crisis year 1946 (vol. 7, 278 pp.), *Foreign Relations* reflected a lessening of American interest (1947: 5, 108 pp.; 1948: 5, 113; 1949: 6, 122). Documents relating to Iran for 1951 – a pivotal year – have not been included in the Near East volume (1984). Instead the reader finds an editorial note: 'Documentation concerning Iran for year 1951 is scheduled for publication in *Foreign Relations, 1952–1954*, volume X'. This final volume for 1952–54 has yet to appear (1988).

Congressional hearings provide a wealth of information. Of note are volumes in the historical series: *Executive Sessions of the Senate Foreign Relations Committee, 1947–1954* (1976); *Mutual Security Programs* of the House Committee on Foreign Affairs; and *Selected Executive Hearings of the Committee 1951–1956: The Middle East, Africa, and Inter-American Affairs* (1980). These hearings reveal congressional antagonism towards Britain and a generally optimistic outlook by Americans who appeared before the committees. Another useful if more general series of hearings was that of the Church Committee (chaired by Senator Frank Church of Idaho, chairman of the Foreign Relations Committee) in 1974: the most useful has been *Multinational Petroleum Companies and Foreign Policy* part 7, *Hearings before the Subcommittee on Multinational Corporations* (1975).

Two international studies also provide background: International Labour Office, *Labour Conditions in the Oil Industry in Iran* (1950); and M. A. Hedayati, *Situation politique et sociale de l'Iran en 1950–1951: Année de la nationalization du pétrole* (Neuchâtel: H. Messeiler, 1951). Hedayati was an International Labour Office representative in Iran.

Muzakirat-i Majlis [Proceedings of the Iranian Majlis] provides contemporary views on United States-Iranian relations. The complete series, from the early years of this century, is available in the Library of Congress. Widespread suspicion of foreign powers and reluctance to favour any bloc stand out.

NEWSPAPERS

The Foreign Broadcast Information Service provides translations of speeches and foreign press editorials from all nations, and is available on microfilm and useful even for foreign language readers; in the case of Iran they provide materials available only at the Library of Congress and a few research libraries. The Library of Congress has provided an excellent, annotated bibliography, *Persian and Afghan Newspapers in the Library of Congress, 1871–1978* (1979), compiled by Ibrahim V. Pourhadi. Only a small part of the Iranian collection has been microfilmed, and reels may be obtained through interlibrary loan. The filming project is continuing. Holdings for the early postwar period reflect vagaries of press censorship, when offending newspapers would be shut down, only to resume publication under a different name. Editorial positions varied widely, from left-wing papers like the Tudeh party's *Mardum* [The People] to such right-wing religious papers as *Parcham-i Islam* [The Flag of Islam]. Many papers are polemical, their editors adhering to philosophies of right or left. A survey of several papers provides the necessary introduction to contemporary Iranian opinion. Particularly useful are *Ettela'at, Kayhan, Khavar, Mard-i Imruz, Sada-yi Mardum*, and *Tulu*. The *Tehran Journal* did not appear until the mid-1950s; the French language *Journal de Tehran* begun in 1935, is a pale imitation of contemporary Persian-language papers.

Cahiers de l'orient contemporain (Paris) provides extracts from Middle East papers and summaries and dates of events not easily found elsewhere. Coverage of Iran in American and British papers between May 1946 and May 1951 is sporadic, Articles by the *New York Times* correspondent Albion Ross are particularly interesting, for Ross seemed to have more understanding of developments in Iran than almost any other foreign journalist. The *Washington Post* published useful articles as well. Initially, the Musaddiq government enjoyed a favourable press in the United States, with American editors conceding the need for some form of nationalisation. In Britain, the *Spectator* and the *Economist* presented a balanced view – at least in the early stages of crisis – while *The Times* and the *Daily Telegraph* opposed Iranian nationalisation.

AUTOBIOGRAPHIES AND MEMOIRS

Iranian authors have contributed a long list of autobiographies and memoirs, including two works by the late shah, Muhammad Reza Pahlavi, *Mission for My Country* (London: Hutchinson, 1960) and *Answers to History* (1980). The first he wrote prior to the White Revolution (1963), the second after he had gone into exile (1979). These reveal little about decisions and present a court history of the postwar years. The shah does make some interesting comments concerning the role of faith and miracles in his life. Accounts by the shah's twin sister, Ashraf Pahlavi – *Faces in a Mirror* (Englewood Cliffs, N.J: Prentice-Hall, 1980) and *Jamais Résignée* (Paris: La Table Ronde, 1983) – must be used with care; her memory is selective. Yet the books detail how much Reza Shah dominated his children, and especially reveal Ashraf's character. General Hasan Arfa, *Under Five Shahs* (London: John Murray, 1964) is an interesting account of internal events, although most of the text deals with the period before 1945. Arfa contributed some useful observations, but as a monarchist his comments on Musaddiq and the National Front should be used with caution. Husain Makki, a leading figure of the National Front, and a historian, has detailed events leading to nationalisation in *Kitab-i Siah* [The Black Book] (Tehran, 1951). Makki participated in many of the events and in spring 1951 he advocated immediate takeover. Fuad Ruhani, *Tarikh-i Milli Shudan San'at-i Naft-i Iran* [The History of the Nationalisation of the Iranian Oil Industry] (Tehran, 1973) is an important study of the turbulent late 1940s and early 1950s. Ruhani was a high official of the Anglo-Iranian Oil Company, one of a handful of Iranian insiders. During the early days of the Musaddiq government he sent weekly summaries of events to Britannic House in London, which were passed to the Foreign Office. Ruhani is more balanced than many other writers on this emotional subject. His book, published in Iran, would have had to meet criticism by the shah's censors. Shahpour Bakhtiar, the shah's last prime minister, has written a lucid account of his days as a member of the National Front, *Ma fidélité* (Paris: Albin Michel, 1985). He includes a sympathetic discussion of Ahmad Qavam. But more important is Bakhtiar's characterisation of Dr Musaddiq; Bakhtiar was a deputy minister in Musaddiq's government. He recognises Musaddiq's weaknesses as well as his strengths; it is a laudatory and yet believable sketch.

For British statesmen there is Clement Attlee, *As It Happened* (London: Heineman, 1954), Emmanuel Shinwell, *I've Lived Through It All* (London, 1973), and the *Diary of Hugh Gaitskell, 1945–1956* (London: 1983), edited by Philip Williams. These three books tell much about politics and relations within the Labour government, but little regarding Iran. Anthony Eden, *Full Circle* (Boston: Houghton Mifflin, 1960) has a useful chapter on the oil crisis, which had occupied him even before he returned to the Foreign Office in October 1951.

American contributions include Dean Acheson, *Present at the Creation* (1969) and President Truman's fascinating diary and other papers edited by Robert H. Ferrell, *Off the Record: The Private Papers of Harry S. Truman* (New York: Harper & Row, 1980). George McGhee, *Envoy to the Middle World* (1983) is an account of an individual who was at the centre of American policy for Iran and the Middle East, 1949–51.

SECONDARY ACCOUNTS

The study of US relations with the Middle East is full of paradox. Despite the diplomatic rupture between the United States and the Islamic Republic of Iran, few historians have turned their attention to US-Iranian relations. Indeed, and with the notable exceptions of Palestine and oil, few have concerned themselves with studying American ties to any of the Middle Eastern states. There is nothing comparable to the outpouring of monographs and other studies detailing American diplomacy in East Asia, studies that have set a high standard for all historians. Studies on US-Latin American relations are only slightly fewer in number. For the Middle East we do not have even an adequate general study or synthesis going beyond 1939 and the work of John De Novo, *American Interests and Politics in the Middle East, 1900–1939* (Minneapolis: University of Minnesota Press, 1963). Available studies on Iran are often the work of political scientists, many of them native Persian speakers (Ramazani, Abrahamian, Ladjevardi), or those who served as representatives of Western governments and institutions in Iran (Cottam, Upton, Elwell-Sutton, Bayne). What is impressive about research on US-East Asian relations is the number of American scholars with facility in languages – Japanese, Chinese, Korean. Arabic, Turkish and Persian should pose no more formidable barriers, and yet diplomatic historians rarely learn them. Perhaps public and private institutions should encourage students to master Middle Eastern languages as they have encouraged them in Eastern European, Russian and East Asian studies.

Few of the fine dissertations on US relations with Iran (or with other Middle Eastern nations) are revised and published. There are at least three first-class dissertations in this category: Richard Pfau, 'The United States In Iran, 1941–47: Origins of Partnership' (Virginia, 1975), Stephen McFarland, 'The Crisis in Iran 1941–1947: A Society in Change and the Peripheral Origins of the Cold War' (Texas, 1981), and Mark Joseph Gasiorowski, 'U.S. Foreign Policy and the Client State' (North Carolina, 1984). Each approaches its subject in an original way, and it is unfortunate they have not reached a wider audience. [Gasiorowski's important article, 'The 1953 Coup d'état in Iran', in the *International Journal of Middle East Studies* (1987) gives promise of future publication.]

One could argue, I suppose, that the paucity of diplomatic studies on the Middle East relates to the recent arrival of the United States in the region, and that neglect might be rectified as archival materials become available from the 1950s, which saw American involvement in Iran, Lebanon, Egypt and the Central Treaty Organisation. But lack of diplomatic studies may mirror a lack of concern for the Middle East. Individuals familiar with Middle East studies recognise the imbalance in institutional support between that area and other regions – Soviet Union, Eastern Europe, East Asia. One need only compare scholarships and fellowships available to students in each of these areas. Despite popular focus on Middle East oil, terrorism, Islamic resurgence, the region as a whole continues to be taken for granted.

There are a few general works on Iran. Julian Bharier, *Economic Development in Iran, 1900–1970* (New York: Oxford University Press, 1971) contains the best available statistics on all sectors of the economy. Two other volumes provide background. Herbert H. Vreeland, ed., *Iran* (New Haven: Yale University Press, 1957) is one of the country survey series. Donald N. Wilber, *Iran: Past and Present* (Princeton: Princeton University Press, 8th edn., 1976) covers a variety of topics including chapters on the Iranian people and their culture. The journal, *Iranian Studies*, published since 1968, is a rich source covering many themes. Of the few scholarly works dealing with US-Iranian relations, the most general – and presently the best survey on the subject – is Barry Rubin, *Paved With Good Intentions: The American Experience in Iran* (New York: Oxford University Press, 1980). This fine book covers a century, with emphasis on the post-1953 years. Although Rubin uses only sources in English, he readily sees the influence of the shah on the United States. An intriguing article, C. D. Carr, 'U.S.-Iranian Relationship 1948–78: A Study in Reverse Influence' in Hossein Amirsadeghi (ed.) *The Security of the Persian Gulf* (London: Croom Helm, 1981), pursues this theme, concluding (perhaps with some exaggeration) that Iran was the tail wagging the dog. Carr promises a full-length study of US-Iranian relations since World War II. The most recent addition to this genre is James Bill's excellent study, *The Eagle and the Lion: The Tragedy of American-Iranian Relations* (New Haven: Yale University Press, 1988). Bill's scholarly interests have taken him many times to Iran, and his attachment to the land and people is evident here. He draws heavily on personal experience, extensive contacts and a variety of Persian materials in addition to archival collections. His criticism of the Pahlavi regime and its American supporters is unrelenting. *The Eagle and the Lion* is especially valuable for the years after 1961; for the earlier period Bill relies on secondary studies. This work will long remain the most detailed and most authoritative account of recent US-Iranian relations. More narrowly focused, and widely influential, is Bruce Kuniholm, *The Origins of the Cold War in the Near East: Great Power Conflict and Diplomacy in Iran, Turkey, and Greece* (1980). The best work linking the three nations of the northern barrier, it represents Cold War orthodoxy. Kuniholm's uncle served in Iran in the early postwar years, and the family has ties to diplomats. He offers information from interviews with diplomats such as Loy Henderson and John Jernegan. Kuniholm may see more uniformity in American policy towards the barrier nations than is warranted. He considers the Azarbaijan crisis of 1946 the turning point in US-Iranian relations, after which the US maintained constant interest in Iran's welfare. A more recent study, Mark Lytle's *The Origins of the Iranian-American Alliance, 1941–1953* (New York: Holmes & Meier, 1987), presents an excellent analysis of relations during the period 1941–47. Lytle's work is mildly revisionist, arguing that US policy-makers overreacted to a perceived Soviet threat and should have encouraged Iran to pursue non-alignment. Still useful is George Lenczowski's *Russia and the West in Iran, 1918–1948* (Ithaca: Cornell University Press, 1949), based on firsthand experience during World War II when the author served as Poland's representative in Tehran. It presents a critical discussion of allied relations and internal developments, dominated by Lenczowski's strong anti-Soviet views.

No single work analyses Anglo-Iranian relations at mid-century, even though for 13 years (1941–54) Iran was vitally important to Britain's international position. Until recently the best study of Labour foreign policy was M. A. Fitzsimons, *The Foreign Policy of the British Labour Government, 1945–1951* (South Bend, Ind.: Notre Dame University Press, 1953). Within the past few years three important studies have appeared. Kenneth O. Morgan, *Labour in Power, 1945– 1951* (Oxford: Clarendon Press, 1984) devotes several chapters to foreign policy, drawing on recently declassified Foreign Office files. Alan Bulloch's magisterial *Ernest Bevin: Foreign Secretary, 1945–1951* (New York: W. W. Norton, 1983) is a massive tribute to its subject and to Bulloch's powers of narration and analysis. Bulloch provides insight into Bevin's Middle Eastern policy that no future historian can neglect. William Roger Louis, *The British Empire in the Middle East, 1945–1951: Arab Nationalism, the United States, and Postwar Imperialism* (Oxford: Clarendon Press, 1984), provides a detailed study of relations in an area of strategic interest to Britain. Broadly based on British documents and private papers, these three books consider Labour's policy in the Middle East favourably, emphasising the region's importance to Britain. Louis stresses the beneficence of a British policy based on non-intervention and partnership. Certainly, if these were the bases of Britain's policy, the message was lost on the Iranians.

Many scholarly studies on postwar Iran devote space to relations with the US and Britain. In the early 1950s, following the overthrow of Prime Minister Musaddiq, many books and articles appeared. Laurence Paul Elwell-Sutton. *Persian Oil: A Study in Power Politics* (London: Lawrence & Wishart, 1955), one of the best, is a masterful account of British intransigence and the coming of oil nationalisation in 1951. Its author had worked for the AIOC and the British government and knew his subject. His book found favour behind the Iron Curtain, where it was translated into Russian (1956) and Chinese (1958). Alan W. Ford, *The Anglo-Iranian Oil Dispute, 1951–52* (Berkeley and Los Angeles:

University of California Press, 1954), based entirely on published materials, provides an account of the crisis that continues as a standard work. Ford understands Iranian nationalism. A pair of articles in the same issue of *Middle East Affairs* (1954) demands attention: Henry C. Atyeo, 'Political Developments in Iran, 1952–54', is required reading; and Benjamin Shwadran, 'The Anglo-Iranian Oil Dispute, 1948–53', presents an excellent review of the complex dispute, concluding that Britain and the United States ganged-up on Iran. These four entries provide skillful analysis without benefit of archival materials. Our understanding of the oil crisis has changed little since their appearance.

General studies of Iran go beyond the early postwar years, and here political scientists have made the greatest contribution. Richard Cottam, *Nationalism in Iran* (Pittsburgh: University of Pittsburgh Press, 1964), a study of politics and political philosophies in the twentieth century, provides convincing analysis of modern Iran. Cottam served in the US embassy in Tehran in the 1950s and writes favourably of Musaddiq and the National Front. Almost alone among American scholars, he spoke out against the excesses of the shah's regime. Currently he is writing a study of US economic relations with Iran. James Bill has also contributed *Politics of Iran: Groups, Classes and Modernization* (Columbus, Ohio: Charles E. Merrill, 1972), which analyses the inner personal tensions promoted by the shah to ensure his control over civil and military leaders. Bill, like Cottam, consistently opposed American policy towards the shah. Marvin Zonis, *The Political Elite of Iran* (Princeton: Princeton University Press, 1971), explores the mechanism by which the shah maintained control, and discusses the fate of those who opposed him. Joseph M. Upton, *The History of Modern Iran: An Interpretation* (Cambridge, Mass.: Harvard University Press, 1960), is a short study of Pahlavi Iran. Upton had many years service in Iran and does not flatter the regime. Publication brought demands from the Iranian court for changes, apparently with no success.

In the 1970s Iran made rapid economic progress, and writers extolled the virtues of the White Revolution and the rule of the shah. A volume of essays entitled *Iran under the Pahlavis* (Stanford: Hoover Institution Press, 1975), edited by George Lenczowski, celebrated the 50th anniversary of the dynasty. L. P. Elwell-Sutton contributed an article, accentuating positive aspects of the reign of Reza Shah. The editor, Lenczowski, likewise praised the 'modernizing monarchy'. Another essay collection, *Twentieth-Century Iran* (London: 1977), edited by Hossein Amirsadeghi, contains an essay by Rose Greaves, '1942–1976: The Reign of Mohammad Reza Shah', which praises the ruler, while Ronald W. Ferrier's essay, 'The Development of the Iranian Oil Industry', sees nationalisation under Musaddiq as misguided. Michael Fischer, 'Persian Society: Transformation and Strain', maintains the countinuing importance of religion and the ulama. Rouhollah Ramazani, especially in *Iran's Foreign Policy, 1941–1973: A Study of Foreign Policy in Modernizing Nations* (Charlottesville: University Press of Virginia, 1975), has considered the movement towards greater independence in foreign relations. This view is interesting in light of the many works – such as Bahman Nirumand, *Iran: The New Imperialism in Action* (New York: Monthly Review Press, 1969) – that claimed the United States dictated Iran's course in international affairs. Ramazani drew heavily on Persian newspapers and such works as Makki, *Kitab-i Siah*.

Since the fall of the shah, scholars have attempted to explain why the revolution took so many people unawares. One of the best of these accounts is Ervand Abrahamian, *Iran Between Two Revolutions* (Princeton: Princeton University Press, 1982), which uses Iranian and Western sources to reconstruct the political groupings of the post-World War II era, providing profiles of nationalist leaders unavailable elsewhere. Abrahamian focuses on the communist party of Iran, the Tudeh, but provides convincing analysis of domestic politics up to the revolution. *Religion and Politics in Iran: Shi'ism from Quietism to Revolution* (New Haven: Yale University Press, 1983) edited by Nikki Keddie, who has written widely on Iranian history, presents two essays useful for understanding the early postwar period: Azar Tabari, 'The Role of the Clergy in Modern Iranian Politics', and especially Yann Richard's 'Ayatollah Kashani: Precursor of the Islamic Republic?' An essay by Thomas Ricks, 'Background to the Iranian Revolution', in Ahmad Jabbari and Robert Olson (eds), *Iran: Essays on a Revolution in the Marking* (Lexington, Ky.: Mazda, 1980), Stresses the popular – and simplistic – notion that the United States created the 'American Pahlavi dictatorship'.

A recent monograph by Habib Ladjevardi, *Labor Unions and Autocracy in Iran* (Syracuse: Syracuse University Press, 1985), analyses the rise and fall of the trade union movement in the 1940s. Working from US and British archives, and Persian oral and written sources, Ladjevardi concludes that a great share of blame for failure attaches to the US and Britain. There is need for more such studies.

Finally, Farhad Diba's *Mossadegh: A Political Biography* (London: Croom Helm, 1986), provides a wealth of information, based in part on unpublished papers of the prime minister. Diba presents a somewhat idealised, but nevertheless useful, account of the nationalist leader, placing him in the context of twentieth-century developments in Iran.

Works concerning US-Iranian relations have fallen into several categories. One considers America largely to blame for the Pahlavi dictatorship (Ricks, Nirumand); another stresses how adroitly the shah manipulated the US (Rubin, Carr, Ramazani); a third (largely pre-revolutionary) praises the Pahlavi accomplishments, seeing no need for blame (Greaves, Ferrier, Lenczowski); a fourth seeks balance, arguing that although the United States did not create the shah, it did contribute to his rise (Cottam, Bill, Rubin). This latter interpretation has gained broad acceptance.

Recently, a trend not to cite references or ascribe information to a source has appeared in works on Iran (Rubin, Gasiorowski, de Villiers). This applies especially to interviews. Admittedly, political conditions in Iran might make it unwise for exiles to be quoted, but this development, carried to extremes, could undermine the exchange of information and the integrity of scholarship. Authors might at least consider providing a list of individuals who contributed information, without specifying their contributions.

For those seeking understanding of events within Iran since 1978 two works stand out. Shaul Bakhash, *The Reign of the Ayatollahs* (New York: Basic Books, 1986) based on Persian sources, including interviews in Iran, is a readable analysis of the revolution, carrying events up to the beginning of 1985. The second volume, *'The Government of God' – Iran's Islamic Republic* (New York: Columbia University Press, 1984), a collaboration of Cheryl Bernard and

Zalmay Khalilzad, begins with an introduction to the political theory of modernisation and revolution but quickly turns to the ideology and structure of the republic. It evaluates — and finds wanting — much of the pre-revolutionary work on Iran by political scientists and sociologists.

Index

Index